ity of the
England

D1582327

This book is a study of the Popular Front and United Front campaigns in Britain in the late 1930s. The author aims to dispel the myth that these campaigns can be understood largely as a ruse engineered by the Communists into which non-Communists were drawn blindly. Instead the author searches for the idea of 'progressive unity' in earlier episodes in the history of the British progressive tradition, including the early life of the Fabian Society, and the agitations against the Boer War, the First World War, and the Treaty of Versailles.

By reassessing the significance of these episodes, and by reconsidering the role of seminal progressive thinkers in the formation of the ideas and political culture of Labour leftism, the author shows that the relationships between liberals and socialists, and between reformists and revolutionaries, had long been both intimate and fluid. By examining the reasons and assumptions behind individual Labour leftists' decisions to support the struggle for progressive unity in the late 1930s, it is shown that the Popular Front was neither an aberration nor a 'stunt', but a reasoned and culturally familiar response to the major political crisis presented by fascism and appeasement.

THE POPULAR FRONT AND
THE PROGRESSIVE TRADITION

THE POPULAR FRONT
AND THE PROGRESSIVE
TRADITION

Socialists, Liberals, and the Quest for Unity, 1884–1939

DAVID BLAAZER

Senior Tutor, Department of History, The Australian National University

CAMBRIDGE
UNIVERSITY PRESS

Published by the Press Syndicate of the University of Cambridge
The Pitt Building, Trumpington Street, Cambridge CB2 1RP
40 West 20th Street, New York NY 10011-4211, USA
10 Stamford Road, Oakleigh, Victoria 3166, Australia

First published 1992

Printed in Great Britain at the University Press, Cambridge

A catalogue record for this book is available from the British Library

Library of Congress cataloguing in publication data
Blaazer, David.
The Popular Front and the progressive tradition: socialists,
liberals, and the quest for unity, 1884–1939 / David Blaazer.
p. cm.
Includes bibliographical references and index.
ISBN 0 521 41383 4
1. Great Britain – Politics and government – 1901–1936. 2. Great
Britain – Politics and government – 1837–1901. 3. Great Britain –
Politics and government – 1936–1945. 4. Coalition governments –
Great Britain – History. 5. Popular fronts – Great Britain – History.
6. Liberalism – Great Britain – History. 7. Socialism – Great Britain –
History. 1. Title.
DA576.B5 1992
320.941 – dc 20 91-42575 CIP

ISBN 0 521 41383 4 hardback

UP

To my parents

Contents

Preface

Writing is a lonely and demanding craft, and it is only natural that writers nearing the completion of a work are given to morose doubts about the real point or value of their efforts. I was struck by these doubts as I neared the completion of the doctoral thesis upon which this book is based. In those early months of 1989, the work seemed to me to be unforgivably irrelevant as politics and aggressively unfashionable as history. To the latter charge I must still plead guilty: the history in this book covers a broad sweep of time; it does not refer to localities, draws on only one oral source, and is neither ethnographic nor deconstructionist. My only consolation here can be that fashions change.

The first problem, irrelevance, is of a different order. 'Irrelevance', in the sense of a lack of any direct application to the problems of the present, is of course not a vice in historical scholarship. Scholars of the diplomacy of the Thirty Years War or the everyday life of twelfth-century serfs are rightly not obliged to demonstrate the immediate utility of their work, but can justify it by pointing to the cultural and intellectual value of the broad historical enterprise itself. Nevertheless, it seemed to me strangely disconcerting that people who within the present century had written with such commitment and urgency as my subjects had done, and who, in many cases, had died within my own lifetime, should seem to have no more direct relevance to my contemporaries than a seventeenth-century pamphleteer. The broad political project on which they were engaged – the search for a form of socialism that could fulfil the libertarian promise of historical liberalism – seemed to have been swept off the agenda, if not by the flabby, opportunistic compromise struck between labour and capital after the Second World War, then certainly by the attack on that compromise launched by resurgent *laissez-faire* ideologues and supported by what pre-Second World

War progressives would have called a collective frenzy of mammon worship which characterised the mainstream of public life in the 1980s. The specific topics which exercised my subjects appeared equally to have been superseded: in international relations the problems of the Balkans and of Mesopotamia seemed, early in 1989, to have been permanently cemented into a form that bore no relationship to the problems of which they wrote; the creation of an international police force under some sort of international government was permanently sidelined by the institutionalised deadlock of the United Nations Security Council; the questions of sectional interest and the common good had sunk under the weight of ever more strident lobbies pursuing ever more particularised demands. In short, the leading figures in this book spoke with voices from another world.

Several European revolutions and a major war later, things are not so clear. Suddenly, we need urgently to understand the contours of Balkan nationality and ethnicity; suddenly, we are obliged again to ponder the role of international capital in Iraq; suddenly, the problems of a just international order and its enforcement have been thrown open to broad public debate. On all of these issues the protagonists of this book have something to say which again is of immediate relevance.

The jury is still out, however, on whether their broader project can or will be resumed. Many of the early hopes that post-communist Eastern Europe would look for a 'third way' now seem to have been dashed by the juggernaut of privatisation as those countries desperately seek sources of capital. On the other hand, the social problems created by that process become ever more pressing. We have not heard the last word from the revolutionary crowds of Berlin and Prague, who most certainly were not moved to their heroism by the prospect of joining an unemployment queue. If fractricidal wars can be averted, and the climate of reason so precious to the progressives can be maintained, it is still possible that their search will become the search, and perhaps even the achievement, of millions.

Acknowledgements

Many people helped me as I researched and wrote the doctoral thesis on which this book is based. I would like especially to thank my supervisors, Dr Philip Bull and Dr Barry Carr of the Department of History, and Mr Robert Manne of the Department of Politics, La Trobe University, for their advice, encouragement, practical suggestions, and their patience and tolerance of a somewhat wayward student. I wish to thank them especially for confining their criticisms to the work's intellectual shortcomings, and not attempting to impose the crippling conventions that now seem to govern much of the Ph.D. industry.

Many other people have assisted me in many different ways. Dr David Boucher gave freely of his time to read and comment on drafts of parts of the work. The members of the history postgraduate seminar at La Trobe University contributed many stimulating comments and challenges to my thinking. More friends, colleagues, and students at La Trobe University than can be named have given intellectual stimulus and moral support. Dr Iain McCalman and other colleagues in the History Department, Faculty of Arts, Australian National University, gave encouragement and moral support while I revised the manuscript for publication. In particular, Ms Maree Beer's assistance checking the proofs made that task both speedy and pleasant. Naturally, the book's deficiencies are all my own work.

I wish to thank also Margot Hyslop, Rosemary Griffiths, and other staff at the Borchardt Library, La Trobe University, for their unfailing helpfulness with many difficult inquiries and requests. I am also indebted to the staff of the following libraries and archives: National Library of Australia; Nuffield College Library; John Rylands Library, University of Manchester; University of Newcastle-upon-Tyne Library; British Library of Political and Economic

Science; Trinity College Library, Cambridge; Labour Party Archives and Labour Party Library; International Institute of Social History, Amsterdam; Bodleian Library, Oxford; Brynmoor Jones Library, University of Hull; Rhodes House Library, Oxford; Manchester Public Library; King's College Library, Cambridge; Public Record Office, Kew. The School of Humanities, La Trobe University, provided a grant which made it possible for me to spend three months in Britain. Louis and Caroline Blaazer, by their extraordinary hospitality and kindness towards a complete stranger, made those months far more comfortable and enjoyable – and therefore more productive – than I could otherwise have hoped. Above all, I wish to thank Renata Grossi, without whose timely applications of sympathy, dynamite, and love this book might well never have materialised. To her and to my parents I also owe special thanks not only for their invaluable assistance with the final preparation of the manuscript, but also for helping to sustain mind, body, and spirit over the long haul.

Abbreviations

BWD	The Diary of Beatrice Webb
COS	Charity Organisation Society
CPGB	Communist Party of Great Britain
CRA	Congo Reform Association
FS corres	Fabian Society Correspondence
FS:EC minutes	Fabian Society Executive Committee minutes
ILP	Independent Labour Party
LLAAM	League of Liberals Against Aggression and Militarism
NEC	Labour Party, National Executive Committee
NS&N	*New Statesman and Nation*
PR	*Progressive Review*
SACC	South Africa Conciliation Committee
SDF	Social Democratic Federation
TUC	Trades Union Congress
UDC	Union of Democratic Control
WEA	Workers' Educational Association

NOTES ON THE TEXT

'Liberalism' and 'Liberal' when capitalised refer to the Liberal Party and its members; 'liberalism' and 'liberal' refer to the political philosophy and its adherents. In some contexts the distinction is so fine as to be meaningless. All works referred to were published in London except where otherwise stated.

Introduction

Contrary to myth, the most numerous and strategically significant group to support the Popular Front campaign in Britain was not the Communist Party but the left of the Labour Party. The success or failure of the proposal to join the 'parties of progress' in a common struggle against the Conservative government depended solely on whether the Labour left could persuade the rest of their party to agree to it. This book is therefore mainly about the Labour left. It aims to show that the left's support for the Popular Front campaign, and to a lesser extent the United Front campaign before it, can best be explained in terms of the left's place in the mainstream of the British progressive tradition. This view implies that the campaigns themselves are best seen as episodes in that tradition, and demands reinterpretation not only of the history of the Labour left in the 1930s, but also of the nature of the United Front and Popular Front campaigns, and of the British progressive tradition itself. The book is devoted equally to each of these three interlocking tasks.

The historiographical and conceptual problems that surround this subject-matter are considerable and require some preliminary discussion. To begin, however, it will be helpful to provide a brief sketch of the United Front and Popular Front campaigns.

(1)

The United and Popular Front campaigns are fairly straightforward episodes, at least in outline. The United Front campaign may be said to have begun as early as March 1933, when the Communist Party of Great Britain, acting on instructions from the Executive Committee of the Communist International, dropped its policy of relentless vilification of the Labour Party and trade union leaders and attempted to interest them in joint activity. This approach received virtually no support from any section of the Labour Party and was quickly rejected by the leadership, who were not only ideologically hostile to Communism, but were also understandably disinclined to work with a body that had spent most of the previous decade denouncing them as class traitors and 'social fascists'.

The Independent Labour Party, however, accepted the Communists' invitation and entered into an uneasy partnership with the CPGB, whose chief aim appeared to be to exploit the new relationship as a device to poach ILP members. This was consistent with the CPGB's earlier tactic of the 'United Front from below' in which the Party had established various political and industrial organisations open to all rank and file workers with the objective of inducting them into their own ranks, and with the effect of disrupting the work of the official Labour organisations and undermining their leadership.

The United Front did not become a contentious issue within the Labour Party until 1936 when the Socialist League – the formally constituted organisation of the Labour left – supported the Communist Party's application for affiliation to the Labour Party. This application was a result of another change of tack by the Communist International, which in 1935 had decided to support the formation of Popular Fronts of all anti-fascists, as opposed to United Fronts consisting only of socialists. The change may be attributed in part to the increasing menace of fascism as Hitler consolidated his power, in part to the Soviet Union's new line in foreign policy which now sought alliances with capitalist states in order to contain Germany, and in part to the successful, spontaneous formation of a United Front in France in 1934. Despite this change in line, however, the Communist International and the CPGB insisted that the broader Popular Front must be preceded by a United Front – that socialists must attain the fullest possible unity before seeking to enlist non-socialist anti-fascists.

The ILP and most of the Labour left supported the United Front, but at first rejected the Popular Front on the grounds that socialism was the only effective means to prevent the spread of fascism. They argued, as the Communists themselves had done, that fascism was merely a particular form of capitalist dictatorship, and that to fight fascism without dismantling capitalism was futile. While the CPGB sought affiliation to the Labour Party as a phase in its Popular Front strategy, the ILP and the Labour left supported the United Front as an end in itself.

When the CPGB's application for affiliation was rejected by the Labour Party conference in June 1936, the supporters of unity fell back on the more limited aim of concerting the electoral and propaganda efforts of the three parties. This too was rejected by the Labour Conference, which reiterated the Party's ban on co-operation with the Communists. In January 1937 the Socialist League defied this ban by publishing, jointly with the ILP and the CPGB, a 'Unity Manifesto' advocating unity of 'the whole Labour Movement . . . to oppose fascism in all its forms'.[1] The Labour Party executive responded first by disaffiliating and then by proscribing the Socialist League. Rather than face the expulsion of its members from the Labour Party, the League dissolved itself.

While some prominent Labour leftists, such as G. D. H. Cole and H. N. Brailsford, were converted to the idea of a Popular Front as early as 1936, and while others never supported it at all, the bulk of them, including Sir Stafford Cripps, chairman of the now defunct Socialist League, began to advocate it in 1938 after Germany annexed Austria. Their main aim was to unify the opposition to the Chamberlain Government's policy of appeasement, which they felt amounted at best to extreme cowardice and at worst to deliberate and sinister encouragement of fascism. The Labour Party declared its opposition to the Popular Front as soon as it was first proposed. Some leaders of the Labour left nevertheless continued publicly to campaign for the Popular Front. As a result, Cripps was expelled from the Party in January 1939 and was followed two months later by five others, among them two MPs, Aneurin Bevan and George Strauss, and a former cabinet minister, Sir Charles Trevelyan.

Considered from any angle the lasting consequences of this conflict were small. The Labour Party dropped its opposition to cross-party co-operation and played an important role in the wartime Coalition Government, and all of the expelled members eventually returned to the Labour fold. Cripps and Bevan were key figures in the post-war Labour Government in which Strauss also served in a junior post. As I have stated, however, my interest in the campaigns is not in their consequences but in their origins, and in what they reveal about the political attitudes and the political heritage of those Labour leftists who took part.

(II)

The Labour left's participation in the United Front and Popular Front campaigns, and indeed the behaviour of the entire non-Communist left throughout the 1930s, is often explained (or rather, explained away) as an aberration engineered by the Communist Party. While all the different breeds of anti- and pro-Communist historians have advanced a wealth of different accounts of this state of affairs (as well as a considerable number of moral judgements), almost all have shared the premise that the non-Communist left's history in this period can be largely, or even completely, understood as a function of the activities and propaganda of the CPGB. Too many studies of the non-Communist left in the 1930s seem to focus on the Communists themselves. The non-Communist left itself is written about as though possessed of neither volition, reason, nor history.

The ideological imperatives of the Cold War are only the most obvious of the many strong historical and historiographical reasons for this tendency.[2] During the thirties the numbers and prestige of the CPGB were at their highest ever. The Party's energetic and frequently effective organisation of the unemployed earned it the support of many working-class people, and the heroism with which the Party rallied to the cause of the Spanish Republic captured the imagination, if not the support, of a wide cross-section of people alarmed at the rapid growth of fascism on the continent and in Britain itself. Most importantly in the present context, a number of causes, chiefly the apparent helplessness of British institutions – including the Labour Party – in the face of the political and economic crises of the time contrasted with the economic and social achievements of the USSR, meant that British intellectuals of the left generally were more favourably disposed towards Soviet Marxism than at any time before or since.

This led many people to take up embarrassingly uncritical positions towards the Soviet Union and the activities of the Communist International and its constituent national parties. When most of these people recanted, either on the signing of the Molotov–Ribbentrop pact in August 1939 or on the onset of the Cold War in the late 1940s, the pattern for much of the subsequent historical understanding of the 1930s was set: left-wing politics in the 1930s had been an enormous confidence trick perpetrated by the Communist International on a generation of young idealists who had been made psychologically and politically vulnerable by sheer despair. There is, of course, a lot of truth in all of this. Specifically, the recantations give an accurate picture of the historical experience of those who wrote them, and probably of a good many other people. For them, Communism had been a god, and it had undoubtedly failed.

These people were not, however, a representative sample of the 'Popular Front' left of the 1930s, nor even of those who were enthusiastic defenders of the Soviet Union. They were for the most part young, and many (W. H. Auden and Stephen Spender are the best known examples) were literary men who lacked both theoretical knowledge and practical experience of politics when Communism first captured their imaginations in the 1930s. Their very youth has contributed to the undue weight given to their experience in conventional understandings of the period. Unlike most of those who were politically experienced in the 1930s, and whose attitudes towards Communism tended to be somewhat more judicious, most of those who were thoroughly and publicly infatuated with Communism in the 1930s lived into the 1950s and beyond to tell and retell their tale.

The most influential exponent of the view that left-wing politics in the 1930s was a gigantic Communist confidence trick has been George Orwell, whose works – especially *The Road to Wigan Pier* and *Homage to Catalonia* – are today without a doubt the most widely read British political texts of the 1930s. Orwell, who joined the ILP in 1938, opposed the Popular Front and had excellent reasons to hate and mistrust the Communists. In May 1937, while on leave from the front in the Spanish Civil War, where he was fighting with the POUM (non-Stalinist Marxist) militia, he took part in the week of fighting that erupted in Barcelona between the Communist controlled police on one side and the Anarchists and the POUM on the other. Indeed he only narrowly escaped the murderous suppression of the POUM by the Communists who libelled the POUM as a fascist front. In England he had a serious dispute with Kingsley Martin, the editor of the *New Statesman and Nation*, who, as a supporter of the Popular Front, refused to publish Orwell's account of the events he had witnessed in Spain for fear of creating friction within the British left.[3] But Orwell's version of the British left's attitude to the Barcelona events is greatly exaggerated. The left-wing press in Britain, although it reprehensibly shied away from reporting the suppression of the POUM, did not retail the Communists' lies about the POUM, and the Barcelona rising itself was fairly reported and analysed in the *New Statesman and Nation* by Brailsford and another writer.[4]

There is, however, a far deeper problem in Orwell's version of the left-wing politics of the 1930s than any particular piece of exaggeration. It is that the recognised political leaders of the non-Communist left, as opposed to the literary 'fellow-travellers', are entirely absent. In Orwell's whole output before the war there is no reference whatsoever to Cripps, Cole, Trevelyan, or Bevan, nor to Harold Laski – another prominent Labour leftist who for a time supported the Popular Front. Brailsford, a journalist and writer who had been active in the Labour Party for three decades, is mentioned only once in a letter in which Orwell disputes a detail of the account of the Barcelona fighting which Brailsford wrote in the *New Statesman and Nation.*[5] Orwell's letter gives no indication that Brailsford's account contradicted the Communists on almost every significant point; still less would one guess that Brailsford wrote one of the two letters of introduction that Orwell carried with him to Spain – letters which put Orwell in touch with the POUM rather than the Communists.[6]

Orwell's work has value as a sincere and powerful revolt against the many deceptions of the 'red decade', but it cannot be accepted as an analysis of the left-wing politics of the 1930s. Even the most casual study of the writings and actions of the leaders of the Labour left reveals a far more complex, and, mercifully, a far less disgusting picture than anything derived from Orwell or the cold warriors can allow. It reveals, for example, that among seasoned members of the Labour left there was a wide variety of attitudes towards the Soviet Union, the Comintern, and the CPGB. It reveals that a significant section of the Labour left was at first hostile to the proposal for a Popular Front, and that different individuals became convinced of the need for a Popular Front at different times and for different reasons. It reveals that many of those on the Labour left who supported Soviet foreign policy in the late 1930s remained critical of that country's repressive practices at home and sceptical of its motives abroad. In short, it reveals that the left's history in this period cannot simply be written as though the Communist Party were a sort of Doctor Pavlov needing only to ring the bells of 'democracy and progress' to produce the required response.

Even to the extent that the non-Communist left's activities and attitudes were influenced by Communist propaganda, they still cannot be understood solely by reference to that propaganda. No matter how skilfully conducted, a propaganda campaign must strike appropriate chords in its listeners if it is to be successful. Indeed, understanding which chords to strike and how and when to strike them is one of the propagandist's most important skills. The successful propagandist must understand the values, anxieties, and idiom of his or her audience, just as the historian must who wishes to understand the operation and importance of a propaganda campaign.

This is merely to reiterate in a different context a principle argued long ago by E. P. Thompson. Discussing the English crowd in the eighteenth century, Thompson protested against the tendency of many historians to assume that there was a simple causal relationship between 'elementary economic stimuli', such as hunger, unemployment, or high prices, and popular disturbances. He argued that in order to understand such episodes we must ask, 'How is [the participants'] behaviour modified by custom, culture, and reason?'[7] This is precisely the question that I wish to pose in relation to the behaviour of the non-Communist left in the 1930s. Just as Thompson disposed of the image of 'the eighteenth-century English collier who claps his hand spasmodically upon his stomach, and responds [by rioting] to elementary economic stimuli',[8] so I hope to dispose of the equally unhelpful (and insulting) image of the 1930s British intellectual who claps his hand to his forehead, and responds – by worshipping Stalin or by working for a Popular Front – to the elementary emotional stimuli of fear and despair.

It might be objected that Thompson was arguing in the context of a particular historiographical problem: the view that 'the common people can hardly be taken as historical agents before the French Revolution',[9] and that it is superfluous to try to do for an intellectual elite what it was urgently necessary to do for a mostly illiterate 'mob' of common people. While this would certainly be a valid point in relation to the intellectual left for most of its history, it does not apply to the 1930s. As I have suggested above, most historians have dismissed the behaviour of the left in the 1930s as an aberration, and have thereby excused themselves from considering the ways in which that behaviour was conditioned by custom, culture, and reason, and have taken the operation of Communist propaganda in the context of despair to satisfy (to echo Thompson again) 'all requirements of historical explanation'.[10] The fact that the subjects of my study were mostly of the intellectual elite makes my task less difficult than Thompson's, but it does not make it less necessary.

(III)

One of the most common consequences of historians' former unwillingness to study the actual words and deeds of the non-Communist left in the 1930s was a failure to distinguish adequately – or even at all – between the United Front and the Popular Front. This was common, as one might expect, in general histories, where fine distinctions are frequently lost;[11] but it was also apparent, as recently as 1975, in more specialised studies. Thus Alfred Sherman, 'The Days of the Left Book Club', Julian Symons, *The Thirties*, Neal Wood, *Communism and British Intellectuals*, and David Caute, *The Fellow Travellers*, all, by one means or another, elided the two campaigns.[12] These texts had other common features: all were written from an anti-Communist viewpoint, and placed the Communist Party of the USSR firmly in the centre of their accounts of the left-wing politics of the 1930s.

The delightful irony of this is that these anti-Communist authors all accepted without question the Communists' central strategic assumption that the United Front was a mere preliminary to the Popular Front, and in their anxiety to demonstrate the Communists' hegemony over the left (incidentally another point congenial to Communist mythology) simply took for granted that the rest of the left shared this view. As I have already suggested and shall show in greater detail in the body of the work, this is by no means true.

More recent writers have recognised that the campaigns were separate but have not fully realised the extent to which they were contradictory. This has less to do with the grinding of ideological axes than with the sheer deceptive simplicity of the apparent historical progression: according to this version of events fascism emerged as a threat in the early 1930s, so Labour leftists sought alliances with other socialists; as fascism became more threatening they sought them with an ever widening circle – first of Liberals, then of 'democratic' Tories. The logical culmination of the whole process – the ultimate Popular Front – was the wartime Coalition Government under the leadership of the anti-Nazi Winston

Churchill, generally viewed though he was as an imperialist and a reactionary.

This notion has a psychological ring of truth, but rides roughshod over the political processes involved. The theoretical assumptions behind the United Front and the Popular Front were in fact contradictory. The United Front strategy was based on the belief that fascism was the form contemporary capitalism inevitably took when in the grip of crisis. Socialism was its only antidote. Liberals and democratic Tories, who supported capitalism, were not merely useless but positively harmful, as they would never consent to the administration of this antidote. Worse still, they would, for all their good intentions, inevitably be forced to support fascist measures in order to maintain the capitalist system. The Popular Front strategy, by contrast, assumed that fascism was a free choice taken by cliques of evil and reactionary capitalists. The main threat of fascism came from those states – principally Germany – whose capitalists had already chosen it. The problem was essentially the military–diplomatic one of standing up to Hitler. There was room in this argument for the idea that there was a clique of capitalists in Britain who desired fascism, and that Neville Chamberlain was their puppet. There was even room for the idea that Churchill's opposition to Hitler stemmed from his desire to defend the British Empire and that he was therefore an unsuitable ally, but there was no room for the idea that every supporter of capitalism must of necessity turn fascist in a crisis. The move from United Front to Popular Front was not, therefore, a logical progression, but a fundamental change in strategy and a correspondingly fundamental change in the left's understanding of the nature of the evil they faced. Even under the most severe threat people do not seek help from among those whom they believe form part of the threat itself. People make choices. And the choices they make are determined, to repeat the phrase, by custom, culture, and reason.

This consideration obliges us to look at the political past of the leading supporters of the United Front and Popular Front campaigns, an exercise which will not only show at once how unremarkable was their advocacy of cross-party collaboration, but will also finally rule out the idea that their actions in the 1930s can be attributed to mere political naïveté.

The oldest prominent supporter of the campaigns was Sir Charles Trevelyan.[13] Born of a famous Liberal family in 1870, Trevelyan entered parliament as a Liberal in 1900, at which time he was a close friend of Sidney and Beatrice Webb and Ramsay MacDonald. He served as a junior minister in the Asquith Government in 1908–14. He resigned his post on Britain's entry into the First World War and immediately helped found the Union of Democratic Control, an organisation of Liberals and members of the ILP who opposed the British government's wartime policies and advocated a negotiated settlement with Germany. In 1920, as a result of the Liberal Party's failures and divisions during the war, Trevelyan, like all the other Liberals in the UDC, joined the ILP, which was then an important constituent body of the Labour Party. He was a cabinet minister in the first two Labour Governments, but resigned from the second in protest at its failure to fund his education portfolio adequately. He retired from parliament in 1931, but when the ILP disaffiliated from the Labour Party in the following year he became a fairly active member of the Socialist League, which was formed out of those members of the ILP who did not wish to leave the main Party.

Brailsford's career could almost be seen as a journalistic equivalent of Trevelyan's.[14] Born into the Liberal non-conformist middle class in 1873, Brailsford, while a member of the Liberal Party, helped found the Glasgow University Fabian Society in 1896. He left the Fabian Society in 1899 when it failed to declare a position on the Boer War, which he opposed. He was active in two organisations against the Boer War, one of which was a coalition of socialists – including revolutionary socialists – and Liberals. As a journalist, Brailsford worked on many different liberal and socialist papers and continued to do so after he joined the ILP in 1907. Like Trevelyan, he was prominent in the UDC and was a founding member of the Socialist League.

G. D. H. Cole and Harold Laski were about twenty years younger than Trevelyan and Brailsford and were both academics.[15] Their careers are therefore different, but reveal some of the same characteristics. Laski came from a middle-class Liberal family, graduated from Oxford in 1914, and immediately began work for the socialist *Daily Herald*. He spent the war years in the USA, but on his return in 1920 immediately resumed his pre-war activity in the Fabian Society and joined the ILP. He also began to contribute to the liberal *Nation*, and became a regular attender at the weekly lunches organised by its editor. It was here that he became friendly with Brailsford and with the assortment of Liberal and socialist journalists who made up the rest of the paper's staff. In 1930, Laski helped found the *Political Quarterly*, a journal which deliberately sought to convey a 'progressive' liberal and socialist point of view.

Cole too was a member of the Fabian Society as a young man shortly before the war, although he soon came into conflict with its leaders when he attempted to capture the Fabian Society for Guild Socialism – a variant of syndicalism of which he was a leading exponent. Although he resigned from the Society over this dispute he helped found the Fabian Research Bureau immediately afterwards. After the war, he, like Laski, although now a prominent member of the Labour Party, became a fairly regular contributor to the Liberal *Manchester Guardian*. Like Laski and the others he was a founder of the Socialist League.

Cripps's career was different again.[16] He came to politics comparatively late in life, after he had established himself in a very successful career at the Bar. His family, however, was political. His father, like many others, had made the transition from the Liberal Party to the Labour Party after the First World War, and as Lord Parmoor was Lord President in the first two Labour Governments. Beatrice Webb was Cripps's maternal aunt. On that side of the family both of his great-grandfathers were active in the Anti-Corn Law League with Richard Cobden. Joseph Cripps, Stafford's great-great-grandfather, spent forty years in the House of Commons where he supported both the Great Reform Act and the repeal of the Corn Laws. Stafford Cripps had deep Christian convictions and considered a career in the Church. He was close to forty when he joined the Labour Party in 1928, partly as a consequence of his family connections, but also because of the influence of the Christian Socialist ideas of R. H. Tawney. By chance he soon became prominent. In 1930, while still without a seat, he was appointed Solicitor-General on the sudden retirement of the incumbent. A safe seat was soon found, and when the Labour Party was trounced in the 1931 election Cripps found himself one of only fifty-two Labour MPs and one of a small handful with any parliamentary ability. Together with George Lansbury and Clement Attlee he formed the triumvirate that led the Parliamentary Labour Party through some of the most difficult years of its history.

Aneurin Bevan was far removed from the plutocratic heights of the Cripps and Trevelyan families, or even the middle-class life of Brailsford, Laski, and Cole.[17] He was a coal-miner who cut his

political teeth on industrial disputes and local government struggles
in a South Wales village. He was converted early to Marxism,
educated at the National Labour College, and elected to represent
his home constituency in 1929. But Bevan, born in 1897, was young
enough for Brailsford's seminal work, *The War of Steel and Gold* (first
published in 1914), to have been influential on his thinking as a
youth. Bevan was a militant whose relationship with the Labour
Party was always problematic. He was a vociferous critic of the
second Labour Government's failure to respond creatively to mass
unemployment, and in 1931 was an active participant in Sir Oswald
Mosley's unsuccessful revolt against the Party leadership, which
ended in Mosley and his closest colleagues leaving the Labour Party
to form the short-lived New Party. Bevan never contemplated this
step,[18] but of those who did follow Mosley, two, Allan Young and
John Strachey, later emerged as supporters of the Popular Front.

With the exception of Bevan all the people here seem obviously
fitted to be supporters of a Popular Front. Brailsford and Trevelyan
had both been members of the Liberal Party and had not turned
their backs on Liberal colleagues when they joined the ILP. The
others either came from Liberal backgrounds or enjoyed good
relations with Liberals or both. On the other hand, if we are to
account for their support for the Popular Front by these biographical incidents, we are left unable to account for their support for a
United Front, which, as we have seen, was in some measure an anti-
Liberal tactic. Similarly, Bevan's biography may help us to understand his support for a United Front, but provides no clue to his
support for a Popular Front. Helpful as they are, these biographies,
considered in isolation, leave much unexplained. The gaps can be
filled only if we consider these individuals' political trajectories as
symptomatic of their participation in the British progressive
tradition.

(IV)

The point may be clarified if stated somewhat differently. The
United Front and Popular Front campaigns were both in large
measure about the relationship between liberalism and socialism.
Were they at bottom irrelevant, or even hostile to each other, or
were they in some sense natural allies, with enough common ground
to warrant practical political co-operation? Far from being a new

question in the 1930s, this was the most constant and important theme in the British progressive tradition for at least seventy years before the Second World War. Whether we consider the progressive philosophical and political discourse, or whether we consider the relationships between the organisations to which the participants in the tradition have belonged, that single theme recurs again and again.

These seventy years – roughly the 1860s to 1939 – form the chronological boundaries of this book. But in order to clarify my claim that the relationship between liberalism and socialism was the dominant theme of the progressive tradition throughout those years, it will be helpful to focus first on a narrower period in which the relationship was most explicitly and continually discussed and debated, and where the main issues involved are therefore clearest.

This period has been given a very thorough treatment in the works of Dr Peter Clarke, who uses the terms 'progressivism' and 'Progressive Movement' to denote a group of people, bound loosely by common ideas, who were prominent in the quarter century before the First World War. Their common ideas were inspired by both liberalism and socialism. On the one hand were the 'New Liberals', whose principal aim was to persuade fellow Liberals that the realisation of their traditional ideals of liberty and equality required a serious revision of their equally traditional distrust of government and faith in the *laissez-faire* doctrines of the classical economists. Among this group were the economist J. A. Hobson, the philosopher L. T. Hobhouse, and the politicians Herbert Samuel and, significantly, Charles Trevelyan. On the other hand were avowed socialists who argued that Liberalism's historical moment had passed, and that Socialism (in the mild and cautious form they advocated), by virtue of its subsumption of all that was valuable in Liberalism, was its only logical successor. Among this group were Ramsay MacDonald of the ILP and the early members of the Fabian Society, including Sidney and Beatrice Webb, Graham Wallas, and William Clarke. H. N. Brailsford moved from the first position to the second early in the new century. Taken together (and, given their close political, social, and quite often familial relationships, that is how they should be taken) these groups constituted the 'Progressive Movement'.

My use of the term progressive for this period is practically identical with Clarke's whose work has opened up many lines of inquiry useful to my own. I differ from him, however, in my understanding of the term in the period after the First World War. In one place Clarke seems convinced that the term can hardly be used at all in this period: 'After the War, progressivism guttered on and flickered out. It was forgotten.'[19] In the richly suggestive concluding remarks of a later work he is less sure.

The election of 1929 blighted progressivism; the combination of capitalist failure and a so-called National Government in 1931 buried it. For after this there could be no presumption of a natural connection between progressive ideas and the Liberal party ... 1914 had been the first and 1931 was the second great dissolution of the progressive movement. It was no longer possible to hold all the items of the progressive political faith. Some salvaged one thing, some another. Archibald Sinclair reported in 1933 that 'progressives are more and more beginning to look to the Labour Party as the only possible alternative to the present Government' ... 'Good Labour' had always provided the troops and there was no shortage of progressive intellectuals in the party already. Some young men who were heirs to the progressive tradition reinterpreted a straight-line theory of progress in the light of the capitalist crash and became Communists. Some progressives stayed in the Liberal party, the traditional home. Others withdrew from active politics.[20]

This argument is repeated in and underlies the narrative structure of Clarke's 1978 study, *Liberals and Social Democrats*. Here Clarke traces progressivism beyond the war to its 'burial' in the early 1930s. The titles of the two chapters devoted to the post-war period – 'Hobson's Choice' (between the Labour and Liberal Parties) and 'The Bleak Age' (the 1930s) – as well as their unmistakable tone of decline, clearly indicate Clarke's views.[21]

My difference with Clarke is partly based on an unavoidable confusion of terms, and is to that extent more apparent than real. Clarke often refers to the Progressive Movement as progressivism; I use the same term to denote the progressive tradition. On the Progressive Movement my quibbles with Clarke are as small as my debts are large. It was, as he maintains, essentially a movement towards a 'middle way' between socialism and 'advanced liberalism' which blossomed around the turn of the century, suffered irrevocable setbacks in 1914–19, and was finished off in 1931.

Where I do differ from Clarke is over his occasional tendency to conflate the Progressive Movement with the progressive tradition. This is more or less valid in the period of the Progressive Movement's heyday, but does not, in my view, hold good either before or after it.

The Progressive Movement, from this point of view, may be seen as the form the progressive tradition took during the period in which the Labour Party grew to supplant the Liberal Party as the chief party of progress.

To place my departure from Clarke in a different perspective, I believe that he has underestimated the thinkers and forces within the Progressive Movement which were, during its life, redefining the progressive tradition itself. Like other traditions, and perhaps more than most, the progressive tradition has been subject to considerable change over time. The content and meaning of progressive ideas and the organisational forms of progressive political activity have – at times gradually, at other times suddenly and dramatically, but nevertheless continually – been reconstituted and rearranged. The crises Clarke mentions – the First World War and the formation of the National Government in 1931 – precipitated great changes in the progressive tradition: during and after the First World War many progressives left the Liberal Party and joined the Labour Party; in 1931 many of the progressives in the Labour Party moved to more uncompromisingly socialist positions than they had previously occupied. The Boer War was another major crisis for the tradition, which precipitated, in the form of Hobson's *Imperialism: a Study*, a major theoretical reassessment of its subject; a reassessment which, as I shall show, formed the basis of Labour left thinking on the questions of imperialism, foreign relations, and, ultimately, fascism.

The contribution made by former Liberals to the development of the Labour left is often overlooked. Indeed, the simplistic left-right schema which has dominated political conceptualisation since the French Revolution provides virtually no way to account for it: the Labour Party is to the left of the Liberal Party, but they overlap a little at the boundary; it is therefore only natural that those who leave the left of the Liberal Party slot comfortably into the right of the Labour Party. This view is particularly congenial to historians in the right-wing Labour tradition who are anxious to claim the political 'middle ground'. It is equally congenial to left-wing historians, to whom the entry of Liberals into the Labour Party constitutes a demonstration of the Labour Party's intrinsic middle-class reformism. Thus James Hinton writes from a left viewpoint that 'the wartime influx of ex-Liberals, coming into the party via the UDC and primarily concerned with foreign affairs, reinforced the middle-class character of the party, militating against any turn towards a more industrially orientated political perspective'.[22]

David Howell, writing more generally of the influence of the New Liberalism on ILP thinking, reveals the assumption upon which this school of thought is based. The positions of ILP propagandists, he argues, 'showed a similarity with those of the more advanced Liberals. From the beginning a major stream in Labour's socialism was in sympathy with the existing order.'[23] This is a *non sequitur*. Howell has not troubled to establish whether any or all of the advanced Liberals themselves were 'in sympathy with the existing order'. Howell does not say so, but it is clear that by the 'existing order' he means capitalist property relations. His claim is problematic, for it fails to distinguish differing schools of thought among the advanced Liberals themselves. While it is true that progressives of differing shades of opinion worked together, the point remains that the differences did exist, and – fatally to Howell's argument – that within progressive and even New Liberal progressive opinion there was a school of thought which strongly questioned the existing system of property rights. Admittedly all of the progressive thinkers we have considered supported liberal democracy, but few regarded it as fully realised. For them, liberal democracy in the form they advocated it was a subversive faith. Its full realisation would mean the transformation of the 'existing order' of hierarchical domination.

Foremost among those New Liberals who questioned existing property rights was Hobson. Hobson, who turned seventy-eight in 1936, played no active role in the controversies of the 1930s. He is nevertheless an important figure in the history of Popular Front leftism, for his theory of underconsumption and his theory of capitalist imperialism – both developed by 1901 – made a distinctive and important contribution to the thought and attitudes of the Labour left. The son of a Liberal newspaper proprietor in Derby, Hobson graduated from Oxford and embarked on a career as a journalist, working at various times on all the great organs of progressive opinion, including the *Manchester Guardian* and the *Nation*. His argument that unemployment resulted from a maldistribution of wealth which left the capitalist with more profit than he could profitably invest, and the worker with too little to buy the products of industry, soon established him as the leading economic theorist of the New Liberalism. He opposed the Boer War, which provoked him to write his enormously influential *Imperialism*, in which he argued that the imperialist and anti-democratic tendencies of British society were connected to the economic structure of contemporary capitalism. He was active in the UDC during the First World War and joined the ILP in 1916. Hobson was held in high regard by all sections of the Labour Party, and is not generally thought of as belonging to the Labour left. Nevertheless, most of his work in the Party consisted of contributions to the ILP's distinctly left-wing weekly, the *New Leader*, and it was on the left that his ideas were best understood and most influential. He was also a founding member of the Socialist League – although he played no active part in it and soon left.

The socialist implications of Hobson's theories were developed further in his later works, and still further in the works of his friend Brailsford. Together, Hobson's and Brailsford's works provide the most explicit theoretical statement of the transition from progressive Liberalism to Labour leftism. They therefore constitute the theoretical fulcrum of this study.

The narrative structure of the study is built largely around the major crises that have confronted the progressive tradition and have precipitated progressives' most thoroughgoing reassessments of their political ideas and their political relationships with one another. These crises were dramatic and unforeseen, but it is important to keep in mind that the changes they wrought are readily understandable in the context of ideas and attitudes present in the progressive movement before they took place. To abandon the Liberal Party, and even to abandon liberalism, was not, as Clarke seems to imply, to abandon progressivism. The progressive tradition is not to be attached to any single political party or to any single political ideology.

A moment's reflection on the sheer diversity of the historical figures to whom the progressive label may legitimately be attached leaves no doubt about this. Even if we confine ourselves to a sample of the people who will appear in this book the range is vast: John Stuart Mill, the utilitarian 'individualist' Liberal who was converted to socialism near the end of his life; Hobson, a Liberal who joined the Labour Party in 1916 and who first fully elaborated the theory that international finance was a root cause of imperialist aggression; Norman Angell, who followed Hobson's migration a couple of years later, but who taught that international finance had made aggression irrelevant; the Liberal Idealist philosopher T. H. Green, who believed that the state was the embodiment of its citizens' highest strivings yet refused to countenance its substantial intervention in economic life; G. D. H. Cole, who denied that the state had any claim greater than other associations within society, yet proposed that it should own the means of production; Brailsford, who consistently denounced the Soviet tyranny; Trevelyan, who was one of its keenest apologists.

In the face of this diversity it is not surprising that progressives themselves have shied away from the task of defining their tradition and have taken refuge in vague, almost spiritual statements of its basis. Thus Asquith, writing in 1902 of the 'attitude of hopefulness, of faith, of confidence', which (he believed) the Liberal Party had shown towards social reforms, argued that 'being possessed at all times by this temper and spirit, rather than the possession at any particular moment of a carefully catalogued creed or programme ... constitutes the mark of the party of progress'.[24]

It is in these terms that we must attempt to characterise progressivism. At its heart is a temper of optimism about human beings and social life that makes conceivable – to use Mill's phrase – the struggle for 'the improvement of mankind'. T. H. Green, in a passage whose echo of Mill must surely be intended, makes the claim for progressive continuity this way: 'The nature of the genuine political reformer is perhaps always the same. The passion for improving mankind, in its ultimate object does not vary. But the immediate object of reformers, and the forms of persuasion by which they seek to advance them, varies much in different generations.'[25] Green's term 'political reformer' suggests another aspect of progressive belief, which is that improvement can be facilitated, if not effected, by institutional change.

This admittedly vague characterisation can only be refined by one further point, which is suggested by W. Lyon Blease. Blease, who was clearly influenced by Green, was specifically concerned with liberalism, but his claims for a fundamental continuity of liberal ends could apply equally well to progressivism, as does his attempt to distinguish liberals from other improvers: 'Even when [the Tory] pursues the good of individuals, he pursues it rather in order to make them better soldiers or workers, that is to say better servants of the state, than to make them better in themselves.'[26] Blease writes with a clear polemical intent, and his claims are perhaps exaggerated. Nevertheless, he provides an important clue to a feature of the progressive temper: the Kantian conviction that improvement is an end in itself and requires no justification.

It is difficult to go further than these generalities while avoiding the danger of constructing a definition which would arbitrarily exclude at least some thinkers who must (if common usage is not to be violated) be included. Rather than try to 'define' the progressive tradition, it is more helpful to regard it as a political discourse carried on through historical time. Progressive thinkers locate themselves in their tradition by their attitudes to earlier thinkers whom they and their contemporaries regard as being in some sense their forebears and fellows. This implies something of a circular process. We know that Harold Laski is a progressive partly because he clearly feels a need in his writing to settle accounts with Mill and Green; we know that Mill and Green belong in the progressive tradition because they are among the thinkers with whom Laski must settle accounts.

'Settle accounts' implies neither dismissal nor full acceptance. A writer of Laski's period who merely repeated Millite formulas would be irrelevant, or worse still, reactionary; one who dismissed Mill's principles without offering cogent reasons for doing so, or without referring to other progressives' reasons for doing so, would *ipso facto* place himself outside the progressive tradition. This last point, however, raises the all-important matter of change. Laski was not obliged to develop his own comprehensive critique of Mill; much of the work had already been done by thinkers whose works in turn became part of the canon with which Laski must settle accounts. Simply, ideas are superseded.

None of this is to imply a smooth, unilinear development. Still less is it to impose some neat deterministic schema on the historical events. It is no part of my project to argue that the emergence of socialism as the main ideology of progressivism, and of the Labour Party as its main political vehicle, was historically necessary, nor even that it was ever finalised. While such an argument could readily account for the United Front – for example as a symptom of progressive Labour leftists' final shedding of Liberal illusions – it would leave little choice but to regard the Popular Front as an atavism, a reversion to the earlier days of the progressive movement. Indeed, some of the opponents of the Popular Front made precisely this allegation. But this would be to abandon the central task of finding out why the Popular Front campaign happened when it did.

The task can only be performed it we remain aware that the history of the progressive tradition did not take place in a sealed room, but in the rough and tumble of politics. The major changes in the progressive tradition, although explicable in terms of the tradition's earlier history, actually took place in the context of profound and usually unforeseen political crises, each of which altered both the intellectual content and the organisational forms of the tradition in different ways.

The important point here is that the recurring question of who belongs with whom in progressive politics, and in what sort of organisation, has, as I shall show in the body of the work, been answered according to different criteria at different times, depending on the exigencies of contemporary politics. The period of the United Front campaign was unusual in the history of progressivism in that the criteria were almost wholly ideological. During the Popular Front campaign they were diverse: concrete agreement on the immediate political objective of ending appeasement; recognition of shared ethical values; the continuing existence of a progressive milieu or network of Liberal and socialist intellectuals who worked harmoniously on journals and in universities, who had common memories of joint political struggles, and who were linked by friendship or even kinship.

(v)

This work is an analytical narrative built around the political crises which have reshaped the progressive tradition. Despite the many advantages of a more thematic structure I have chosen narrative because it is best suited to my purpose, which is not merely to point out the obvious parallels between the behaviour and attitudes of Labour leftists in the late 1930s and progressives in earlier crises, but to demonstrate that those parallels exist because the former were the direct political descendants of the latter, even when they were not the same individuals. I aim to demonstrate that the progressive tradition endured, that it never went away. To do so it is necessary to discuss some quite familiar events. The point is to reinterpret them so as to show that they signify – among other things – the central continuities of the progressive tradition. In particular, it is necessary to show continuity across such events as the First World War and the decline of the Liberal Party, which are frequently taken as the nemesis of progressivism. To that extent I have found it necessary to recount some old tales. Throughout, I have tried to strike the right balance between boring the specialist and confusing the non-specialist.

Any short work that aims for a new perspective on seventy years in the history of something as complex as the British progressive tradition is bound to be somewhat selective in its subject-matter. Some important issues and events must be treated illustratively rather than exhaustively; others – apparently less significant – must be discussed in considerable detail. In order that the reader may more readily understand the reasons for the selection and ordering of the events and issues I will discuss, it is desirable to chart the course in advance.

The narrative begins at the moment when the question of the relationship between liberalism and socialism first emerged in the British progressive tradition. This means discussing two developments within Liberalism: the emergence of liberal arguments for state intervention in the economy, and the emergence of a liberal 'collectivist' philosophy. Here I revise orthodox conceptions of the historical relationship between 'collectivism' and 'individualism' by separating them from the concepts of 'state intervention' and '*laissez-faire*', with which they are respectively usually associated. This argument has the negative purpose of levelling the historiographical ground. To put it simply, I regard the orthodox dichotomy between 'individualism' and 'collectivism' to be false and misleading in that it introduces a notion of rupture in the progressive tradition for which I believe there is no warrant, and which seriously handicaps any attempt to show the intimacy of the relationship between liberalism and socialism. The positive purpose of the argument is to show that both 'collectivism' and 'state intervention', which are generally associated with socialism, emerged in the British progressive tradition first of all as liberal ideas. I then consider the ways in which collectivist and individualist ideas freely contended, and sometimes merged, within the thought of the 'New Liberals' and Fabians of the 1880s and 1890s.

The intermingling of collectivist and individualist ideas was reflected in the organisational forms of progressivism in the quarter century before the First World War, when progressives of the Liberal Party and the ILP took part in collaborative activity as a matter of daily routine. Here I offer a new interpretation of the role of the early Fabian Society by arguing that it was not the agent of a novel 'collectivist' doctrine, but the most important of a number of meeting grounds of progressives with various party affiliations and diverse philosophical views. It was in this milieu that the political habits and attitudes of some of the leading advocates of the United Front and the Popular Front – most importantly Brailsford and Trevelyan – were formed.

The Boer War is the first of three episodes I discuss (the other two are the First World War and the appeasement policy) in which a crisis in foreign policy precipitated a major reassessment of the organisational structure and the ethical and intellectual content of progressivism. It caused serious divisions within existing organisations, and led some progressives to contemplate the formation of a new, anti-imperialist party. Ethically, it was the moment at which the majority of the pre-war progressive movement affirmed its commitment to the anti-imperialist principles of forebears such as Bentham and Cobden. Intellectually it was the occasion for Hobson's major restatement of the anti-imperialist position, born of the necessity for anti-imperialist progressives to find an intellectual basis for their opposition to the war that was consistent with their thought on domestic policy. Hobson's most significant conclusion was that capitalism as then constituted was incompatible with democracy and other Liberal values. This argument was taken a step further by Brailsford, who argued that these anti-democratic and anti-liberal tendencies were endemic to capitalism *per se*. This line of thought was central to the post-war Labour left, in which Hobson and Brailsford were intellectual leaders.

The other important contributors to the Labour Party's post-war thinking on international relations to be discussed are E. D. Morel and Norman Angell. Their ideas coincided with Hobson's and Brailsford's on those points where the latter were most in accord with earlier Liberal thinkers, but Angell's theories contradicted Hobson and Brailsford by arguing that contemporary capitalism was a force making for international harmony.

Hobson, Brailsford, Angell, and Morel, as well as others such as Trevelyan and MacDonald, joined in 1914 to form the Union of Democratic Control, the most important organisation of opposition to government policy during the First World War. I argue that the UDC was a characteristically progressive organisation in that it united its participants in a common cause regardless of their ideological and theoretical standpoints. The most noted historical significance of the UDC is its role in conveying Liberal opponents of the war into the Labour Party. This process snowballed after the war, bringing into the ILP not only those Liberals who were in the UDC, but also many others who opposed the post-war settlement, and still others who simply deserted the sinking Liberal ship. A consequence was that most, although not all of the participants in the pre-war progressive milieu were henceforward to be found in the Labour Party. My purpose in discussing these events is to show that progressives' decisions to change or not to change their party allegiance were not determined by any fundamental ideological considerations, but by differing assessments of the parties' ability to promote progressive ideals. These differences were not sufficient to provoke a serious rupture among progressives. It will be shown not only that the habits of cross-party co-operation survived among the seasoned veterans of pre-war progressivism, but that some of the men who came to prominence within the Labour Party after the war slotted comfortably into the enduring progressive milieu. Harold Laski and G. D. H. Cole fit into this category.

I then analyse the intellectual leadership of the inter-war Labour left, among whom are Laski, Cole, Brailsford, and Hobson. The analysis has three main purposes. The first is to show the profound influence of Hobson's thought not only on the Labour left, but also – via Lenin's adoption of much of Hobson's critique of imperialism – on the Communist Party. The second is to show the points at which the ideas of the Labour left conflicted with those of the mainstream of the Labour Party. The third is to show the tensions between the socialist and liberal elements in Labour leftists' thought. These appear most sharply in their attitudes to the USSR and, less importantly, the CPGB, which seemed to embody many of the Labour leftists' socialist ideals while repudiating many of their Liberal ideals.

My account of the United Front campaign is based on the idea that the common ground between Labour leftists and Communists on imperialism led them also to analyse fascism in very similar terms. This analysis was at odds with that of the Labour leadership, with the result that the Labour left's strategy for combating fascism was far more compatible with the Communists' than with that of their own Party. This fact was the basis of the Labour left's willingness to work with the Communists and their desire for unity between the

Communist and Labour Parties. The United Front campaign's anti-Liberal aspect is explained in terms of the Labour left's move towards a more militant posture in consequence of the collapse of the second Labour Government and the inability of British institutions to find any solutions to the economic and social problems of the 1930s. These failures of the system served on the one hand to strengthen Labour leftists' conviction that capitalism was incompatible with the realisation of their ideals, and on the other to increase their attraction to the USSR, which appeared to be making enormous social and economic progress. I conclude by describing and analysing the Popular Front campaign, concentrating particularly on the transition from the United Front to the Popular Front and showing that this cannot be explained merely as a blind following of the Communists' lead. I account for the transition by arguing that the Popular Front campaign was much more preoccupied with foreign policy than the United Front campaign had been. Like the earlier crises in foreign policy (the Boer War and the First World War) it forced progressives to consider their relationships with one another in terms of ethical values and immediate ends rather than ideology. On this basis the proposed alliance with Liberals made excellent sense. Anti-imperialism, however, remained an important value for progressives. One of the purposes of the Popular Front was to forestall the need for a war against Germany under imperialist Tory leadership. This was an important taboo which was not overcome until the very eve of the war. My analysis of the debates within the Labour Party between the supporters and opponents of the Popular Front shows that the latter's incessant appeals to party loyalty were ineffective because the participants in the progressive tradition had always subordinated party considerations to the advance of their ideals, which they now perceived to be under dire threat.

CHAPTER I

The progressive side of politics

Progressive thought in Britain in the four decades preceding the First World War exhibited an extraordinary eclecticism. This is not to say merely that many different views were current which could be classified under the umbrella term 'progressive'; in any democratic society such a statement is a truism. Rather, it is to say that there existed a 'Progressive Movement', which to its participants was a vital reality, and within which many different political and philosophical opinions were freely held and discussed. This discussion was not simply a contest of rival orthodoxies. Indeed, orthodoxies – in the sense of monolithic systems of anthropological, philosophical, social, and political belief requiring the adherent's unqualified acceptance – are difficult to detect in the progressive milieu of the late nineteenth and early twentieth century. It is not merely that Fabians, New Liberals, and others co-operated within the Progressive Movement, but that within each of these groups there existed Idealists and Positivists, ideas derived from thinkers as diverse as Mill and Marx, a baffling range of socialisms and non-socialisms, and an array of 'individualisms' and 'collectivisms' so complex as to call into question the very usefulness of these terms themselves.

The terms are nevertheless deeply entrenched in academic discussion of the period. The major argument of this chapter is that the important unifying themes of progressive discourse before the First World War are frequently obscured by notions of antithesis and rupture which arise principally from the conventional use of the terms socialism, collectivism, individualism, *laissez-faire*, and state intervention. It is crucial to dispose of such notions in order fully to apprehend the theoretical eclecticism and the organisational fluidity of pre-war progressivism, and therefore, as I shall argue, to understand the theoretical and cultural basis of those post-war attempts to unify progressivism of which the Popular Front campaign was the

25

most explicit and important. Before we turn to a consideration of the ideas, activities, and organisational affiliations of British progressives before the First World War, it is necessary to attempt to resolve these conceptual difficulties, for they are, as I have suggested, serious obstacles to our understanding.

(I) INDIVIDUALISM AND COLLECTIVISM IN THE PROGRESSIVE TRADITION: A TERMINOLOGICAL ANTITHESIS

More than most political labels, the term socialism has been so widely used and abused for so long that its use by historians is fraught with difficulty. These difficulties are probably nowhere more acute than in the British context before the First World War, where the term was used by both friends and critics to describe a very broad range of opinions and programmes, many of which would not today be considered socialist. In 1909, Thomas Kirkup, the first English historian of socialism, while considering socialism to be 'one of the most elastic and protean phenomena of history', criticised as 'neither precise nor accurate' the 'growing tendency to regard as socialistic any interference with property undertaken by society on behalf of the poor, the limitation of the principle of *laissez-faire* in favour of the suffering classes'.[1] At the end of the nineteenth century, this type of 'interference' was so widely advocated that to describe it as socialist is to rob that term of virtually any analytic value. Most present-day writers share Kirkup's disapproval of this loose terminology. Many – among them Willard Wolfe, who cites Kirkup to justify his rejection of the term 'socialism' – have sought escape from these difficulties by adopting the term 'collectivism' to describe this type of interference.[2] While it is certainly wise to use some means to distinguish this type of interference from a programme of full social ownership, the term collectivism is poorly equipped for the task. Contemporaries often used the term interchangeably with socialism, and like socialism, collectivism was itself used to cover a wide range of political programmes from minor state interference to complete social ownership. The difficulty cannot be resolved by such a simple semantic trick as Wolfe has proposed.

Further consideration of these and other relevant terms reveals that the semantic problem is far deeper and more complex than Wolfe has realised, or than the customary usage of 'collectivism' would suggest. Moreover, consideration of the political milieu in which the terms were commonly used suggests that the difficulties are not merely semantic, but stem from a too rigid conceptualisation of the politics of the period.

The semantic aspect of the problem lies in an inadequate ordering of the terms most frequently used to discuss the political ideas of this period. Many writers, of whom Wolfe is but one, have used the term collectivism to signify state intervention as though the two were synonymous. Similarly, many writers have equated individualism with *laissez-faire*. Although it is an obvious historical fact that individualist thinkers usually advocated policies of *laissez-faire* while collectivist thinkers usually advocated state intervention, we should not on these grounds simply conflate these terms. It is true that contemporaries often did so, but there is no more reason to follow them in this than there is to imitate their unhelpful use of 'socialism'. In any case, not all contemporaries were happy with this conflation. In a passage which is helpful largely because it exposes the enormous and intricate web of complexity surrounding the whole problem, Ramsay MacDonald – a key participant in the Progressive Movement before the First World War – expressed his dissatisfaction with the widespread use of 'individualism':

I do not like to use this word because it is so misleading. When used as the antithesis of Socialism, the word means mechanical or anarchist individualism; Socialism is itself a theory of individualism because only under Socialism will men be free. For convenience, however, I use individualism in the popular slip-shod way as the opposite of Socialism, because no other word will serve my purpose.[3]

MacDonald's 'solution' is unsatisfactory. Nevertheless, he has clearly shown that the conventional use of the terms 'individualism' and 'collectivism' ultimately conceals more than it reveals about nineteenth-century British politics, for it constructs a simple antithesis which cannot account for the important historical processes of the period. It cannot account for the gradual process whereby many individualist Liberals came to be among the most enthusiastic and influential advocates of systematic state intervention, nor can it adequately comprehend the eclecticism of British progressivism before the First World War, which has been discussed above and which will constitute the subject-matter of this and the following chapter. Still less does it help us to understand the ideas of the thinkers and activists we will encounter later in our study.

Harold Perkin has argued that the conventional antithesis

between collectivism and individualism in nineteenth-century his-toriography is false and misleading. Instead, Perkin proposes two types of individualism and no less than seven types of collectivism. He distinguishes between the two types of individualism thus:

The first, most typically held by Adam Smith, held that the social harmony required if the individuals' interests were not to conflict to the point of social breakdown would be provided by a 'hidden hand', meaning the natural tendency of men's self-interests to supply each others' needs ... The other version ... was that of the *artificial* harmony of interests: men's self-interests were not naturally harmonious ... they could only be made so by the contrivance of governments ... [it] assumed that state intervention was a continuing necessity. It is easy to see why the second [version] should ... lead easily and imperceptibly to more state intervention.[4]

Perkin places these two versions of individualism on a continuum with six of the seven types of collectivism he describes, which range from 'state intervention to prevent obvious moral nuisances or physical dangers not previously considered criminal', to 'the national-isation of the means of production, distribution, and exchange'. The important dividing line in nineteenth-century politics, he claims, was not that between individualism and collectivism, but that between this last form of collectivism and the sixth: 'state provision of a few marginal services'.[5]

   Unfortunately, Perkin's important argument is contained in a rather flimsy conceptual package. Not only is he unable to account for the 'great gulf' that undoubtedly existed between these last two types of 'collectivism' in the nineteenth-century mind, he also seems unsure of how to make use of his two versions of 'individualism' as becomes apparent when he describes them as 'two forms of *laissez-faire* individualism'.[6] Perkin's difficulties stem from the fact that the terms in which his definitions are offered are oddly mismatched. While he defines individualism theoretically, he defines collectivism merely by describing particular types of legislative proposals.

   Perkin's treatment of the problem is nevertheless an advance on many of its predecessors. His insistence on a theoretical definition of individualism enables him to be suitably dismissive of Brebner's claim that 'Jeremy Bentham was the archetype of British collec-tivism.'[7] That Brebner could make this claim is a consequence of precisely that conflation of the terms collectivism and state interven-tion that the present discussion is intended to refute. John Stuart Mill, as well as Bentham, are both regarded as collectivists simply on the strength of their advocacy of state intervention in certain areas of social and economic life. But when Brebner explains these thinkers' justification for this advocacy, the shortcomings of his approach are clearly revealed: 'Bentham argued that individual interests must be *artificially* identified or made one by the omnipotent lawmaker, employing the felicific calculus of "the greatest good of the greatest number".'[8] The crucial point here is that for Bentham, as well as for Mill, the fundamental postulate of social and political thought was the discrete individual engaged in 'the pursuit of happiness'. The fact that both conceived the maximisation of that happiness as a good which could sometimes be secured by the action of the state was neither consequent to nor inconsistent with their individualism but additional to it. This is equally true of Adam Smith's belief in the 'hidden hand' and his consequent support for *laissez-faire*.

Put simply then, individualism is the philosophical belief that each human being is in principle a discrete phenomenon. For the individualist, social life is purely contingent: human beings find it 'expedient' to interact with one another for economic benefit, mutual defence, intellectual enrichment, or simple conviviality. 'Liberty' in this context consists in each individual's right to choose freely the extent and content of these interactions, guided only by its own sense of expediency, and constrained only by every other individual's identical right. It must be emphasised, however, that while a concern for liberty has invariably been fundamental to the structure of belief of liberal individualists, such a concern is not a corollary of the individualist conception of man.

At this level, individualism is clearly antithetical to collectivism which can be defined as the belief that the human being is constituted socially, and that there is no human state, actual or conceivable, that is independent of or prior to human society. In this conception it is of course impossible to generate clear distinctions between the interests of the individual and the interests of the society – except perhaps as dialectical moments. Here too it must be stressed that this idea has no necessary bearing on the question of the state, although it is clear that the terms in which individualist thinkers treat the question are, to the philosophical collectivist, largely meaningless.

The debates between collectivism and individualism were an important feature of British nineteenth-century philosophy, just as disputes over desirable levels of state intervention were an essential component of politics. But between the philosophical ideas of individualism and collectivism and the programmatic notions of *laissez-faire* and state intervention must lie many more specific economic, social, and political postulates. As D. G. Ritchie observed in 1902 when writing on the question of state intervention: 'From a man's philosophical speculations we cannot always predict his attitude in practical politics.'[9]

Today, when the participants in international, party political, academic, and other disputes often claim that their differences have some fundamental philosophical basis, Ritchie's claim may seem to smack of either naïveté or an unattractive lack of rigour. It is nevertheless an important key to understanding British politics before the First World War. Failure to grasp this is at the heart of post-Second World War historians' attempts to couch the political disputes and developments of the period in terms of a simple philosophical antithesis.

A brief consideration of some of the key thinkers in nineteenth-century politics shows that a wide range of views could be argued within both a collectivist and an individualist philosophical framework. It shows also that the increasing popularity of interventionism and the development of collectivist ideas – although related – were not parallel. Neither development was simply a function of the other.

State intervention in the interests of the working class was an established practice in Great Britain before the economic restrictions of the mercantilist era were properly done away with. Much of this intervention could be justified within the framework of *laissez-faire* economics on the grounds that it was intended to protect the position of women and children only, who, it was argued, were not and could not be free agents in any meaningful sense.[10] *Laissez-faire* economists remained adamant in their opposition to state intervention to protect the position of sane adult males; indeed, such opposition was one of the defining characteristics of their faith. In 1844, when the Political Economy Club debated whether 'legislative interference between the Master and the Adult labourer, to regulate the hours of work [is] expedient', there was only one vote in favour,[11] but there is no inconsistency in the fact that of the opponents of such intervention, not one had ever publicly questioned the principle that children ought to be protected. This in no way diminishes their *laissez-faire* credentials, for even concern for the well-being of children was not permitted to undermine the sanctity of the principle of non-interference in adult relationships. Work in textile mills was so organised that it was virtually impossible to legislate for children without *ipso facto* restricting the working hours of adults. Accordingly, the classical economists either opposed such legislation outright, or, as in the case of Althorp's Act of 1833, sought its amendment in order to avoid this consequence.[12]

Among those present at that meeting of the Political Economy Club were many of the figures usually associated with *laissez-faire* individualism. Nassau Senior, Robert Torrens, Thomas Tooke, J. R. McCulloch, all, as one would expect, recorded their votes against the question. Perhaps more surprising is that Edwin Chadwick shared their view. Chadwick is frequently taken these days as an archetype of the mid nineteenth-century bureaucratic humanitarian reformer.[13] This is not without justification: Chadwick was actively involved in proposing and implementing many measures of state intervention, most notably in the field of public sanitation. How is this to be reconciled with his apparently unbending attitude to the question of labour legislation? A clue is provided by the fact that while Chadwick is the best known, and was possibly the most determined of *laissez-faire* thinkers to be interested in reform of this type, he was not the only one. All of the classical economists admitted that there were essential public needs that were unlikely to be provided for by any but public bodies.[14] It was all a question of 'expediency', a notion admitting of so many possible interpretations that a very wide range of views could be held within its ambit. *Laissez-faire* was not identical with the later anarchist individualism of Herbert Spencer, but a guiding principle 'which the great Reformers applied broadly and rationally, not with the stupid narrowness attributed to them by modern critics'.[15]

The core of *laissez-faire* individualism, then, is not to be found in an unbridled hostility to the state, despite the fact that its proponents always demanded an extremely rigorous demonstration of the 'expediency' of any proposed measure of state intervention. Rather it is to be found in their absolutely unshakeable commitment to freedom of contract, which lies at the heart of their objections to legislation to restrict the conditions of labour of adult males. This belief was a direct consequence of their individualist conception of liberty. For as long as the relationship between master and man was viewed as a contract freely entered by self-willing beings, no interference with it could be justified.

The best known individualist advocate of state intervention is John Stuart Mill. Early in his career, while still a staunch advocate of *laissez-faire*, Mill nevertheless recognised that it was the political programme of a time, and not a basis for the organisation of society: 'The laissez-faire ... principle, like other negative ones, has work to do yet, work namely of a destroying kind, and I am glad to think it has strength left to finish that, after which it must soon expire: peace to be with its ashes ... for I doubt much that it will reach the resurrection.'[16] This differentiates Mill sharply from the classical economists, for whom *laissez-faire* was a scientific discovery, and may go some way towards accounting for the acute tensions that appear in Mill's thought on the questions of the role of government, liberty, and justice. Those tensions could conceivably be resolved within the framework of *laissez-faire* by the same logic as applied above to account for Chadwick's social reforming tendencies. Sometimes, however, Mill, if only fleetingly, seems to provide justification for a repudiation of the *laissez-faire* notion that the employer–employee relationship is a free contract: 'No longer enslaved or made dependent by the force of law, the great majority are so by force of poverty; they are still chained to a place, to an occupation, and to conformity with the will of an employer.'[17] This is to ground labour relations in their social context – an enterprise that is not only beyond the scope of *laissez-faire*, but also fatal to it.

Although the passage just quoted was written after Mill's 'conversion' to socialism, it is important to note that in one absolutely critical passage written before his 'conversion' Mill subverted the *laissez-faire* doctrine still further. It appears among the famous 'exceptions to the laissez-faire principle' at the end of *Principles of Political Economy*:

Let us suppose ... that a general reduction of the hours of factory labour ... would be for the advantage of the work-people ... A workman who refused to work more than nine hours while there were others who worked ten, would either not be employed at all, or if employed, must submit to lose one-tenth of his wages. However convinced, therefore, he may be that it is the interest of the class to work short time, it is contrary to his own interest to set the example ... But suppose a general agreement of the whole class: might not this be effectual without the sanction of law? Not unless enforced by opinion with a rigour practically equal to that of law.[18]

By arguing that men's free pursuit of their own self-interest can be effectually restricted by the social context in which they make choices, Mill has introduced a form of reasoning alien to *laissez-faire* thought. By doing so he has overturned the notion of the sanctity of contracts in any sense that would be acceptable to the classical economists.

Mill cannot, however, be regarded as a collectivist. Despite his suggestion that the law should sometimes prohibit people from acting in their immediate individual interest in order to enforce their collective interest, Mill was not in practice willing to entrust such a function to any government: 'the depositaries of power who are mere delegates of the people, that is of a majority, are quite as ready . . . as any organs of oligarchy . . . to encroach unduly on the liberty of private life'.[19] Here Mill flatly denies any notion of a general will. Where a collectivist might see a society or a nation, Mill sees a mere majority. This is important, for it indicates a major difference between Mill's thought and that of the collectivist thinkers to whom our attention will shortly turn. Unlike them, Mill was unable to ascribe an independent life, existence, or volition to anything except individual human beings.

Mill's conversion to socialism in 1869 did not entail a wholesale repudiation of his previous thought. Rather, it was based on the fullest possible development of his earlier denial of the absolute sanctity of the rights of private property, which led him finally to claim that 'Society is fully entitled to abrogate or alter any particular right of property which on sufficient consideration it judges to stand in the way of the public good.'[20] In the same work, however, Mill still held it to be an 'indispensable condition' of progress 'that human nature should have freedom to expand spontaneously in various directions both in thought and practice; that people should both think for themselves and try experiments for themselves'.[21] Even when advocating socialism, Mill adhered simultaneously to collectivist economic premises and individualist social premises. More importantly for the present discussion, Chadwick's and Mill's thought, taken together, indicates some of the diversity of views on the question of the role of the state that could be taken within a philosophical framework of individualism, and suggests the limitations of 'individualism' as a *political* category. An examination of the political ideas of some philosophical collectivists of the late nineteenth and early twentieth centuries shows that 'collectivism' has similar limitations.

Collectivist ideas first appeared in the English liberal tradition in the work of T. H. Green, but the adoption of such ideas by many liberal advocates of state intervention is probably attributable to the pressures placed on their cause by an extreme *laissez-faire* reaction. As has been noted, this reaction, which found its philosophical voice in Herbert Spencer, was far more vehement in its opposition to the state than the classical economists had ever been. Regrettably for the individualist humanitarian reformers, Spencer was able to appropriate to himself the intellectual heritage of individualism. The tensions between the *laissez-faire* and interventionist articulations of individualism had always been present: Spencer's greatest success was to make every act of state intervention appear to be a violation of individualism *per se*. In the increasingly populist political context created by the Second Reform Act, interventionist liberals found themselves caught between the devil of Spencer's self-proclaimed individualist purity and the mysterious deep blue sea of collectivist philosophy. T. H. Green took them wading.

Green was the first English thinker 'to argue the theory of the reality of the common good'.[22] The theory led him directly to overturn the individualist notion of freedom. No longer could freedom be seen as the mere freedom from individual restriction that previous liberal thinkers had placed at the centre of their faith. For Green, the growth in freedom was to be measured 'by the greater power on the part of the citizens *as a body* to make the most and best of themselves'.[23] Society and the individual are thus indivisible. Each person is dependent on every other to maintain an environment in which the individual struggle for self-perfectibility can be carried on.

In this intellectual context, it was easy for Green to argue that 'Freedom of contract ... is valuable only as a means to ... the liberation of the powers of all men equally for contributions to the common good.'[24] As Green well knew, to argue thus was to storm the very citadel of *laissez-faire*, as is shown by his almost casual observation that the sale of labour might need to be controlled in order to prevent its 'being sold under conditions which make it impossible for the person selling it ever to become a contributor to the social good in any form'.[25]

Far from being an object of suspicion, the state, in Green's philosophy, was potentially the very embodiment of society's – and *ipso facto* the individual's – highest aspirations and ideals.[26] Green did not believe that any actually existing state attained this potential. Merely to posit it as an ideal, however, placed an enormous obligation on Green and his followers, for it was the task of the reflecting citizen to assist the process (implicit in history) by which the state would become the perfect instrument of the common good.[27]

Although Green's thought was collectivist in that it posited a fundamental identity of personal and social ends, whose realisation could only take place through each other, his views on state intervention were far from clearly defined. In practice he showed enthusiasm for state intervention in only two areas: the drink trade and land ownership. The former could be justified because alcohol was itself a hindrance to true freedom; the latter because land, unlike other forms of property, was finite, and because its ownership and inheritance were still subject to remnants of feudal custom and law.[28] Otherwise, Green had no objection to the appropriation of property, or even to inequalities in property resulting from inheritance or unearned increment, because he did not believe that either would 'lessen for anyone else the possibilities of ownership'.[29]

As we have seen, Green acknowledged that in Victorian Britain capitalism sometimes did function so as to prevent universal ownership of property. Accordingly, he advocated restrictions on the conditions of the sale of labour so as to prevent this. Nevertheless, Green did not detect any intrinsic feature of capitalism that threatened the common good. Fred Inglis has argued that Green 'lacked the intellectual apparatus of economics', and that 'The deep lack in his metaphysics of ethics was a credible theory of capital's contracts and obligations.'[30] It is to these deficiencies that we must look in order to account for Green's lack of ardour for state intervention. Any attempt to argue that the latter constitutes proof that Green was 'really' an individualist renders his philosophical ideas incomprehensible. Furthermore, it leaves no scope to account for his well-documented influence on the subsequent development of collectivist theories of state intervention.[31] As Plant and Vincent (echoing Richter) maintain:

Green's theories, by direct implication, contained an adequate defence of state intervention in the name of human freedom, to secure that freedom from want without which the moral life could not be lived . . . On the other count, if self development were based upon a free market there was no precise limit to the acquisition of property.[32]

The most important of Green's followers to adopt the latter view was Bernard Bosanquet, the guiding spirit of the Charity Organisation Society. The COS, which dominated social work in London from the mid 1870s,[33] based its approach to social improvement on the improvement of the individual by his own efforts, guided and assisted by voluntary organisations. The direct alleviation of material hardship was only a secondary aspect of the work of the COS. On the whole, the COS believed that 'doles' were harmful, except when specifically designed to tide over victims of specific, temporary reverses.

Although the COS deplored most forms of state intervention, it nevertheless conceived of poverty as a social problem, whose solution – although reached by treatment of the individual – must be sought by the community as a whole, and would constitute a significant contribution to the common good. Plant and Vincent have encapsulated Bosanquet's own attitude to this question admirably: 'The individual must be allowed, through his independence, to make his own will a reality, for only through this "it may be possible for him consciously to entertain the social purpose as a constituent of his will".'[34]

Bosanquet's reluctance to seek solutions to social problems in state action stemmed not from individualism, or from any belief that the interests of the state and individual were opposed, but from the belief that 'So far from promoting the performance of actions which enter into the best life, [the state's] operations, where effective, must directly narrow the area of such actions by stimulating lower motives as regards some portion of it.'[35] This belief fundamentally conditioned the COS's approach to poverty. In practical politics it meant that the philosophical collectivist Bosanquet was closer to the *laissez-faire* views of the classical economists than was the individualist Mill.

It is therefore not surprising that the individualist views of Mill and the collectivist views of Green were both extremely influential in the formation of progressive opinion of many shades in late Victorian and Edwardian Britain. To hold that this period marks progressivism's 'collectivist' break with an 'individualist' past, or even that the period is characterised by a struggle for supremacy between individualism and collectivism, renders incomprehensible the ideas of the leaders of progressive opinion – both liberal and socialist – in the period. As we shall see, all of these leaders were committed in varying degrees to state intervention, and although some based their commitment on fundamentally individualist premises and others based it on collectivist premises, most had intellectual and ethical debts to both. Furthermore, what philosophical differences there were had no discernible effect on the organisational affiliations of these individuals or on their ability to co-operate with one another politically.

(II) PROGRESSIVE IDEAS IN THE LATE NINETEENTH CENTURY

It is with the emergence of the New Liberalism that we may first properly speak of collectivism as a significant political force within the Liberal Party. Its proponents were the first Liberal politicians and journalists to employ explicitly collectivist justifications of the type suggested by Green's philosophical work for extensions of state intervention. In doing so, however, the New Liberals were as anxious as Green had been to emphasise the continuity of their ideas with those of the earlier, individualist liberalism. New Liberals tended to argue that they had not changed liberalism, but merely enriched its central concept of liberty. Green's student, Asquith, was explicit about this: 'A more matured opinion has come to recognise that Liberty ... is not only a negative but a positive conception ... It is in this fuller view of the true significance of Liberty that we find the governing impulse in the later developments of Liberalism.'[36]

This still left the problem of explaining why the earlier liberals had not stumbled across this 'true significance'. The explanation offered by Samuel was fairly typical: 'The whole machinery of government has been vastly changed and improved. A new system has been called into being – mainly through the efforts of the early Liberals themselves – and the State of today is held worthy to be the agent of the community in many affairs for which the State of yesterday was clearly incompetent.'[37] This line of argument makes a mockery of Mill's reservations about state action (which, it will be remembered, applied as strongly to democratically governed states as to oligarchies) and illustrates the rather cavalier treatment that the New Liberals were sometimes wont to give the earlier liberalism in order to claim their pedigree.

The New Liberalism was not entirely incompatible with the imperatives of its predecessors, for although the notions of the common good and positive freedom introduced by Green were genuine innovations, they were not necessarily opposed to the traditional values of individual freedom of thought, speech, and enterprise. In the estimation of New Liberals, these individual freedoms were themselves essential components of the common good. In a passage which Freeden describes as 'an ingenious combination of innovation and traditionalism',[38] Hobson put the matter thus:

The unity ... of socio-industrial life is not a unity of mere fusion in which the individual virtually disappears, but a federal unity in which the rights and interest of the individual shall be conserved for him by the federation. The federal government, however, conserves these individual rights, not, as the individualist maintains, because it exists for no other purpose than to do so. It conserves them because it also recognises that an area of individual liberty is conducive to the health of the collective life. Its federal nature rests on a recognition alike of individual and social ends, or, speaking more accurately, of social ends that are directly attained by social action and of those that are realised in individuals.[39]

With arguments like these, the New Liberals strove to lay to rest 'the pernicious fallacy of [the] antithesis of state and individual'.[40]

The New Liberalism, for all its debts to Green's Idealism, was also compatible with utilitarianism. Hobson believed that Green himself had failed to transcend utilitarianism,[41] but in the eyes of some Idealist New Liberals this was to Green's credit. Ritchie argued that Green's apparent tendency to fall back on practically utilitarian criteria of political judgement was conscious, but that Green had 'a logical justification for applying the test of social well-being to which the Utilitarian, with his Hedonist starting-point, has no claim, and that, having defined the ends as the realisation of a permanent self-satisfaction, he escapes the difficulties attending the balancing of pleasures and pains'.[42]

To suggest that Green's thought was important to the New Liberals is to imply neither that Green's was the only influence on them, nor that his influence extended no further than the Liberal Party itself. Some New Liberals were hostile to Idealism, and traces of Green's thought can be detected even among the ranks of those Fabians who were not simultaneously New Liberals.

For Hobhouse, Idealism was a German import that had 'swelled the current of retrogression', and was 'one expression of the general reaction against the plain, human, rationalistic way of looking at life and its problems'.[43] During the First World War Hobhouse devoted an entire book to the repudiation of Idealism, which he held responsible for the crimes of German militarism. It is interesting to observe, however, that while Bosanquet was flailed unremittingly, Green, as a man 'of real humanity, genuinely interested in progress',[44] was largely exempted on the grounds that his conception of the common good 'far from overriding the individual, assumes his participation as an individual, and, far from ignoring his rights, jealously preserves them as conditions under which he is a free and rational being to achieve a good which is his own as well as the good of society'. While Hobhouse believed that Green departed 'notably from the Hegelian model',[45] his indulgence is indicative of a typically progressive disinclination to make enemies on the strength of theoretical disagreements.

Hobhouse's claim to have discovered a philosophical basis for his support of Britain's involvement in the First World War is dubious. The Idealist philosopher Sir Henry Jones, who was an ardent supporter of the war effort, was naturally severely critical of Hobhouse's book,[46] but Jones in turn incurred the wrath of Hobson – a critic of Idealism and opponent of the war – for his justification of conscription. His Idealist argument that 'the State had a right to compel ... It owned us, we belonged to it', Hobson condemned as 'the pure milk of Prussianism'.[47] But this is to anticipate; the question of the relationship between philosophical and general political ideas and the issues of war and peace belong more properly to later chapters.

Hobson, although he acknowledged Green as an indirect influence on his own early intellectual development, contended that Idealism provided no adequate apparatus with which to understand capitalism. Hobson's attack on Idealism, like Hobhouse's, was also directed chiefly at Bosanquet's version of it, although Green did not escape unscathed. To Hobson, the COS's view that indiscriminate doles to the poor weakened their character was an outrageous hypocrisy:

Are there no other forms of private property which should stand in the dock with 'doles' to the poor? How about gifts and bequests to the rich? Do they too not come 'miraculously'? Are they 'affected by your dealings with them'? Are they 'definite material embodiments of their owners'? ... Mr Bosanquet in his theory of private property has chosen to take his stand by 'origin'; his test of valid property is the way it comes into the possession of its holder. Why do the Charity Organisation Society and their philosophers constantly denounce small gifts to the poor, and hold their peace about large gifts to the rich?[48]

This condemnation of Bosanquet, and *ipso facto* of Green's defence of inheritance and unearned increment, is based on a field of inquiry which to these Idealists was *terra incognita*: economic analysis of capitalism as a system. Such analysis was the core of Hobson's life work. His first serious intellectual project was the production (in collaboration with A. F. Mummery – a businessman whose chief claim to fame was his prowess as a mountaineer) of *The Physiology of Industry*, whose main object was to demonstrate that 'an undue exercise of the habit of saving ... impoverishes the community'.[49] Here was laid out the basis of the economic theory of underconsumption which Hobson spent the rest of his life elaborating. At the heart of the theory lay the idea that pervades the book: the interests of the community can clash with the interests of the individuals who constitute it.[50]

The biographical accident that led Hobson to begin his life's work with a critique of an aspect of capitalism serves partly to account for his unique contribution to the New Liberalism. He shared with other New Liberals a horror at the human misery and waste that they could all see, as well as a desire to refashion the Liberal Party into a political force that could systematically right these wrongs. But Hobson was unique in bringing to the task a coherent analytical framework through which society could be considered not only as a moral, but also as an economic whole. This analysis led Hobson to a striking conclusion: 'A clear grasp of society as an economic organism completely explodes the notion of property as an inherent individual right, for it shows that no individual can make or appropriate anything of value without the direct continuous assistance of society.'[51]

Hobson's use of the term 'organism' was not a casual figure of speech. The 'organic metaphor' was a crucial part of Hobson's and other New Liberals' social outlook. In common with most political and social philosophies of the late nineteenth century, the New Liberalism sought for itself a 'scientific' basis. In turning to biology New Liberals were, paradoxically, inspired by Spencer's use of Lamarckian evolutionary theory to justify his extreme *laissez-faire* doctrines.[52] New Liberal theorists extrapolated an evolutionary argument which placed themselves as social reformers on the side of biology by positing that both mind and social consciousness were themselves products of evolutionary processes. Ethical thought was thus seen as evolving. As Hobhouse argued, 'The turning-point in the evolution of thought, as I conceive it, is reached when the conception of the development of humanity enters into explicit consciousness as the directing principle of human endeavour.'[53] Ritchie extended this idea by arguing that the process by which ideas evolved was also natural: 'The process by which we accept and reject opinion is not merely *analogous to* natural selection. It is that same process in a higher sphere ... The element of consciousness differentiates intellectual selection from biological natural selection.'[54]

The New Liberal notion of the organic nature of society differed from Spencer's principally in that it attributed consciousness to the social organism. The medium of this consciousness was (as it was for Green and Bosanquet) the state.[55] This idea was a modernisation of the notion of the general will, as Hobson made clear:

That the habit of common thought and action among the members of a nation can take place without creating and establishing a common consciousness, a common will and common obligations, cannot for a moment be admitted ... This is the doctrine of the general will, as I understand it ... But what I seek to establish is the admission that a political society must be regarded as 'organic' in the only sense which gives a really valid meaning to such terms as 'the will of the people' ... The common social life thus formed has conscious interests and ends of its own which are not merely instruments in forwarding the progress of the separate individual lives, but are directed primarily to secure the survival and physical progress of the community regarded as a spiritual whole.[56]

The organic and evolutionary arguments taken together gave the New Liberalism its vitality as an ideology of social reform, for this collective mind as manifested in the state was itself subject to evolutionary process as was the individual mind. The name of this evolution was Progress.

While it is important to remember that not all New Liberals subscribed to all of these ideas *in toto* – some of them for example ascribed no reality to the general will – the importance of collectivist ideas in much New Liberal thought should now be apparent. It is therefore time to consider a question that the New Liberals frequently asked themselves. Were they socialists?

The multiplicity of uses to which the term socialism was put during this period has already been mentioned. New Liberals' answers to this question were obviously determined to a great extent by their own individual interpretations of the term. Some New Liberals were content to proclaim themselves socialists on the slightest justification, although they remained staunch advocates of economic competition and private ownership of the means of production. Arnold Toynbee, in a lecture entitled 'Are Radicals Socialists?', provides a good example of this attitude:

The Irish Land Act ... means ... that the Radical party has committed itself to a socialist programme. I do not mean the Socialism of the Tory Socialist; I do not mean the Socialism of Robert Owen; but I mean that the Radicals have finally accepted and recognised the fact ... that between men who are unequal in material wealth there can be no freedom of contract.[57]

This was more frequently the usage of the New Liberals' conservative and traditional liberal opponents. New Liberals themselves tended to be more careful in their usage of the term, and keen to distinguish their own views from socialism. Samuel, for example, argued that the sole 'line of cleavage' between those people whom bravado led him to describe as the 'liberal majority' and the ILP was 'the identity of the principles of the ILP with those of Socialism, and a disbelief that the socialist remedy for economic ills is an effective one'.[58] Here Samuel is employing a 'maximalist' interpretation of the term. On this interpretation, all New Liberals would certainly have denied any suggestion that they were socialists. Many, however, adopted an interpretation of the term that was somewhere between Toynbee's and Samuel's, not using socialism as a term applicable to any form of state intervention in the economy, but neither insisting that the nationalisation of the means of production, distribution, and exchange was the only programme that warranted the title. All New Liberals, and most other progressives, were opposed to 'pure' state socialism. A contributor to the *Progressive Review*, reporting sympathetically on the propaganda of the German Social Democratic Party, was keen to inform readers that 'The accusation of "State socialism" which is frequently brought against them seems to be almost ludicrously untrue.'[59] The accusation, we may assume, appeared to the writer to be a serious barrier between his subject and his audience.

While state socialism was unacceptable to New Liberals this did not mean that members of organisations which officially advocated it were beyond the progressive pale. This was partly because New Liberals' rejection of state socialism was not a matter of fundamental principle. State socialism was seen as likely to lead to economic stagnation and over-bureaucratisation of daily life, and to be based on an oversimplified (because too materialistic) vision of human nature, but it was not seen as *morally* indefensible. The property rights which state socialism denied were not absolutes in New Liberal thought, however important they were to the common good. And while state socialism was undesirable as a general practice, New Liberals could and did make a strong case for its application to many of society's largest enterprises. It was all a matter of degree, which was determined not by principle, but by expediency. In any case, state socialists were rather difficult to find in progressive intellectual circles. Although the ILP held a formal commitment to the socialisation of the means of production, distribution, and exchange, few among its leaders advocated this as an immediate programme or even a sufficient one. As Samuel put it after listing his own objections to state socialism: 'In these qualifications there is little with which the more thoughtful members of the ILP would disagree.'[60]

Surveying the progressive landscape seven years later, Hobhouse put this point on a more general level: 'I venture to conclude that the differences between a true, consistent, public-spirited Liberalism and a rational Collectivism ought, with a genuine effort at mutual understanding, to disappear.'[61] There were, in Hobhouse's view, two obstacles to this desirable harmony, each of which arose from 'distortions of Liberalism and Socialism'.[62] On the Liberal side, 'The principle of liberty may be converted into an unlovely gospel of commercial competion in which ... the promptings of self-interest [are] invested with the sanctity of a stern duty.'[63] On the socialist side,

All the interest is concentrated on the machinery by which life is to be organised ... All the sources of the inspiration under which socialist leaders have faced poverty and prison are gone like a dream, and instead of them we have the conception of society as a perfect piece of machinery pulled by wires radiating from a single centre, and all men and women are either 'experts' or puppets. Humanity, Liberty, Justice are expunged from the banner, and the single word efficiency replaces them.[64]

Although Hobhouse did not specify, his last criticism was clearly directed against the 'collectivism' of the Fabian Society. As such, it is in accordance with the conventional scholarly interpretation of the society's political stance and historical role. That interpretation is substantially correct in relation to the period after the Boer War, which is when Hobhouse's criticism was advanced. Before the Boer War, however, the society's stance was far more eclectic. The Fabian Society, at least for the first fifteen years of its existence, was not the exclusive purveyor of a distinctive doctrine of centralist, collectivist, mechanical state intervention and control. Rather, it was the key ensemble of progressives of almost every shade of opinion. As I shall show in the following chapter, the membership of the Society, and the ideas discussed within it, overlapped extensively with those of the other progressive ensembles of the period.

A brief consideration of the political and intellectual backgrounds and ideas of the early members of the Society reveals that from its inception in 1884 as a splinter from 'a group of middle class suburban Utopians' called the Fellowship of the New Life,[65] the Fabian Society was a striking example of progressive eclecticism. Among its early members were two, Hubert Bland and F. Keddle, who were also members of the Marxist Social Democratic Federation. Another, Edward Pease, was a Quaker who traced his views to the influence of Mill, Comte, and Henry George.[66] Yet another, Charlotte Wilson, was an avowed anarchist and follower of Kropotkin. The society soon attracted some remarkable recruits. Within thirty months of its founding, the six people who together with Bland were to govern the Society during its early formative years, and who – perhaps even more importantly – were to bring the Society spectacularly into the public view with the publication of their *Fabian Essays in Socialism*, had all joined.

On the face of it, it was an unlikely collaboration. When Shaw joined the Society he was an idiosyncratically inclined recent convert to Marxist economics. His friend Sidney Webb was a positivist and 'Millite Liberal',[67] whose 'intellectual grandfather' was Bentham.[68] Webb's colleague in the Colonial Office, Sydney Olivier, had been active in the Christian Socialist movement, while Olivier's agnostic friend Graham Wallas was a 'secularised evangelical'[69] who had heard and rejected Green's Idealism while at Oxford, and whose intellectual attachments were to Aristotle and Darwin.[70] William Clarke, who had been a member of the Fellowship of the New Life, was an admirer of Mazzini, and seems to have discovered Marx at about the same time as he was converted to Idealism through the influence of his flatmate J. H. Muirhead (an Idealist philosopher and member of the COS) and Muirhead's friend Ritchie.[71] Annie Besant, 'by far the most widely known and influential Fabian' of the 1880s had attained her prominence through the National Secular Movement.[72]

These seven very different minds did manage, between 1885 and 1888, to hammer out something of a unified doctrine, which found its fullest expression in a series of lectures which were adapted under Shaw's editorship into the *Fabian Essays*. The diversity of the essayists' ideas are nevertheless apparent in the essays: Wallas doffs his cap to Darwin,[73] Clarke describes the expansion of capitalism in terms strongly reminiscent of Marx,[74] and Bland betrays his Tory background with the alacrity with which he treads on Liberal corns.[75] But the striking feature of the essays is their common rejection of Utopianism and 'Catastrophism' and their belief in 'the necessity for cautious and gradual change'.[76]

This belief entailed a particular method of historical and social investigation: 'Starting from the present state of society, it seeks to discover the tendencies underlying it; to trace those tendencies to their natural outworking in institutions, and so to forecast, not the far-off future, but the next social stage.'[77] A corollary of this was a political practice: 'All we can do is consciously co-operate with the forces at work and thus render the transition more rapid than it would otherwise be.'[78] The three quotations given here have been from Shaw and Besant, but the themes are echoed by all of the essayists, and it is when touching on them that they most frequently refer explicitly to one another.[79]

The claim that socialism as a practice grew naturally from existing institutions enabled the Fabians to claim that socialism as an ideology grew naturally from individualism. In Olivier's essay the two claims are impossible to separate:

Socialism appears as the offspring of Individualism, as the outcome of individualist struggle, and as the necessary condition for the approach to the individualist ideal. The opposition commonly assumed in contrasting the two is an accident of the now habitual confusion between personality and personalty, between a man's life and the abundance of things that he has. Socialism is merely Individualism rationalised, organised, clothed, and in its right mind.[80]

Perhaps the most clearly distinctive achievement of the early days of the Fabian Society was the development of a 'Fabian' economic theory. This was the work of Webb, Shaw, Olivier, and Wallas who, as Wallas described it,

From the beginning of 1885 ... had all four belonged to a little reading circle in Hampstead for the study of *Das Kapital*. We expected to agree with Marx, but found ourselves from the beginning criticising him. Webb and Olivier [understood] the Ricardian law of rent. It was on this point that we first definitely disagreed with Marx ... This led us to abandon 'abstract labour' as the basis of value, and to adopt Jevons's conception of value as fixed by the point where 'marginal effort' coincided with 'marginal utility'. It was this rejection of Marxism which made possible our partial 'permeation' of Liberal and other non-socialist political organisations.[81]

Wallas's observation tells only a part of the story. While it is true that a determined and unanimous commitment to Marxism would have placed a barrier between the Fabian Society and the vast majority of Liberals, including New Liberals, it is important to note that individual proponents of Marxist ideas were not ostracised by progressives of any party affiliation. Furthermore, the theoretical underpinnings of 'permeation' went well beyond this mere negative. So far I have discussed the New Liberalism and Fabianism separately, but it should now be clear that this is slightly inappropriate. New Liberals and Fabians shared essentially the same sources of theoretical inspiration and the same willingness to seek their inspiration from an extraordinarily wide range of thinkers and systems within the progressive tradition, whether individualist, collectivist, socialist, evolutionist, secularist, or Christian.

The habit of theoretical eclecticism was one of the most enduring legacies which nineteenth-century progressivism was to leave to its successors. It had a profound effect on the attitude many progressives later took to the question of the Popular Front. The road was far from smooth, and many strains were placed on progressive eclecticism in the intervening years, strains which in some measure altered the definition of progressivism itself. The habit of latitudinarianism in organisational matters which was eclecticism's natural corollary was subjected at various times to strains no less severe. Indeed, even as progressives greeted the new century, they found themselves in the grip of a crisis which threatened to tear all their organisations apart from top to bottom.

CHAPTER 2

The colours of the rainbow

The focus of the present chapter is the progressive milieu of the 1890s. Its purpose is twofold: first, it aims to show how the lack of sharp theoretical dividing lines within progressive thought was reflected in a lack of sharp dividing lines between the 'ideologies', or even the membership, of progressive institutions; secondly, it considers the major crisis within progressivism precipitated by the Boer War. More broadly, it aims to show on the one hand how co-operation across lines of party and 'ideology' was an established progressive habit, and on the other how war, above all things, was capable of changing such organisational boundaries as did exist, and even of forcing a redefinition of progressive ideas.

The history of progressivism in the 1890s is to a large extent the history of the Fabian Society. This is not to say, however, that it must be the history of 'Fabianism', if by that term we understand the propagation of mechanical schemes to extend state intervention. 'Fabianism' was the doctrine and practice of Shaw and the Webbs, and, influential as it was, it did not represent the sum total of opinion within the Fabian Society, nor even among the original Fabian essayists. 'Fabianism' and the Fabian Society were not, before 1900 at least, coextensive terms.

The argument of the previous chapter should make it unnecessary to say that the significance of the Fabian Society does not lie, as is often supposed, in its introduction of collectivism to unsuspecting Liberals. Rather, it lies in the fact that the Fabian Society was the epitome of progressivism; just as the *Fabian Essays* contained all of the ideas that preoccupied progressives of the time, so the Fabian Society was able to contain progressives of every shade of opinion. In this the Society closely resembled the other institutional locations of progressivism. The progressive newspapers and magazines, the various discussion groups, even the Liberal Party, were open to differing progressive viewpoints.

(1) FABIAN PERMEATION AND THE PROGRESSIVE MILIEU

In May 1890, the Fabian Executive instructed Pease, its secretary, to compile a register of members of the Fabian Society showing their 'particulars [sic] qualifications for work'.[1] The resulting register, which was completed sometime in the middle of 1891, is much more than a reconnaissance report for the strategists of Fabian permeation. It is a unique window on the progressive milieu, which better than any other single document extant reveals the complex interweaving and overlapping of progressive organisations which characterised the late Victorian and Edwardian period.

The register shows, among other things, the organisations in which the members of the Fabian Society had influence, and the periodicals to which they contributed. We may assume that the individual Fabians were members of most, although possibly not all, of the organisations in which they claimed influence. Whether members or not, the register reveals that many of the Fabians had a very wide range of contacts and interests, from secularism to Christian Socialism, from the SDF to the COS.

The register shows some almost incredible juxtapositions. Of the eight Fabians who claimed influence in the SDF, three also claimed influence in various local Liberal associations, a fact which suggests that at least some of the members of the SDF were not as inflexibly sectarian as their leaders. One of these three, Dr Augustus Walker, also claimed influence in the New Road Literary Society, the Christian Kingdom Society, the Chit Chat Club, the Irish Nationalist League, and the Salvation Army Auxiliary League.[2] Although Walker had his fingers in an unusually large and varied assortment of pies, he was not altogether a freak. By and large, the register reads like a catalogue of compulsive joiners. Of the 206 people on the register, 46 claimed influence in two or more bodies outside the Fabian Society, and of these a dozen claimed influence in more than five.[3]

Only in a very limited sense can this wide net of Fabian influence be seen as a consequence of the Society's policy of permeation.[4] As Dr McBriar has pointed out, 'permeation' was a flexible term, which in its general meaning denoted the Fabians' willingness to address their arguments for socialism to virtually any organisation, in the hope that some of them 'would be willing to accept at least a grain or two of Socialism'.5 In its more particular meaning, 'permeation' was a political tactic directed specifically towards transforming the existing Liberal Party into a socialist party, rather than setting about the task of creating a new and separate party.

In its second, more particular meaning 'permeation' was the subject of a good deal of dispute within the Fabian Society. Opinions on the question turned on judgements about the relative strength of existing tendencies within the Liberal Party.6 In favour of the tactic was the obvious fact that, as we have seen, many Liberals were already, without the assistance of Fabian missionaries, moving towards positions that were as 'socialistic' as those advanced by the Fabians themselves. Against it was the equally obvious fact that many within the Liberal Party remained unequivocally hostile to any forms of state intervention that went beyond those specifically endorsed by the classical economists, or at the very most by the pre-socialist Mill.

The debates over permeation in this particular sense have been ably discussed by McBriar.7 For the moment we are more concerned with the more general meaning of the term, upon which the more particular meaning was partly predicated. The principles under-lying permeation in this general sense were best summed up by Shaw in 1896, the year which in many respects was the high-water mark of permeation's success:

The Fabian Society ... has no distinctive opinions on the Marriage Question, Religion, Art, abstract Economics, historic Evolution, Currency, or any other subject than its own special business of practical Democracy and Socialism. It brings all the pressure and persuasion in its power to bear on existing forces, caring nothing by what name any party calls itself, or what principles, Socialist or other, it professes.8

This view did not create the permeating tendencies of the Fabians. It merely allowed the Society to capitalise on the established habits of progressives. By opening its ranks to all progressives regardless of their existing affiliations, the Fabian Society was able to establish itself as the pivotal ensemble of the progressive network – as the largest formally constituted organisation in which Marxists and advanced liberals, radical clergymen and Comtean positivists, single taxers and land nationalisers could all rub shoulders together. Permeation in this general sense, being to a large extent descriptive, caused no controversy within the ranks of the Fabian Society. Indeed, given the diverse sources of inspiration of the early Fabians discussed in the previous chapter, it is difficult to see how the Society could have been established on any other basis.

These observations apply only to a slightly lesser extent to permeation in its more particular sense. Even if it were only a narrow policy of 'entrism', permeation of the Liberal Party would have been impossible but for the relaxed rules and norms of that Party's local organisations. But permeation was a two-way street, for as well as encouraging Fabians to join Liberal organisations, it also enabled, and even encouraged, Liberals to join the Fabian Society. This was the trajectory of many prominent Fabians. William Clarke, for example, on joining the Fabian Society in February 1886, gave his address as the National Liberal Club,[9] and D. G. Ritchie, a Liberal, was inducted into the Society without his prior knowledge.[10]

Almost from the inception of the Fabian Society, its Executive can be seen struggling for permeation on two fronts. On the one, it worked assiduously to damp down disputes within and beyond Fabian ranks in order to maintain the ambience necessary for permeation to remain viable, and in order to keep the Society sufficiently latitudinarian to capitalise on that ambience. On the other, it worked actively to create broad formal alliances between organisations.

This is not to say that the Executive blandly acquiesced in every political tendency to emerge within the Society, nor that it was prepared to co-operate with anyone on any terms. In the late 1880s and early 1890s there were important struggles between the anarchists and the state socialists within the Society, and between the reformists within the Society and the revolutionaries outside it – principally those of the Social Democratic Federation and the Socialist League.[11] Nevertheless, the manner in which these disputes were conducted by all sides was such that they did not lead to an irrevocable burning of bridges. In 1886, for example, in response to the growing strength of the anarchists within the Society, the Society organised a series of meetings which were attended not only by Fabians but also by members of the SDF and the Socialist League. At one of these, Annie Besant brought matters to a head by moving 'That it is advisable that Socialists should organise themselves as a political party' in order to achieve their ends, to which William Morris of the Socialist League replied by moving an amendment that concluded that 'it would be a false step for Socialists to attempt to take part in the Parliamentary contest'.[12] The debate was heated, and resulted in a fairly decisive victory for Besant's motion, but it is important to note that although the meeting was officially a meeting of the Fabian Society all present were permitted to vote.

Even with this victory to their credit, the Executive did not feel bound to expel the anarchists from the Society, and in fact went out of its way to allow their continued participation by forming, early in 1887, a Fabian Parliamentary League, 'which Fabians could join or not as they pleased'.[13] Seven years later, after the Fabian Parliamentary League had 'merged silently and painlessly into the general body',[14] the Executive was still inclined to be conciliatory. When, in October 1893, a poorly attended meeting of Fabian group secretaries resolved that 'The Executive Committee be requested to instruct that members of the Society who are avowedly opposed to collectivist socialism be requested to resign their membership',[15] the Executive steadfastly refused to take action.[16] The leading proponent of anarchism within the Fabian Society, Charlotte Wilson, remained a member, albeit for the next twenty years an inactive one.[17]

Moving the motion to form the Fabian Parliamentary League, Besant 'expressed the conviction that the contemplated League would furnish an instrument whereby the forces of Radicalism and Socialism might be united in criticism and in initiation of practical steps towards their common goal'.[18] The formation of the League may thus be seen as a move on the second front of permeation as well as the first. Not only was the Executive working to preserve the broadest possible basis of unity in the Fabian Society itself, it was also working to create bases for unity beyond its own ranks.

Relations with the SDF, and especially with Morris, remained fairly cordial, for all the obvious tensions between their ideas and those of the Fabian Society. In 1890 Morris lectured the Fabian Society on Gothic Architecture, and one of Morris's lectures to the Hammersmith Socialist Society was printed posthumously as a Fabian Tract in 1903.[19]

In 1893, the Fabian Executive was requested by the membership to enter into negotiations for 'socialist unity' with the SDF and Morris's Hammersmith Socialist Society. The negotiations failed, largely because the Fabian Executive had resolved beforehand that unity was 'not possible',[20] but the very fact of the membership's request, and the fact that such negotiations were possible, alerts us to the existence of the friendly contacts between these organisations which were as much a feature of the progressive politics of the time as were their frequent sharp exchanges.[21] Indeed, the Fabian Society's minutes amply back up Shaw's claim that

The [SDF] rank and file . . . are for the most part our very good friends, as they shew by the freedom with which they help us and invite us to help them in any convenient way without the slightest regard to the denunciations of us in which *Justice* [the SDF's organ] periodically indulges. On our side we take no offence and bear no grudge, knowing too well how often our success has been made easy by their exertions in breaking ground for us.[22]

A part of Shaw's purpose in the *Early History* was to demonstrate that permeation of the Liberal Party was over, and that the Society was moving rapidly towards a policy of independence. His remarks came at a rather sticky patch in the Fabian Society's history, for pressure from sections of the membership to participate in the formation of an independent socialist party was bearing hard on the Executive, as is shown by its acquiescence in entering into negotiations with the revolutionaries of the SDF and the Hammersmith Socialist Society.

The period reveals the inherent difficulties of the Executive's position. It was a relatively easy matter to preserve the Society as a stream into which the minor currents of radicalism and socialism could be drawn; as the 1891 register of members shows, these currents tended to eddy together of their own accord anyway. It was a much larger task to keep directing the Fabian stream into the broad river of liberalism while the latter gave no guarantee of ever reaching the open ocean of socialism.

The first major crisis in the Executive's policy came in 1893. The occasion was the publication of 'To Your Tents O Israel', a bitter Fabian attack on the Gladstone administration's failure to honour its pledges to improve the wages and conditions of government employees. It argued that the Liberals' 'progressive' Newcastle programme adopted prior to the election of 1892, 'had been taken up merely to catch votes, and that the Cabinet as a whole had neither a touch of its spirit in them nor any intention of even pretending to live up to the letter of it'.[23] The only solution lay in independent labour representation organised and financed by the trade unions themselves.

This marked a considerable shift from the position taken up in the *Fabian Election Manifesto* of the previous year, which had warned against the dangers of independent candidatures splitting the Liberal vote, had exhorted socialists to 'always vote, Labour candidate or no Labour candidate', and had expressed extreme pessimism about the capacity of the working class to field viable candidates.[24] Although 'To Your Tents O Israel' tried valiantly to convey the impression that the shift was a long anticipated Fabian deep strategy, it seems more likely that its immediate cause was, as Beatrice Webb confided to her diary, the tactical fright given the Fabian Society by the formation of the Independent Labour Party ten months earlier.[25]

'To Your Tents O Israel' and the Fabian tract into which it was later incorporated caused the resignations of some half-dozen members of the Fabian Society. The most prominent of these, H. W. Massingham, then editor of the *Daily Chronicle* – an influential organ of advanced liberalism – wrote an enraged letter of resignation to Pease, denouncing 'the reactionary proposals concerning the trade unions'.[26] To Shaw he wrote a long letter which included something of a confession of faith:

I have been a permeator all my days, a collectivist Radical working on journalistic lines and that is what I remain. It is Fabianism which has changed and I who remain the Fabian declining (even at the risk of being called a camp follower of the Liberals) to turn a somersault as you have done, to wreck our influence with the Radicals.[27]

Writing to Sidney Webb a fortnight later, he forecast 'the final collapse of the labour movement', and concluded that he thought it 'unlikely that we shall ever work together again'.[28]

D. G. Ritchie also left the Fabian Society over 'To Your Tents O Israel'. His letter of resignation reveals a great deal about the attitude of Liberal Fabians to the work of the Society. It also neatly sums up the way in which the Executive dealt with the obvious contradictions of permeation:

If the Society is to adopt the political policy of the SDF and to become a society for the propagation of Keir Hardies, I do not care to be connected with it ... I had hoped that, with an occasional fling at official Liberalism – to please the gallery – the Society intended to continue with its useful work of permeating Liberalism with Socialism ... and on the other hand its no less useful work of turning useless or mischievous *intransigent* Socialists into practical Socialist Radicals.[29]

To a letter from Pease asking him to reconsider, Ritchie replied, 'much as I regret it in many ways, I am more in my proper place – possibly even more useful to the interests we have in common – outside the society than in it'.[30]

From Ritchie and Massingham in a moment of crisis we pass to Herbert Samuel in a moment of perfect calm. In May 1892, Samuel – who was never a member of the Fabian Society – wrote to Pease declining to contribute to Ben Tillet's election fund because of his lack of confidence in Tillet's ability. Although Samuel claimed that he would donate as much as possible were Tom Mann the candidate, he went on to explain his own attitude to independent labour representation in the following terms:

Nor do I think it would be an advantageous thing were everyone holding advanced views in politics to leave the Liberal Party. It is as necessary to work upon the views of that party from within as from without, and it is to that work that I intend to devote myself. Consequently it is impossible for me to support a man who is running in direct opposition to the Liberal Party.[31]

Underlying all these arguments is a rooted objection to class representation. This, more than any practical difference over the question of 'socialism', was the main barrier between many New Liberals and the ILP. It was, as we shall see, a very important factor in keeping a number of Liberals out of the Labour Party after the First World War. As a number of commentators have argued, New Liberalism can be interpreted as an attempt to 'contain' the growth of labour representation by imposing upon the Liberal Party an ideology of social reform that would, on the practical level, meet working-class grievances sufficiently to keep workers loyal to the Liberal Party, and, on the ideological level, produce a corporate ideology that would counteract the growth of class consciousness.[32] There is certainly evidence for this contention in Massingham's, Ritchie's, and Samuel's comments, but, to anticipate the argument of later chapters, it is important to note that a good number of Liberals did not shrink from joining the Labour Party as soon as they were convinced that it, and not the Liberal Party, was the effective vehicle of their hopes for a just and rational social and economic order.

But Massingham's, Ritchie's, and Samuel's letters have points in common apart from their reservations about independent trade union representation. All describe their organisational affiliations as vocational choices. These choices, furthermore, appear to have been

Table 1. *Departures from the Fabian Society 1891–7*

	i Members in 1891	ii Members in 1891 but not in 1897	iii Col. ii as percentage of col. i
All members	206	85	41.5
Members with any other affiliation	155	58	37.5
Members with no other affiliations	51	27	53.0
Members with Liberal/radical affiliations	96	36	37.5
Members without Liberal/radical affiliations	110	49	44.5

Sources: Fabian Society membership book, n.d. (1891). Fabian Society membership list, 1897.

based largely on considerations of congeniality of particular political arenas, which in turn influenced their judgements concerning the arena in which they were personally likely to be the most effective. The lack of any clear philosophical dividing line between socialism and advanced liberalism, as well as the openness and heterodoxy of the organisations concerned, made the choices easy, for in practice they made little difference. For the same reasons it was a simple matter for the Bristol and Clifton Christian Socialists to drop the word Christian from their title and replace it with Fabian,[33] or for a group of socialists at Glasgow University, having failed to excite much interest in their attempt to establish an ILP branch, to succeed a few weeks later in establishing a branch of the Fabian Society.[34]

This was as true after 'To Your Tents O Israel' as it had been before, for the very simple reason that 'To Your Tents O Israel' resulted in no discernible change in Fabian practice, apart from the fact that the ILP was duly 'permeated' and Pease, as Fabian delegate to the ILP executive, participated enthusiastically. Even Massingham was collaborating with the Webbs only four months after his resignation,[35] which suggests that he quickly recognised that 'To Your Tents O Israel' was, to use Ritchie's terms, a fling to please the gallery.

Most Liberal Fabians seem to have understood this at the time. Comparison of the register of 1891 with the Fabian membership list of 1897 reveals that those Fabians who claimed influence within Liberal organisations left the Fabian Society at a slightly lower rate

(37.5%) than those who did not (44.5%).[36] As Table 1 shows, however, this discrepancy does not imply that the Fabian Society became relatively less attractive to progressives with non-Liberal affiliations. The discrepancy is entirely accounted for by the fact that those who claimed no influence whatsoever outside the Fabian Society left at a somewhat higher rate (53%) than the average (41.5%). Among all those who claimed influence outside the Fabian Society, the rate of departure (37.5%) was effectively the same for those who claimed influence in Liberal organisations and those who claimed influence elsewhere.[37] Insofar as any factor can be said to have influenced people to leave the Fabian Society in this period it was not a specifically ideological one. Rather, the Fabian Society seems to have been more likely to have had a lasting appeal for those who, in one way or another, were generally enmeshed in the progressive milieu. The Fabian Society's openness went beyond the mere fact that its membership was drawn from the whole gamut of progressive organisations, for non-membership of the Society did not preclude close collaboration with it. Samuel, for example, although never a member of the Fabian Society, wrote four Fabian Tracts on local government in 1894;[38] and in 1895, he, along with his close friend Charles Trevelyan – another Liberal who was not a Fabian – and Ramsay MacDonald, then secretary of the ILP, was described by Beatrice Webb as one of a 'certain set of young people all more or less devoted to the Fabian Junta' – that is to herself, Sidney and Shaw.[39]

The unlikelihood that the Fabian Society could ever confirm Ritchie's fears by adopting the policy of the SDF, or propagating Keir Hardies, is well illustrated by Beatrice Webb's reflections on an 'informal conference' in January 1895 (more than a year after the publication of 'To Your Tents O Israel') between the Webbs, Pease, Shaw, Ramsay MacDonald, Frank Smith (who, like MacDonald, was a member of both the ILP and the Fabian Society), Hardie, and Tom Mann:

It was melancholy to see Tom Mann reverting to the old views of the SDF and, what is worse, to their narrow sectarian policy. Keir Hardie ... deliberately chooses this policy as the only one which he can boss ... [Mann] is possessed with the idea of a 'church' – of a body of men all professing exactly the same creed and all working in exact uniformity to exactly the same end. No idea which is not 'absolute', which admits of any compromise or qualification, no adhesion which is tempered with doubt, has the slightest attraction to him.[40]

For Beatrice Webb 'sectarianism' was not merely tactically unsound, it was emotionally and intellectually repugnant. The rapid growth of the Fabian Society in the 1890s, and the corresponding stasis of the SDF, was at least in part due to the fact that permeation appealed temperamentally as well as tactically to large numbers of participants in the progressive politics of the period.

(ii) THE DISCOURSE OF PROGRESS

While the Fabian Society remained the pivotal political organisation or progressivism in the 1890s, it was not the sole, or even the principal channel for the energies of many of the decade's most prominent progressives. The progressive culture of the 1890s was not primarily organisational but literary. Peter Clarke's observation that 'The New Liberalism lived by ideas'[41] applies equally well to progressivism in general.

The ideas were expressed mainly in a rich periodical literature. Like the membership of progressive organisations, the lists of contributors to progressive journals overlap considerably. While particular individuals had their own preferred vehicles, and while each periodical tended to prefer some tendencies of progressive thought to others (the *Speaker*, for example, was more sympathetic to the concerns of traditional liberalism than was the *Daily Chronicle*), none of them existed merely to propagate an orthodoxy. Rather, their purpose was to promote discourse that reflected differing, but broad and overlapping bands of the progressive spectrum.

Some magazines, of which *Nineteenth Century* is the most conspicuous example, did not confine themselves to progressivism, but were open to the entire range of liberal and socialist opinion. Its regular contributors included William Gladstone and Edward Dicey (arch-opponent of 'collectivism') on the one hand and Peter Kropotkin and Michael Davitt – the veteran of Irish nationalism and socialism – on the other. Among occasional contributors were Tom Mann, H. H. Champion (erstwhile comrade of Hyndman and pioneer of independent labour representation), John Burns, Keir Hardie, and Annie Besant. Beatrice Potter contributed an article in 1890, as did her childhood mentor Herbert Spencer. Her brother-in-

law, Leonard Courtney, and Joseph Chamberlain, with whom she
had earlier been infatuated, each contributed three articles in the
course of the decade. After her marriage to Sidney Webb, Beatrice
co-wrote, with Helen Bosanquet and another woman, an article on
'Commercial Laundries' for the Industrial Sub Committee of the
National Union of Women Workers. Presumably the collaboration
was happier than was their later work on the Royal Commission on
the Poor Law.[42]

Other weekly and daily papers with a more distinctively progressive bent were Massingham's *Daily Chronicle*, Lawrence Hammond's
Speaker, and, of course C. P. Scott's *Manchester Guardian*. On all
of these papers the same names recur: Massingham, Hobhouse,
Hobson, William Clarke, Harold Spender, H. N. Brailsford, Henry
Nevinson, Hammond. It is scarcely an exaggeration to say that
every one of these progressive journalists worked on all of the above
papers at some time between 1890 and 1900.

While all of these journals naturally reflected the unifying themes
of progressivism, one short-lived journal took this a stage further
by explicitly attempting to create unity. The *Progressive Review*,
launched in 1896, was the project of the Rainbow Circle, a discussion
group formed two years earlier in order to find an intellectual basis
for progressive unity.[43] Among the circle's members were three of the
Fabian essayists, Olivier, Clarke, and Wallas, as well as Ramsay
MacDonald, Herbert Burrows of the SDF, and the New Liberals
Trevelyan, Samuel, Hobson, and R. B. Haldane. The review's
contributors represented, if anything, a still broader range of
opinion. They included – apart from the members of the Rainbow
Circle itself – Keir Hardie, Sir Charles Dilke, Henry Salt, Havelock
Ellis, Sidney and Beatrice Webb, and MacDonald's friend, Eduard
Bernstein, the German SPD leader.[44]

In the first edition of the *Progressive Review*, William Clarke stated
its task, which was to find 'The synthesis, the unity of principle and
of policy which shall give solidarity of structure, singleness of aim,
economy of force, consistency of action to this medley of multifarious
effort'.[45] Clarke went on to explain that the *Progressive Review* would
work to this end even in its editorial methods: 'Since it is our purpose
to impose unity of thought and endeavour upon the work of criticism
and construction which we essay, and not merely to collect a number
of detached personal judgements, it has seemed best ... to preserve
in an Editorial section a strict practice of anonymity.'[46] Thus the

primary object of the review was to act as a vehicle for a unified discourse which was to be limited only by the wide parameters of the category 'progressive'.

The issues canvassed in the pages of the *Progressive Review* would have been as familiar to readers of the progressive press as the names of its contributors. Its articles on Irish Home Rule, labour representation, the continuing crisis of the Liberal leadership, municipalisation and nationalisation, workmen's compensation, and the decline of individualism would have appeared just as at home in the *Contemporary Review* or the *Speaker* as they did in the *Progressive Review*, which differed from them only in the emphasis it gave to reports on foreign progressive movements, and to the prospects and problems of progressive unity.

The moment of the *Progressive Review*'s foundation seemed propitious. Not only did the Rainbow Circle appear to be pursuing its object fruitfully,[47] but the appearance earlier in the same year of Fabian Tracts 69 and 70 seemed to suggest that the Fabian leadership was as intent as it had ever been on creating synthesis among progressives. Tract 69, Sidney Webb's *The Difficulties of Individualism*, shows Webb closely attuned to New Liberal modes of thought. First he incorporated some of the biological thinking that was, as we have seen, so important to many new Liberals: 'We have learnt to think of social institutions and economic relations as being as much the subjects of constant change and evolution as any biological organism.'[48] Next Webb acknowledged liberalism's traditional distrust of arbitrary power in terms that were to become stock phrases of Labour politicians: 'Irresponsible personal authority over the actions of others – expelled from the throne, the castle, and the altar – still reigns, almost unchecked, in the factory and the mine.'[49] Green was given a passing nod with a reference to 'the expansion of the sphere of government in the interests of liberty itself',[50] and finally, Webb dressed up an argument of Mill's in the latest evolutionary garb by claiming that in the struggle for survival 'No individual can safely choose the higher plane while his opponent is at liberty to fight on the lower.'[51]

Webb's tract's immediate successor was Shaw's *Report on Fabian Policy*, which not only proclaimed the Fabian Society's complete indifference to any question other than 'its own special business of practical Democracy and Socialism', but also took pains to court liberals by insisting that 'The Fabian Society does not suggest that the State should monopolise industry as against private enterprise or individual initiative.'[52]

The ILP too, while not diminishing its commitment to the independent parliamentary representation that was its *raison d'être*, seemed bent on opening its ranks to diverse shades of opinion – a development which delighted MacDonald: 'The most important thing from my point of view is that all oaths and bindings upon members [have been] withdrawn ... It takes away the little Bethel tint from the party and gives everyone liberty of action. It is now as good as the Fabian.'[53]

These high hopes and good intentions were not sufficient to prevent the cleavage that was soon to appear in progressive ranks over the issue of imperialism. The problem was not, perhaps, entirely unforeseeable. Some indication of the difficulties it was to cause appeared in the *Progressive Review* even in 1896, when on the one hand one contributor wrote of 'the great work of colonial expansion',[54] while another asserted that 'Liberalism and Imperialism are, in the nature of things almost antagonistic – certainly not too friendly – forces.'[55] Imperialism was one of the rocks on which the *Progressive Review* foundered in 1897, the others being finance, Hobson's illness, Clarke's depression, and a personal antipathy between Clarke and MacDonald.[56]

In the month of the *Progressive Review*'s collapse, Clarke resigned from the Fabian Society. This too was partly due to the depression that was both cause and effect of his growing disenchantment with politics of all kinds.[57] This depression, although partly temperamental and personal, had its roots in a general downturn in progresssive fortunes attendant on Gladstone's resignation in 1894 and the Liberal Party's electoral defeat of the following year. Gladstone's departure from public life revealed the Liberal Party's lack of any coherent political position. As various cliques of Liberals rushed to fill the void, the Webbs came to align themselves increasingly with those MPs who seemed most determined to turn their backs on the Gladstonian past. These were the 'Liberal Imperialists' grouped around Rosebery, Haldane, Asquith, and Grey. Among the lesser lights of this group were Samuel and Trevelyan. Under these circumstances it is not surprising that Clarke, who had formed the view that 'The real crux of politics is not going to be Socialism and anti-Socialism, but Jingoism and anti-Jingoism',[58] felt himself unable to take 'much interest' in Fabian affairs.[59]

The collapse of the *Progressive Review* and Clarke's departure from the Fabian Society were merely harbingers of the real crisis which emerged on the outbreak of the Boer War. Among progressive organisations, only the ILP survived the crisis unscathed – not because of its new-found tolerance, but because alone among progressive organisations it was united in its response.

(III) IMPERIALISM: THE REAL CRUX OF POLITICS?

Peter Clarke has suggested that the Boer War was 'the context of the separation of the New Liberalism from Fabianism'.[60] The claim needs both qualification and elaboration; not only was the separation far from total, but there were other equally important separations within both Fabian and New Liberal ranks. Just as importantly (as Clarke has also observed) the Boer War created new and somewhat surprising alliances, many of which endured.[61] In short, the Boer War was a crisis in the full sense of that overworked term. It was the first time since the birth of the Fabian Society and the emergence of the New Liberalism that Britain had been at war, and therefore the first time that progressivism in its late nineteenth-century form had been obliged to give serious attention to questions of foreign policy. This marked a turning point which not only redefined the relationships between organisations and creeds, but also precipitated redefinition of the creeds themselves.

The Fabian Society's status as the pivotal organisation of progressivism was severely and irreparably compromised – although not entirely destroyed – by the South African imbroglio. As usual, the Executive tried bravely to contain the damage, and in this it was probably as successful as circumstances allowed. The majority of the Executive tried at first to shy away from the issue altogether on the grounds that the Society was insufficiently informed to make a judgement. Olivier responded angrily to this and demanded that the issues be fully canvassed and the Fabians' position declared.[62] This was attempted at a meeting on 8 December 1899, but the results were so unsatisfactory that Olivier resigned from the Executive within the week.[63]

The two motions that were put at this meeting contained the essence of the opposed positions on the war taken by progressives both inside and outside the Fabian Society. The first, put by S. G. Hobson,[64] condemned the war as a commercial and militarist escapade, and declared that 'The phase of Imperialist expansion that has overrun this country of recent years, and is the chief cause of the war, has distracted the attention of the nation from domestic progress, [and] has debased the conscience and lowered the democratic spirit of the English people.'[65] Shaw's motion, which was more ambiguously framed, was predicated on the belief that the war was a result of 'a lofty and public-spirited Imperialism', but carried the warning that it was necessary to insist that 'the advance in liberty and good government for which we are professedly fighting shall not be lost sight of in the hubbub of party recrimination, theatrical patriotism, and financial agitation'.[66] Hobson's motion was defeated narrowly. Shaw's – despite the support of a majority of the Executive – was defeated by a two-thirds majority.

The Society was thus left without a declared position on the biggest political question of the day. As it was clear that there was no hope of the Society's declaring in favour of the war, the Executive's next best option was to preserve this status quo by falling back on the principles of Tract 70 and declaring that the war was 'outside the special province of the society'.[67] When MacDonald proposed a postal ballot designed to establish whether the members favoured the Society taking a position on the war, and if so, whether the position should be for or against, the Executive, possibly fearing a further demonstration of the strength of anti-imperialist feeling, allowed only the first question to be put.[68] On this question, the members decided by 259 votes to 217 that the Society should take no official stance on the war.[69]

This was precisely the possibility that had most frightened Olivier at the outbreak of the war:

If the society should suppose or the executive should suppose that the question of this war in South Africa does not concern it . . . it will mean that the dry-rot that has collared the Liberal Party, and has shown us the Heaven-sent figures of Haldane, Grey, Asquith etc. distended, for all future efficiency, with political sawdust, whilst old bituminous mummies like Morley and Courtney are regurgitated alive out of the tomb – has also got well hold of the Fabian Society, and that really there is no further reason for its continued separate existence.[70]

The full irony of Olivier's warning was realised as the controversy over the war developed, and as the alliances it created became more peculiar. Nevertheless, the decision not to pronounce on the war was the least divisive course the Society could have taken. Although about two dozen members resigned in consequence, many who were ardent opponents of the war kept up their membership, apparently satisfied that the Society had at least not come out in support of the war.

Among those who resigned from the Fabian Society once the result of the ballot was known were several prominent members including MacDonald and his wife, Henry Salt, Mrs Pankhurst, Pete Curran of the ILP, Walter Crane, and H. N. Brailsford.[71] Some of them became active in anti-war organisations. Salt and Crane joined the South Africa Conciliation Committee, and Brailsford joined both it and the League of Liberals against Aggression and Militarism.

Altogether, five Fabians joined the LLAAM and twenty-one joined the SACC. Brailsford, the Rev'd Dr John Clifford (a Christian Socialist), and H. D. Pearsall joined both, giving a total of twenty-three members of the Fabian Society whose opposition to the war was strong enough to drive them to organised activity. Thirteen of these people, however, stayed in the Fabian Society through the crisis and were still members in 1904.[72] This is especially significant given the fact that of the 807 people on the Fabian membership list in 1897, 454, or 56% had left by 1904. Thus, among some of the most committed Fabian opponents of the Boer War, the rate of departure from the Society (43.5%) was slightly below the average.

Both of these organisations were predominantly Liberal in composition, the League more so than the Committee. Both were curious coalitions of New Liberals and socialists such as Hobson, Massingham, and William Clarke on the one hand, and traditional 'Gladstonian' Liberals like Courtney and Harold Spender on the other. Their membership overlapped considerably: of 743 members of the SACC and 251 members of the LLAAM, 98 people were members of both. Twenty-two of the forty-two-strong Executive committee of the LLAAM were members of the SACC.[73]

Not surprisingly, the propaganda of the two bodies was virtually indistinguishable. Both emphasised the atrocities involved in the British conduct of the war, compared British policy in South Africa unfavourably with the Gladstonian tradition of foreign policy, and stressed the financial and human cost of the war and the damage it did to the prospects of social reform at home. The principal difference between the two organisations was that while the League worked 'To press forward in the councils of the Liberal Party the policy of peace, retrenchment, and reform which has been handed down to us by the greatest leaders of that Party',[74] the SACC aimed its propaganda at the wider public.

The war led to still more unlikely alliances outside the formal anti-war organisations. Both the ILP and the SDF opposed the war, and their opposition led them to give public support to men like Courtney, whose opposition to all forms of state intervention had previously marked them as opponents, and whose presence within the Liberal Party had constituted a powerful argument for the establishment of the Independent Labour Party. As a result of the war Ramsay MacDonald even found himself the recipient of advice and practical assistance from the Quaker radical George Cadbury.[75]

The crisis gave rise, in the minds of some progressives, to the idea of completely redrawing the landscape of progressive politics. Stanton Coit, the leading figure of the Union of Ethical Societies, proposed to MacDonald the formation of 'a new party – "The Democratic Party" ... into which men like Hobson would throw themselves',[76] and Morris's old friend Walter Crane, writing to MacDonald of his disgust at the imperialism of the Fabian Executive, concluded, 'The SDF and the ILP are at all events thoroughly sound on this question. It would be a good thing to unite with them and the other organisations who are working against the war and the policy which dragged us into it.'[77]

The most serious initiative in this direction came through the *Ethical World*, of which Coit and Hobson were editors. The *Ethical World* was the organ of the South Place Ethical Society – another important location of progressive activity. In common with the other Ethical Societies, of which the London Ethical Society (dominated by Bosanquet, Muirhead, and R. B. Haldane) was perhaps the most important, South Place sought to replace deism with a secular and rationalist basis for ethical belief.[78] It served as a venue for political lectures and discussions on a broad range of progressive themes. Its three salaried lecturers, whose task was to take the ethical message to the provinces, were themselves a tribute to the political diversity of the Society. Hobson was one; the others were the New Liberal J. M. Robertson and Herbert Burrows of the SDF – all members of the Rainbow Circle.[79] Other members of South Place included Massingham, Clarke, and MacDonald.

Among the contributors to the *Ethical World* in its first two years (1888-9) were its editors Hobson and Coit, and Bosanquet, Muirhead, MacDonald, Burrows, Robertson, and W. S. Sanders, who was simultaneously a member of the Fabian Society and the SDF. In 1900, with the closing off of some sections of the progressive press to 'pro-Boer' opinion, a flood of new writers appeared in its columns. Conspicuous among them was Massingham, who had lost the editorship of the *Daily Chronicle* over his stance on the war. Others included Clarke, Walter Crane, Kate Courtney (wife of Leonard and sister of Beatrice Webb), S. G. Hobson, H. M. Hyndman, Herbert Spencer, Keir Hardie, and Edward Carpenter. The paper generally reflected the 'pro-Boer' stance of its editors, but even here it is important to note that some supporters of the war such as Shaw and D. G. Ritchie, who wrote a number of articles supporting the war, also made their first appearance in 1900.

It was Massingham who led the attempt to refashion progressive politics during the war. His proposal for a 'Democratic Convention' of 'Co-operators, Trade Union leaders, Socialist and Independent Labour men, the youngest and more progressive of the Free Church ministers, the Irish voters, and the pick of the radical Club men'[80] to organise a common fight in the next election met with a chorus of approval from representatives of all the bodies he mentioned. A. E. Fletcher, Massingham's predecessor as editor of the *Daily Chronicle*, set out the arguments in terms very similar to the arguments for a Popular Front which we will encounter at the end of this study. Fletcher explained that ILP leaders had objected to the idea on the ground that there were no Liberal MPs worth having as members of a Democratic Party. He conceded the point, but went on to argue that it would not be difficult

to name at least a score of Radical members ... who, while unwilling to accept the Marxian programme[!], would gladly co-operate with the Socialists for definite ends at elections. The next General Election will turn upon the foreign and colonial policy of the Government, especially as considered in reference to its postponement of progressive legislation at home, and I think it would be great folly on the part of the leaders of the various sections of the Progressive Party, whether Radical Democrats or Social Democrats, if they opposed each other's candidates who are pledged up to the hilt against the South African iniquity.[81]

The Liberal leadership, unlike the Fabians, could not, as aspirants to the government of the empire, simply claim that the issue was not their concern. The result was farcical, as different sections of the Party and its leadership gave private utterance to mutually hostile positions, while publicly swearing their mutual loyalty. The atmosphere within the Party became, if anything, more bitter than that within the Fabian Society, as is illustrated by the differing treatment the Liberal Imperialists and the Fabian Executive gave to Emily Hobhouse, who was one of the most energetic and effective publicisers of British atrocities in the war. While the 'Limps' tended to disparage her evidence, to the point where her brother, L. T. Hobhouse, felt obliged to write rather sharply to Trevelyan defending her standing as 'an extremely candid and scrupulous person',[82] the Fabian Executive was happy to distribute bills advertising her meetings at a meeting of the Fabian Society.[83]

The decisive moment for the Liberal Party came when its leader, Sir Henry Campbell-Bannerman, condemned the British 'methods of Barbarism in South Africa' in a speech to the National Reform Union in June 1901. Campbell-Bannerman had previously avoided making any strong statement in order to prevent exacerbating the divisions within his Party. His now famous speech was the signal for a vigorous attack on the 'pro-Boers' (as the opponents of the war were half inaccurately dubbed) by both the Liberal Imperialists and Sidney Webb. Until Campbell-Bannerman's speech, Webb had occupied a 'middle position' of resignation to the regrettable necessity of the war.[84] In July 1901, however, he accepted an invitation to a dinner held to honour Asquith for his open breach with Campbell-Bannerman. Webb's logic in accepting the invitation was simple: 'Haldane and Asquith are at least not hostile to our views: the others are. I will go.'[85]

A week after this dinner, at which both Asquith and Rosebery made speeches denouncing 'Gladstonianism', Beatrice Webb analysed the new political situation in her diary:

Rosebery's business is to destroy Gladstonians. Whether or not he is to become a real leader depends on whether he has anything to put in the place of a defunct Liberalism. Mere Imperialism will not do ... Now supposing he fails ... to be constructive, then he leaves the field open to Asquith, Grey, and Haldane with a great deal of the rubbish cleared away ... Meanwhile GBS [haw] writes urging us to plunge in with Rosebery as the best chance of moulding home 'policy'.[86]

Sidney Webb's response to Shaw's urging appeared in the *Nineteenth Century* in September, under the eccentric title 'Lord Rosebery's Escape from Houndsditch'. It was clearly based on an analysis similar to Beatrice's. After attributing the Liberal Party's electoral failures to the irrelevance of the Gladstonians' 'atomic conception of society' in a society which had 'become aware . . . that we are not mere individuals but members of a community',[87] Webb went on to put an analogous argument on imperial questions.

For the very reason that these races are assumed to have ends which differ from, and perhaps conflict with, those of the British Empire as a whole, it is asserted that they must, in justice, be allowed to pursue those ends at whatever cost to themselves and to their neighbours . . . What, in the name of common sense have we to do with obsolete hypocrisies about peoples 'rightly struggling to be free'? Our obvious duty with the British Empire is deliberately so to organise it as to promote the maximum development of each individual state within its bounds.[88]

Webb was correct to point out that the most prominent opponents of imperialism had traditionally been staunch individualists and supporters of *laissez-faire*. Jeremy Bentham had urged Britain to give up its colonies on the grounds that it had no right to govern foreign peoples and that the financial cost of keeping colonies was 'ruinous'.[89] But the man who gave his name to the tradition of anti-imperialism and 'non-intervention' was Richard Cobden. Intellectually, Cobdenism was intimately connected with *laissez-faire*. Its central plank of international free trade was based on the view that the state had no right to interfere in any economic transaction, whether it crossed national boundaries or not. If left to itself international trade would find a natural equilibrium from which all nations would benefit. The other main components of the Cobdenite tradition flowed from the traditional Liberal 'individualist' distrust of the state. Imperialism and an aggressive foreign policy required a large army and navy, which was objectionable not only because it entailed high taxes, but also because it increased the power of the state; in particular, it increased the power and prestige of the aristocracy who traditionally dominated the services and who thereby had a vested interest in war.

While Gladstone and other Liberal individualists subscribed to these views, they sometimes allowed moral zeal – the desire to impose what they regarded as justice – to override them in the practical conduct of foreign policy. The Gladstonian legacy on foreign and imperial policy was therefore highly ambiguous. While Gladstone often appealed to the rhetoric of national rights, his actions in foreign policy provided plenty of precedents for British intervention in other nations' affairs, conspicuously, the British invasion of Egypt in 1882, which Gladstone justified in terms of Britain's 'duty' to restore order.[90]

To a true Cobdenite, such justification was entirely specious. As early as 1858, John Bright, Cobden's friend and close political ally, denounced such departures from what in his opinion were true Liberal principles: 'The idea is now so general that it is our duty to meddle everywhere, that it really seems as if we [Liberals] had pushed the Tories from the field, expelling them by our competition.'[91] This was no casual complaint. It was Bright himself who provided the most concrete demonstration of the distance between Cobdenism and Gladstone's foreign policy by resigning from Gladstone's cabinet over the invasion of Egypt.

Webb therefore used too broad a brush when he attributed the attitudes of the 'pro-Boers' to Gladstonianism. It was not true that by opposing the Boer War 'the majority of the Socialist leaders proved to be . . . mere administrative Nihilists – that is to say, ultra-nationalist, ultra-Gladstonian, old-Liberal to their fingertips'.[92] Rather, it meant merely that no coherent socialist or New Liberal argument against imperialism had as yet been devised. This lack was soon remedied, as we shall see in the next chapter, but the fact that the 'pro-Boer' progressives did allow themselves, temporarily, to be identified with outmoded political views alerts us to the supremely important, quintessentially Gladstonian characteristic of their position. It was ethical.

Webb recognised this and mocked it: 'Moral superiority, virtuous indignation, are necessaries of political life to them: a Liberal reform is never simply a social means to a social end, but a campaign of Good against Evil.'[93] This was the truth, and by putting it this way Webb amply demonstrated the nature of the rupture among the progressives. This became still clearer as he went deeper into the question of ends and means. Underlining his proximity to the Liberal Imperialists, Webb quoted Asquith to justify his demand for a programme of National and Imperial 'Efficiency'.

What is the use of an Empire if it does not breed and maintain in the fullest sense of the word an Imperial race? What is the use of talking about Empire if here, at its very centre, there is always to be found a mass of people, stunted in education, a prey to intemperance, huddled and congested beyond the possibility of realising in any true sense either social or domestic life?[94]

Here Webb was clearly nailing his colours not only to the Liberal Imperialist mast, but more generally to the mast of 'National Efficiency', a catchcry that enjoyed a considerable vogue among prominent politicians of all parties, among them Lloyd George, Winston Churchill, Joseph Chamberlain, and the Liberal Imperialists themselves. The advocates of National Efficiency based their arguments principally on instrumentalist considerations of Britain's future as an economic and military great power, and drew extensively on Bismarckian models of social reform.[95]

Here we are face to face with a key distinction between progressivism and its rivals. As we saw in the first chapter, one of the defining characteristics of the progressive tradition was the pursuit of 'improvement' for its own sake rather than as the means to produce – in Blease's phrase – 'better servants of the State'. The Liberal and Fabian Imperialists placed themselves on the wrong side of this line; a fact which Webb's claims to theoretical consistency only emphasised. The opponents of the Boer War were, as we have seen, a political ragbag held together only by their shared ethical convictions that Britain's attempt to suppress a small nation was wrong, and militarism was inherently evil. The fact that the progressive tradition's loudest opponents of empire and militarism – men like Bentham and Richard Cobden – had also been among its staunchest 'individualists' was irrelevant. The important point was that the mainstream of the Progressive Movement responded instinctively to the crisis with a thundering affirmation of the progressive tradition's ethical opposition to imperialism. Those like the Webbs and Asquith, whose instincts did not produce this response, were henceforward peripheral to the tradition. They are, therefore, peripheral to the remainder of this study.

The Boer War, and the Fabian Junta's attempt to seek alliances with the Liberal Imperialists, was the context in which 'Fabianism' first began to take its now customary (and often pejorative) meaning. It was distinguished from other brands of social reformism less by its collectivism – for as we have seen, the non-Fabian varieties had that in full measure – but by its instrumentalism; its willingness to subsume the traditional ethical concerns of progressivism to 'its own special business of practical Democracy and Socialism'.[96] The principles of Tract 70 were thus Fabianism's greatest weakness as well as its greatest strength.

The commitment of the Fabian leaders – especially Shaw and the Webbs – to an instrumentally conceived version of state socialism strengthened in the ensuing years, and cost them the support of many progressives as it led them to take up positions offensive to the Liberal conscience on questions such as education and free trade. This did not alienate only Liberals; on many issues – not only free trade and education, but temperance reform and Irish Home Rule – the Liberal conscience was identical to the progressive conscience, and, for that matter, the ILP conscience. As Graham Wallas put it when a Fabian Tract repudiating free trade[97] provoked his resignation from the Society: 'On the issues which divide the Liberal and Conservative Parties I am a Liberal.'[98]

Important as these developments were, they did not immediately bring an end to all co-operation between imperialist and anti-imperialist progressives. Although the Fabian Society's membership began to decline for the first time in its history after the Boer War, this was both slight and temporary. Although a significant number of important members left over the war, many more stayed, and the Society did not split. Although the leadership's relations with other progressives both inside and outside the Society were severely strained, they were not terminated. Networks of social intercourse, as well as co-operation in projects like the London School of Economics, continued to bind the Fabian 'Junta' to the progressive milieu. More significantly, the Fabian leaders' serious differences with the ILP and the SDF over the war did not prevent their participating together – in the midst of the crisis – in the formation of the Labour Representation Committee, an event, incidentally, which appears to have caused no heartache for Fabian Liberals.

The Boer War also gave a new and sharper definition to the New Liberalism. New Liberalism was always a flexible term, and prior to the war several of the Liberal Imperialists, as advocates of systematic state intervention, had been identified with it. Henceforward, men like Asquith and Samuel were no longer to be considered as belonging in the same camp as opponents of the war, although again, this did not prevent men like Hobson and Hobhouse, together with the ILP, lauding the Asquith Government's social reforms or supporting it in its struggle with the Lords in 1909-11. If the Boer War was the context of the separation of the New Liberalism from Fabianism, it was also, to the same degree, the context of its separation from what was to become the dominant strand of official

Liberalism. More importantly, it was the moment at which anti-imperialism first emerged as a defining characteristic of the new, 'collectivist' progressivism, a characteristic which was to determine the shape of progressive alliances until 1940.

CHAPTER 3

Imperialism and war

Progressives' anti-imperialist instincts, however powerfully felt, could not in themselves bring about lasting changes to the contours of progressivism. To do so they required organisational and theoretical expression. The lasting effects of the Boer War on the progressive milieu and its organisations can only be seen as detrimental: relationships between individuals were strained; debates in the Rainbow Circle were heated and repetitive; the Fabian Society was severely and irreparably debilitated, but neither side of the struggle was able to produce a new, permanent organisation or alliance to replace existing ones. On the pro-war side the Fabian Junta's attempt to 'permeate' the Liberal Imperialists quickly proved a failure, destroyed by, among other things, the Fabians' support for the Education Act of 1902.[1] On the anti-war side, organisations like the SACC and the LLAAM lasted only as long as the war itself; and it is hardly necessary to add that the spectacle of SDF militants defending Morley's meetings was never to be repeated once the war was over. The hopes of men like Massingham and Coit for a new organisation of anti-imperialist 'democrats' came to nothing. Moreover, the Fabian defections apart, the Boer War gave rise to no substantial change in the composition or relative strengths of the major political organisations to which progressives adhered.

It took the far graver crisis of the First World War and its aftermath to precipitate major changes in the organisational balance of progressivism. The most important vehicle of opposition to the Government's wartime policies, the Union of Democratic Control, like the SACC, began as a committee of Liberals and ILP members who, from differing viewpoints, opposed the Government's war policy. This time, however, the coalescence was permanent. Within two years of the cessation of hostilities the entire leadership of the

UDC was in the ILP, as were many other Liberals, who gave up on their old Party in the post-war years.

The consequences of the Boer War for the development of progressive ideas were both profound and lasting. From within the ranks of the New Liberalism, Hobson was to produce *Imperialism: a Study*,[2] a statement of a progressive anti-imperialist position which was to shape progressive opinion for decades to come. Hobson's political biography neatly epitomises the contrast between the two wars: while the Boer War moved him to theoretical innovation it did not force him out of the Liberal Party; while the First World War saw him leave the Liberal Party for the ILP it did not lead him to adopt any new theoretical position. Other Liberal thinkers who contributed ideas to the opposition to the First World War and the Treaty of Versailles described a similar trajectory. Like Hobson, their theoretical positions were established before that war began; like Hobson, it took the war itself to move them into the ILP. In short, the theoretical apparatus with which progressives constructed their criticisms of the Government's foreign policy during and immediately after the First World War was available before hostilities commenced, but for many progressives the voicing of those criticisms made their position in the Liberal Party untenable. It was in the context of this organisational change that the new ideas precipitated by the Boer War had their full political effect.

The theoretical developments of 1900–14 and the organisational developments of 1914–21, which together determined the shape of inter-war progressivism and thus the ways in which progressives understood and acted on the rise of fascism and the threat of war in the 1930s, are the subject of this and the following chapter. The ideas involved are complex and the events untidy. In order to make sense of the discussion therefore, it will be useful to begin with a brief outline of some of the major points, and to foreshadow the picture of progressivism that will emerge from it.

During the years 1914–20 progressives reiterated their anti-imperialist and anti-militarist commitment. This was not the exclusive property of those who opposed the war, nor even of those who joined the Labour Party after it. Rather, as I shall show in the next chapter, it was the common characteristic of those who opposed the punitive and imperialistic character of the post-war settlement.

By 1920 most of these people were members of the Labour Party, and of those within the Labour Party almost all were members of the

ILP, which had worked closely with Liberal progressives in the UDC, and which was the first party to declare its opposition to the terms of the peace. The ILP's formal commitment to socialism did not deter many Liberals from joining, largely because the range of views on socialism among ILP members within the pre-war ILP was about the same as the range within the broad progressive milieu in which most of the ILP leaders were participants.

Nevertheless, the left of the Labour Party had always had its home within the ILP, and had been a powerful force there. But the war transformed this left. Before the war it was distinguished from the rest of the ILP largely by the militancy of its rhetoric. After the war it was distinguished also by its commitment to a particular analysis of imperialism, which derived ultimately from the thought of Hobson, who joined the ILP during the war. Thus, one of the principal components of the thought of the inter-war Labour left was derived from a leading New Liberal theorist of the pre-war progressive milieu.

Pre-war progressivism supplied ideas not just to the Labour left, but to the whole of the ILP. The ideas of Edmund Dene Morel and Norman Angell – both Liberals – were also incorporated into the ILP repertoire during and shortly after the First World War. As we shall see, however, Angell's and Morel's ideas, unlike Hobson's, did not imply any sort of socialist critique of contemporary society. This is not to suggest that there was a neat division between Hobsonites and others within the ILP; people from all sections of the Party borrowed freely from the arguments of all three men, as did those opponents of the peace who chose, for reasons we shall examine in the following chapter, to remain within the Liberal Party. The point remains, however, that Hobson's theory of capitalist imperialism was far more influential on the left of the ILP than elsewhere, and became one of the central defining characteristics of the labour left.

Progressives carried more than theories into the Labour Party. They took also a set of habits and attitudes towards organisations and the conduct of political activity and discourse. Indeed, the very fact that they transferred their allegiance to the Labour Party owed a great deal to the attitudes and habits discussed in the earlier chapters. These too had a profound effect on the nature of the post-war left, for they meant that even those progressive Liberals who later formed a part of the Labour left kept up a fairly constant intercourse with those who remained in the Liberal Party. Indeed, the progressives of the Labour left worked more closely and harmoniously with their fellows in the Liberal Party than with the right wing trade unionists who were nominally among their comrades.

The present chapter deals with the theoretical aspects of the processes just sketched. It analyses the main streams of progressive thought on foreign policy issues developed in the years between the Boer War and the First World War. It identifies the differences between them, shows the basis on which their proponents came to work together in the UDC, and thereby provides a basis for an understanding of the theoretical content of post-war progressivism.

(i) THE HOBSONIAN SYNTHESIS

The most important theoretical work to emerge from the controversy over the Boer War was Hobson's *Imperialism: a Study*. It contained an apparently coherent critique of imperialism which harmoniously combined liberal and socialist values and arguments, in much the same style that his work on domestic economics and politics had done. This was a huge achievement; simultaneously Hobson revivified and redefined the Cobdenite strand of the liberal tradition in foreign policy.[3] More importantly for the purposes of the present study, he provided the basis, directly and indirectly, of both left-wing Labour and Communist thought on imperialism in the inter-war period. This common heritage in turn provided the basis for these groups' broadly overlapping analyses of fascism in the 1930s, and thus one of the main intellectual pillars of the campaign for a United Front. It is therefore essential to consider Hobson's work and its influence in depth.

Imperialism was the culmination of a number of anti-imperialist texts which Hobson had been producing since before the outbreak of the Boer War. It synthesised Hobson's own underconsumptionist ideas on economics[4] with the ideas on imperialism he had developed in two theoretical articles and in his mostly empirical book, *The War in South Africa*. Most of these ideas were fairly familiar, at least in outline. Hobson's arguments concerning the rights of small nations, the nexus between imperialism and protection, the financial burden of imperialism, and the innate antagonism between militarism and democracy were all drawn from the repertoire of nineteeth-century liberalism.5 In Hobson's works, however, some were restated with new premises which would have been surprising or even shocking to Cobden or Gladstone.

Hobson's argument for the rights of small nations, while it reaffirmed a belief dear to liberalism, arrived at its conclusion by a route that was distinctly new. His reformulation of the argument was necessitated by Webb's attack on the anti-imperialist position and first appeared in an article published only a month after 'Lord Rosebery's Escape from Houndsditch'. As we have seen, the burden of Sidney Webb's attack on the opponents of the Boer War was that their arguments were based on outmoded, individualist attitudes to questions of empire. Webb hoped to undermine the position of socialist and New Liberal opponents of the war by showing that it was based on ideas that they themselves had long rejected. Hobson's task in 'Socialistic Imperialism' was to make the argument impervious to such an attack by placing it on new foundations consistent with the collectivist philosophy and the organic evolutionism espoused by the leading progressive thinkers of the day.

Hobson began by accepting that mere 'priority of occupation' did not confer on any group the right 'to neglect or abuse resources, the utilization of which might be an urgent need to the world at large',[6] any more than the rights of the individual included the right to act in socially harmful ways. In principle this was a clear departure from Cobdenism (or, as Webb would have it, 'Gladstonianism'); for Cobdenites, the rights of nations in international society were as axiomatic as the rights of the individual within each individual nation. For Hobson, however, unlike Webb, the analogy stopped at this point, for while the individual state may be regarded as an expression of the general will of its citizens, 'there exists no organized or recognized mode of expression of the general will of nations'.[7] The British Empire could no more claim to substitute itself for such a mode of expression than an individual in an ungoverned territory could claim the right to coerce his neighbours.[8] Such a claim could only be justified in exceptional circumstances, and then only if it could be demonstrated that some good would result to others beside the nation or the individual employing force. In South Africa it was clear that British force was being applied to serve exclusively British interests.[9]

Hobson also repudiated the argument that the expansion of empires was a path towards the development of internationalism by

arguing that 'The forcible breaking down of small national boundaries, and the welding of huge empires out of the pieces, retards the
process of world-civilisation by crushing the external expression of
the social nature of man in their largest and most valuable forms.'[10]
Hobson's argument on this point was analogous to his argument on
the relationship between the individual and the state. The relationship was not one of hostility, but of dynamic interdependence:
'Internationalism is not the negation but the expansion of the
national spirit ... Sound national forms and feelings are essential to
the slow gradual growth of an internationalism which shall develop
for itself in due time valid laws and institutions.'[11]

This line of reasoning led Hobson to the view that diversity among
nations was as necessary and desirable as diversity among individuals. In reply to 'those who chatter about absorbing nations, as a
big screw factory absorbs little ones',[12] he had a number of counter-
arguments. First was the argument that all institutions (nations and
screw factories alike) have an optimum size, which they exceed at
their peril.[13] Second, he argued that social and political concepts are
not exportable commodities, but vary fundamentally from place to
place.[14] This diversity was not arbitrary, nor was it merely a
manifestation of a contrast between 'backwardness' and 'progress'.
Rather, it was based on biological necessity: 'a nation in being is
better adapted to its territorial environment than any other nation
seeking to subjugate it, and should be left free to utilize its land and
grow its own political institutions'.[15]

In Hobson's view these were the genuine organic arguments on
the issue of imperialism. Arguments like Webb's were mere crass
mechanism: 'To substitute bonds of iron for the organic ligaments of
international goodwill, and to pretend that this process is sanctioned
by laws of social evolution is the grossest possible abuse of scientific
method and of scientific terminology.'[16] While Hobson, like Webb,
claimed a scientific rationale for his conclusions concerning small
nations, the practical political consequences of his argument were
identical with those of the traditional Liberals whose stance Webb
had described as 'sentimental hypocrisies': large, powerful nations
had no warrant to interfere in the affairs of their smaller, weaker
brethren.

Hobson's argument that imperialism was harmful to the political
health of Britain itself, while more traditionally liberal in both form
and conclusion than his argument concerning small nations, was

nevertheless an argument that was entirely consistent with socialism.[17] We have already seen it employed within the Fabian Society
by S. G. Hobson.[18] The harm resulted from two processes. On the
one hand, the task of governing the empire was inherently so arcane
that no effective popular control could be exerted over it. This led
inevitably to 'the subordination of the legislative to the executive,
and the concentration of executive power in an autocracy'.[19] On the
other hand, imperialism created 'a larger and larger number of men
trained in the temper and methods of autocracy as soldiers and civil
officials in our ... Empire, reinforced by a number of merchants,
planters, engineers, and overseers, whose lives have been those of a
superior caste'.[20] On their return to England, these men often
attained local and national influence, where their habits and
attitudes led to 'infringements of the liberties of the subject and ...
the abrogation of constitutional rights and usages'.[21] These traditionally liberal arguments led Hobson to a traditionally liberal
conclusion on this aspect of the question: 'Imperialism and popular
government have nothing in common: they differ in spirit, in policy,
in method.'[22]

Hobson advanced an equally traditional liberal argument concerning the relationship between imperialism and free trade. In
Hobson's work the argument is explicitly intended as a reassertion of
a liberal truth which time had done nothing to undermine. The
stated economic justification of imperialism was that it provided the
imperialist country with new markets. In the slogan of the day, trade
followed the flag. Although, as we shall see, Hobson rejected this
claim,[23] the belief itself entailed that contemporary imperialism was
protectionist as it 'naturally strives to fasten to the mother country
the markets of each new territorial acquisition'.[24]

Hobson's attitude to free trade was the most straight-forwardly
Cobdenite aspect of his thought. Until the 1930s, when his faith
wavered,[25] it was also one of his most passionate commitments, the
one which led him eventually to leave the Liberal Party.[26] His belief
that 'Imperialism repudiates Free Trade'[27] appears to have inspired
his first anti-imperialist work. 'Free Trade and Foreign Policy',
which he wrote in 1898, was a condemnation of the British Government's policy of 'forcing doors open and forcibly keeping them
open'.[28] Hobson singled out the Liberal Party for special attack, as it
endorsed imperialist policies while claiming to be true to free trade
principles. His attack demonstrates the ambiguity of Liberalism's

record on imperial questions. Implicitly it was an attack upon the practices of Gladstone, but to drive it home Hobson quoted Cobden, one of 'the prophets of the middle century'.

It is because I want to see Free Trade, in its noblest and most humane aspect, have full scope in this world, that I wish to absolve myself from all responsibility for the miseries caused by violence and aggression, too often perpetrated under the plea of benefiting trade . . . We have nothing to hope from measures of violence in aid of the promotion of commerce with other nations.[29]

A commitment to the principles of free trade was the most important and the least controversial of the many beliefs that British socialists and trade unionists shared with British Liberals. Its enduring importance to both can be seen in the formation of the first Labour Government in 1924. An election called by a Conservative Government seeking a mandate for protection left no party – Labour, Liberal, or Conservative – with a parliamentary majority. Although the Conservatives were the biggest single party, and although many Liberals had profound reservations both about Labour's policies and its competence to govern, the Liberals decided to support a minority Labour Government in order to maintain free trade.[30] Shaw's ambiguous assertion of the virtues of protection in 1902 was virtually the only occasion before the First World War on which a British socialist openly departed from the free trade gospel, and that, as we saw, cost the Fabian Society one of its founders. Hobson was on strong ground here, for regardless of whether there is a necessary theoretical relationship between socialism and free trade, the latter was just as much a sacred cow for British socialists as it was for British Liberals.

In Hobson's view, the policy of protectionist imperialism was a failure, even when considered on its own terms. In both 'Free Trade and Foreign Policy', and in an entire chapter of *Imperialism*, Hobson presented statistics demonstrating that trade did not 'follow the flag',[31] but rather, that the growth of the empire had been accompanied by a reduction in the total volume of British trade with its colonial possessions.[32] In the same period, British trade with foreign countries and self-governing colonies had increased. Hobson, like Bentham and Cobden before him, pointed to the immense financial cost of maintaining the huge military and administrative establishment necessary to defend and police Britain's empire. Only one conclusion could follow: imperialism was 'unsound business', undertaken at the behest of an influential minority: 'The business interests of the nation as a whole are subordinated to those of certain sectional interests that usurp control of the national resources and use them for their private gain . . . Irrational from the standpoint of the nation [imperialism] is rational enough from the standpoint of certain classes in the nation.'[33]

The charge was not new. Liberal and socialist opponents of the Boer War had made it repeatedly in their discussions of that conflict. Courtney – a Gladstonian – held that 'But for the gold fields and those who came to exploit them we should never have had this war.'[34] Similarly, the ILP maintained that the war had 'been brought about by a swindling horde of home and foreign exploiters for their own ends',[35] and Edward Carpenter warned the 'British Public' not 'to be fooled in this way by a few millionaires and gold-grubbers'.[36] Hobson viewed the war in virtually identical terms: 'We are fighting in order to place a small international oligarchy of mine-owners and speculators in power at Pretoria.'[37] Like the other critics of the war, Hobson could not restrain himself from resorting to a theory of a specifically Jewish conspiracy in order to account for the events, although unlike the other critics, Hobson appeared to feel uneasy in doing so.[38] His statement that, 'It is difficult to state the truth about our doings in South Africa without seeming to invoke the ignominious passion of Judenhetze',[39] reveals a delicacy sadly lacking in other writers.

Reliance on conspiracy theories was the greatest weakness of Hobson's early comments on the war, as it was generally of the anti-war case. The existence of conspiracies – even where they do exist – is always difficult to prove. But it did not take Hobson long to elevate his argument to a higher plane. Between the writing and the publishing of *The War in South Africa*, Hobson was reaching toward the idea that the relationship between finance and imperialism was not a contingency of the South African situation, but the outcome of a fundamental change in the international economic and political order.

I would insist upon the supreme importance of recognising the dominance everywhere exercised by the new confederacy and interplay of two sets of forces, conveniently designated by the titles International Capitalism and Imperialism . . . The large establishment by members and classes belonging to one nation of permanent investments of capital in another country is a patent breach of the old order, destroying the very roots of the old national sentiments.[40]

It was in furnishing an explanation for the apparent ease with which the as yet small group of international capitalists had come to dominate British politics that Hobson developed an analysis, and proposed a solution, that – to liberals at least – were novel:

It is admitted by all business men that the growth of productive powers in their country exceeds the growth in consumption, that more goods can be produced than can be sold at a profit, and that more capital exists than can find remunerative investment. It is this economic condition of affairs that forms the taproot of Imperialism. If the consuming public of this country raised its standard of consumption to keep pace with every rise of productive powers, there could be no excess of goods or capital clamorous to use Imperialism in order to find markets.[41]

This was the key argument of *Imperialism*. In advancing it, Hobson transcended earlier liberal and socialist arguments against the Boer War (including his own) and, by synthesising them with his under-consumptionist economic theory, converted them into a generalised critique of modern imperialism *per se*.

This argument naturally recommended itself to socialists. Indeed, before the publication of *Imperialism* it had actually been advanced, in a rudimentary form, in an ILP pamphlet which bore marked similarities to Hobson's earlier works on the subject. It argued the case for small nations in much the same way as Hobson had done, pointed to the relationship between imperialism and militarism and the harmful effect of militarism on democracy and denied that trade follows the flag. It then proposed an alternative to the economics of imperialism: 'If the home market were properly cared for, trade would prosper.'[42]

Imperialism was popular among socialists, but it was not a socialist text. It was an underconsumptionist text. It was crucial to Hobson's argument that the excessive accumulations of capital that gave rise to imperialism were not an inherent feature of the capitalist system, but an anomaly that could be corrected. While there were powerful groups – the military, arms manufacturers, aristocrats with unemployed younger sons, financiers, monopolists – whose interests would be permanently damaged by the end of imperialism, the vast majority of the population, including most capitalist manufacturers and traders, would be far better served by the increase in domestic prosperity that would result from a general increase in wages and a return to free trade. Hobson was emphatic that no economy could benefit as a whole from an imperialist policy: 'A completely socialist State which kept good books ... would soon discard Imperialism; an intelligent *laissez-faire* democracy which gave duly proportionate weight in its policy to all economic interests alike would do the same.'[43]

This was important to *Imperialism*'s persuasive force. As Bernard Porter has pointed out, the argument that imperialism brought general economic gain to the whole community was one of its best established and most widely employed defences.[44] Hobson's achievement was simultaneously to deny that imperialism made economic sense, while finding on the one hand that there were features of the existing economy that gave it force, but on the other that those features were irrational and removable within the framework of capitalist economy. The problem was not, at root, a problem of the economic system, but of the political control of that system: 'Secure popular government, in substance and in form, and you secure internationalism: retain class government, and you retain military Imperialism and international conflicts.'[45] Hobson, at least at this point of his life, had no desire to argue that class government was inherent to capitalism.

The most substantial work of the pre-war years to incorporate the Hobsonian critique of imperialism was H. N. Brailsford's *The War of Steel and Gold*. Brailsford was a member of the ILP and a convinced socialist, but his political and journalistic activities were typical of the progressive milieu we have examined in previous chapters. Brailsford was a founder of the abortive Glasgow University ILP and then of the more successful Glasgow University Fabian Society until the Boer War precipitated his resignation. In 1904 Brailsford, who was a member of the Society of the Friends of Russian Freedom, was fined £100 for his part in procuring false British passports for a group of Russian revolutionary exiles to return to Russia. His fines and legal costs were paid with money lent by, among others, Shaw, Gilbert Murray, and C. P. Scott, editor of the *Manchester Guardian*, to which Brailsford was then a casual contributor.[46] He joined the ILP in 1906 and two years later became a leader writer on the *Nation* under Massingham's editorship. His closest colleagues there were L. T. Hobhouse and Lawrence Hammond. In the years 1910–14 most of his time outside journalism was taken up with his work on the

Conciliation Committee. This body's ambitious, unrealised objective was to find a proposal for the enfranchisement of women simultaneously acceptable to the Asquith Government and the various women's suffrage groups. It did not, however, seek to fuse the women's groups, believing, as Brailsford did, that 'each method and each policy has its uses'.[47] The composition of the committee illustrates the extent to which many of the wounds of the Boer War had healed. Apart from Keir Hardie and Philip Snowden, who as members of the ILP had been bitter critics of the war, it included the Liberal Imperialists Sir Edward Grey and Winston Churchill.[48] Conversely, Brailsford's work on the (suffrage) Conciliation Committee left him with a profound distrust of Lloyd George, a former leader of the 'pro-Boers'.[49]

Brailsford's work on imperialism first appeared in a series of articles in the *Nation* in 1912.[50] *The War of Steel and Gold* was, however, the first systematic and detailed working out of his views. Brailsford's purpose was somewhat different to Hobson's. Whereas Hobson had formulated a critique of imperialism principally in order to show its roots in the British economy and its pernicious effects on British domestic politics, Brailsford's main purpose was to use the Hobsonian analysis to show the effects of imperial rivalry on the relations between the European powers. The central contention of the book was that 'The questions which divide rival Powers . . . are all incidents in the effort of modern finance to find openings in distant regions, to lay its rails in Mesopotamia or to exploit the tropical produce of Angola.'[51]

Like Hobson, Brailsford saw underconsumption as the driving force behind 'finance's' need to export its capital, but his analysis differed from Hobson's in a number of important ways. As a socialist, Brailsford could not accept Hobson's argument that the process was due to the workings of 'certain sectional interests that usurp control of the national resources', for this argument is based on the profoundly Liberal assumption that the 'natural' posture of the state in capitalist society is one of neutrality. For Brailsford the relationship was far more subtle and far more insidious.

The explanation of the solidarity between the diplomatist and the financier in most modern empires is not to be sought in any crude labels. For each of them it is part of the providential order of the universe that patriotism should profit the governing class. That is why it is commonly the sincerest of all the disinterested emotions. It would be as false to say that the diplomatist is the sordid tool of finance, as it would be to say that the financier is the disinterested purse-bearer of patriotism. They belong to the same social world; they each submit to the same vague influences which cause the world to turn its interest now to this corner of the earth, and again to that.[52]

Brailsford's difference from Hobson on this point may be explained not only by his socialism, but also by the fact that unlike Hobson, he was a specialist on international questions. His reputation and his livelihood as a journalist were based chiefly on his expertise in that field, which is clearly apparent in his work. It was probably this specialised knowledge which led Brailsford to observe that 'political and sentimental impulse' was on occasion the initiator of colonial expansion.[53] While such an empirical observation would have weakened Hobson's position, it strengthened Brailsford's; the point remained that 'Capital moves with the flag – sometimes before it and sometimes after it.'[54] The capitalist state, of its very nature, served capitalist ends, and there was rarely a need for any clique of capitalists to prod its machinery into action.

While the socialist conclusion that 'The evils of the process are a necessary inevitable accompaniment of capitalistic civilisation' followed inexorably from Brailsford's analysis, it was characteristic of the man that he had reforms to propose, 'so that the minimum of injury shall result to ourselves, to native races, and to our European neighbours'.[55] These reforms were identical in spirit to the measures Hobson had proposed to bring capitalist imperialism to an end. The most important was that foreign policy and the movement of capital must be subjected to public scrutiny and democratic control through parliament. Brailsford believed that this would be effective because 'The veil of secrecy [over the conduct of foreign policy] means too often a claim to do beneath it what no man who respected his own honour, or cared for the good opinion of his fellows, would dare to do in public.'[56] Thus Brailsford, in spite of his distinctively socialist analysis and conclusion, was as convinced as Hobson that imperialism, at least as it then operated, was incompatible with existing social and political ethics.

It was especially incompatible with liberal ethics. It is clear that Brailsford's work was directed as much to a liberal as a socialist audience, and that he wrote in order to fulfil his own part in the task he explicitly set for 'Socialist idealists'. That task was to impose 'a constructive policy of ... reform upon the present generation of

Liberals' in the field of foreign policy, as Brailsford believed had already been done in domestic policy.[57] It was doubtless for this reason that Brailsford jabbed remorselessly at a particularly tender Liberal nerve, the Entente with Russia: 'We have helped to restore [Russia's] solvency and revive its prestige, while it hanged its Socialists, dissolved its Dumas, imprisoned its Jews, defiled the free soil of Finland, and erected its gallows in the cities of Persia. Nowhere has the Triple Entente served a Liberal thought.'[58]

Here we find the core of Brailsford's belief and the key to a large part of his life's work. Contemporary capitalism was irreconcilable with the liberal ethics to which he always subscribed. *Mutatis mutandis* capitalism must be abolished. The task was to convince Liberals of the need, and until they were convinced to enlist their democratic sympathies for projects of immediate reform.

(II) MOREL, ANGELL, AND THE PACIFIC REASON OF TRADE

Very many Liberals remained unconvinced of Brailsford's or even Hobson's arguments, among them some of the staunchest opponents of militarism and some of the most trenchant critics of the conduct of British foreign policy. Most of these Liberals in fact focussed their attention on the works of Norman Angell and E. D. Morel, whose criticisms sat more comfortably with the traditional Liberal defence of the rights of property. Of these two, only Morel was enmeshed in the progressive milieu, although it appears that Angell may have been influenced by the evolutionary organicist thought of some New Liberals.

Morel's fame and his interest in foreign policy both arose from his work in exposing and agitating against the horrors of King Leopold of Belgium's merciless exploitation of the Congo Free State, which first came to Morel's attention in the course of his duties in a Liverpool shipping firm with a substantial trade in West Africa.[59]

Two considerations moved Morel. The first, in point of time, was the rights of British traders, which he believed were being infringed by King Leopold's exclusionist economic administration; the second, but by far the most important and enduring, was his concern for the well-being of the native Africans. His concern took a form unusual in early twentieth-century Europe, for Morel, who was profoundly influenced by the pioneering anthropologist Mary Kingsley, saw the best solution of the natives' difficulties not in 'improving' them by

Christian philanthropy, but in allowing them freely to develop on the basis of their own institutions, customs, and culture.

In Morel's view the only legitimate catalyst of African development was trade. The fundamental evil of the Leopoldian system was that by appropriating the land and its products, Leopold had denied the Africans not only their fundamental right to their own property, but also their only possibility of development. Before contact with Europeans the native had no incentive to give labour 'to other purposes than those of sustaining life in conditions as comfortable as his needs and ambitions dictate'.[60] His society therefore remained economically and culturally static. Anywhere the African had been presented with European goods he had 'voluntarily grafted upon himself extra labour' in order to produce for exchange. To trade with the African was therefore the only method by which Europeans could stimulate African development that was either morally or anthropologically sound:

To insist upon the principle of trade relationship between the European and the Negro in his own home as the basic principle in that relationship is synonymous with declaring that the Negro must be treated (not as a half-babe, half-saint, to be petted and veneered with an outward culture altogether foreign to his ideas, leaping over twelve centuries in a few years) as a Man with the rights of a Man – not as a brute beast.[61]

Such arguments were pure 'Kingsleyism', but they also bore a close resemblance to Hobson's insistence that nations were best left to develop their own institutions,[62] and although Morel specifically disavowed any interest in the dispute between free trade and protection (presumably so as not to alienate any part of his potential audience), his belief that trade was 'the pivotal element which unites all societies, the link which binds together in a practical sense the various branches of the human family'[63] evinces the same Cobdenite passion with which Hobson castigated the Liberal Imperialists.[64]

Morel never developed a critique of imperialism. Until 1910 the Congo was his sole obsession, and in his propaganda he sometimes held up other imperialist ventures as ideals against which to condemn King Leopold's system. Furthermore, Morel's thought on the Congo never led him to criticise or even to analyse European social, political, and economic structures. The Leopoldian system was just that: a system created by one wicked man who – a few henchmen aside – was its sole beneficiary.[65] Apart from this tiny clique, Belgians derived no benefit from the system, which, by precluding trade, gave rise to no demand for Belgian products. Ideally, trade should and did follow the flag. King Leopold's crime was to make this impossible. Far from being the product of any inherent feature of Belgian capitalism, Leopold's rule could only be sustained by trampling on Belgian as well as Congolese interests and by violating Belgium's constitution. The durability of King Leopold's 'puppet government' was due entirely to historical accident.[66] Analysis of Leopold's regime therefore required no further search for underlying causes, and criticism of it implied no criticism of imperialism itself.

Morel's work for Congo reform led him instead to a critique of the conduct of British foreign policy. He believed that the British Government had a clear duty to act decisively against King Leopold's rule in the Congo. On moral grounds this duty sprang from Britain's 'tradition as emancipators of the races of Africa'.[67] On political grounds Britain's duty sprang from the fact that it was a co-signatory to the Convention that had originally given King Leopold control of the Congo, a Convention whose terms he had clearly breached.

In 1904, Morel, together with Roger Casement, launched the Congo Reform Association with the object of mobilising international, and especially British, public opinion against King Leopold. Among the CRA's Executive Committee were Trevelyan, MacDonald, and the Rev'd John Clifford (the Fabian and Christian Socialist), as well as scions of such renowned Liberal and radical families as Gladstone, Cadbury, and Wilberforce. The main proposal of the CRA was that the Belgian Government should wrest the Congo Free State from Leopold's grasp by annexing it to Belgium. The British Government was sympathetic to this proposal, although Morel, paradoxically, was not, preferring instead that the Congo Free State should be placed under the supervision of an international commission.[68] When the Belgian Government annexed the Congo in 1908, and the Leopoldian system continued unchecked, Morel's worst fears were confirmed. While Morel became more bellicose on the issue – even going so far as to advocate that the British navy should confiscate Belgian cargoes from the Congo – the British Government appeared reluctant to press the issue any further.[69]

It was almost inevitable that Morel, with his unshakeable faith in the justice and urgency of his cause, would not only suspect some extraneous hidden motive, but would also regard any such motive as *ipso facto* evil. The hidden motive he detected was a desire on the part of Grey, the Foreign Secretary, to conciliate Belgian opinion so as to keep Belgium out of the arms of Germany.[70] Moreover, as Morel had recently discovered, the French Government itself was hostile to further action on the Congo question, fearing possible pressure on its own practices in the French Congo. That Grey should be influenced by such considerations was due, in Morel's opinion, solely to the Anglo-French Entente concluded in 1904.

Morel therefore turned his attention to the broader questions of European diplomacy. To the Entente itself he had no objection, but Grey's behaviour over the Congo led him to suspect that the Entente in fact was 'an arrangement with secret clauses, a sort of military convention, which necessitates on our part a state of perennial antagonism and suspicion in our relations with another great Power'.[71] This pointed the way to the theme of all of Morel's future work. With the death of King Leopold in 1909 and the accession of King Albert, who appeared determined to dismantle Leopold's system, Morel temporarily appeared in danger of becoming a crusader without a cause. He now chose to devote his considerable skills as a publicist to combating the evils of 'secret diplomacy'.

The first main object of Morel's attention was the Agadir crisis of 1911, an episode from which he drew conclusions very different from those of Norman Angell, as we shall see. In Morel's view, Britain had 'not treated Germany fairly' in this crisis,[72] and had risked war in order to enable France to carry out its 'long-matured design of acquiring a Protectorate over the greater part of Morocco'.[73] British policy could only be explained by its 'unsanctioned secret commitments to France and Spain'.[74] This way of conducting diplomacy, Morel believed, 'would not be tolerated for twenty-four hours by the British people if they realised the true position', for it was,

in the interest neither of the British nor the French *peoples* that they should be fettered in their intercourse with other peoples; or committed by their Governments to a definite course of action in advance. Such commitments play into the hands of certain interests in Britain, France and Germany, who, whether they be actuated by motives of honest conviction, or inspired by class or personal interests, or merely governed by fixed and narrow ideas, are the enemies of peace.[75]

Morel's criticisms thus resembled Hobson's and Brailsford's, but only at the points where their ideas coincided with much earlier liberal ideas. His references to class interests were only superficially akin to their arguments. Morel actually said very little about the relationship between class interests and foreign policy, and what he did say suggests that he saw the relationship as incidental to the fundamental evil. In Morocco, for example, the French Government had used 'international finance' as a 'convenient lever' to achieve its purpose. Diplomacy and finance exerted on each other a mutually corrupting influence, but this was a by-product of the system of secrecy, and not, as Brailsford maintained, the central dynamic of foreign policy, rooted in the very structure of capitalist society. Morel found the origin of the evil in the Foreign Office itself. Behind its veil it had nurtured a system of entrenched incompetence beyond the scope of the Foreign Secretary himself to control. Morel's main target was not class interests, but the 'disorganised condition of our own Foreign Office, the personal rivalries which obtain within it, its extraordinarily faulty intelligence system, the way in which the embassies abroad have got out of hand through the absence of a strong directing head at home'.[76] Morel thus never became a critic of imperialism as Hobson and Brailsford understood the term. Indeed, he regarded British imperialism as on the whole beneficial to the natives who were his main concern. He did, however, share Hobson's and Brailsford's opposition to secret diplomacy, seeing it not, as they did, as one of the major outworkings of an inherently undemocratic system of imperialism, but as the fundamental cause of a foreign policy that was, above all things, irrational.

Angell's influence extended well beyond progressive circles. His *The Great Illusion* was enormously popular. It went through ten printings in various English editions, and was translated into ten languages within two years of its first publication in 1909. It prompted the spontaneous establishment of a number of 'Norman Angell societies' devoted to the discussion and propagation of Angell's ideas, and a 'Norman Angell Monthly', *War and Peace*, whose contributors included Conservatives and Liberals, among them Hobson.[77] It was widely and sympathetically discussed by leading politicians, economists, soldiers, and philosophers, and even, it appears, King Edward VII.[78]

Angell's purpose was altogether different from that of either Hobson or Brailsford. He barely even mentioned the issues that were of central importance to them, for he was a critic not of imperialism, but of war. When he discussed the British Empire he discussed only the self-governing dominions; the problems of India or of the British possessions in tropical Africa appear not to have exercised his mind at all.

Angell's argument, in outline, was extremely simple: in the modern world each nation was so dependent on every other that war was economically self-defeating: 'Military and economic power give a nation no commercial advantage . . . it is an economic impossibility for one nation to seize or destroy the wealth of another, or for one nation to enrich itself by subjugating another.'[79] The almost universal belief in war as an effective instrument of policy was therefore the 'Great Illusion' of the book's title.

Although Angell spent very little time in Britain during the pre-war years, and was not closely associated with the New Liberal thinkers discussed in earlier chapters, he relied very heavily upon the collectivist and biological arguments that were dear to many of them. Angell's organicist ideals were probably derived in the first instance from Spencer, as were those of many of the New Liberals, but it is interesting that he gives Spencer the same twist as Hobhouse did:

The individual in his sociological aspect is not the complete organism. He who attempts to live without association with his fellows dies. Nor is the nation the complete organism. If Britain attempted to live without co-operation with other nations, half the population would starve. The completer the co-operation the greater the vitality; the more imperfect the co-operation the less the vitality ... The higher the organism the greater the elaboration and interdependence of its parts, the greater the need for co-ordination.[80]

This was an evolutionary process. Human history demonstrated that 'Man's pugnacity ... under the forces of mechanical and social development [is] being transformed and diverted from ends that are wasteful and destructive to ends that are less destructive, which render easier that co-operation between men in the struggle for their environment which is the condition of their survival and advance.'[81]

None of this made Angell a socialist, even in the sense that, say, L. T. Hobhouse might be termed a socialist; and despite his use of biological metaphors and arguments Angell's views were in one important aspect the pure milk of Cobdenism. He was convinced that the development of capitalism itself had been the major driving force of the pacific developments he described, and that it would necessarily continue to move society in this direction in the future.

This placed his ideas in direct opposition to those of Hobson and Brailsford. Not only did Angell deny that finance aimed to 'interfere with politics',[82] he also held that finance, by virtue of it being the most sophisticated and delicate mechanism of the new pacific order, had an entirely beneficial effect on international relations. This too he argued biologically:

The Stock Exchange and the bank rate . . . enable the organism [society] to realize instantly what cruder and less-developed organisms could not realize at all, for the simple reason that they possessed no nervous systems. Banking provides the organism with its sensory nerves, which means, surely, the capacity to co-ordinate its acts and perform them with a realization of their effect.[83]

Angell's main evidence for this argument was the 'Agadir crisis' of 1911, in which he believed war between France and Germany had been averted by the beginnings of a financial crisis that had forced the German statesmen to realise that Germany depended on French credit, and therefore on French prosperity and confidence, for its own economic survival.[84]

Angell's belief in the essential mutualism of the international capitalist economy implied another opinion hostile to Hobson and Brailsford: the impossibility of tribute. On this topic, Angell confined his discussion to the exaction of large indemnities from one industrial nation to another, and remained strangely (but consistently) silent on the tropical empires. Despite this limitation, Angell's view is extremely important, for it formed the basis of a good deal of the later criticism of the reparations provisions of the Treaty of Versailles. The core of his argument was 'that the population as a whole of any nation receiving a large indemnity must suffer from any consequent disturbance in the credit of the paying nation'.[85] He argued further that tribute must ultimately be levied in goods, and that the effect of this would only be to disrupt the markets of the receiving nation, thereby causing widespread unemployment.[86]

The greatest difference between Angell on the one hand and Hobson, Brailsford, and Morel on the other is to be found not in any one of Angell's specific arguments, but in the general tendency of his entire project. His task, as he saw it, was to convince all people – rich and poor, governing and governed – of the sheer folly of war. He simply assumed that the proof of this would suffice to make war impossible, for he did not believe that there was any large or powerful group with a vested interest in the perpetuation of militarism. For Angell it was axiomatic that 'the general trend of [Government] policy must sooner or later be determined by the interests and the necessities of the mass of the people from which it derives its power'.[87] The neutrality of the modern capitalist state, which Hobson and Morel saw (for differing reasons) as a corrupted ideal, and which Brailsford regarded as impossible, Angell took simply as given.

The considerable differences between Brailsford and Angell were made plain in their reviews of one another's works. Brailsford's criticism of Angell boiled down to two points: Angell had failed to distinguish the interests of classes from the interests of nations, and had unjustifiably assumed that what was true of the relations between modern industrial nations held good for the whole world. The latter point was the simpler. Angell was correct to ridicule the idea that, say, Germany could or would conquer, loot, and colonise England as the Normans had done, but other countries, 'still in an agrarian phase of development' – the Russians in Persia, or the Balkan countries – manifestly could and did benefit from such actions.[88] Brailsford's main criticism was much closer to the theoretical heart of the analysis he had propounded in *The War of Steel and Gold*. He explicitly accepted Angell's claim that in the modern world no nation as a nation could benefit from war, but this missed what for Brailsford was the central point that modern nations were class societies: 'The Lancashire operative and the suburban clerk are certainly no richer because the navy enables us to control without owning Egypt. But the bondholders who despoiled the Khedive Ismail are immensely the richer.'[89]

The political power of the bondholders was the decisive element in international relations, so while Angell was correct to maintain that 'Germany' did not trade with 'England', but that individual German firms traded with individual English firms, he was wrong to conclude that nationality was therefore of no consequence in the modern world, because 'Capitalists do act in national groups abroad, and do receive from diplomacy, not merely protection, but active support in their schemes of expansion.'[90]

Angell flatly rejected Brailsford's main premise. The problem lay squarely with the masses: 'it is the old prejudices and popular international rivalries which prevent the international financiers from acting in common'. The capitalists were not, however, entirely blameless. Given that the prejudices of the masses made it impossible for them to co-operate across national boundaries they had little choice but to 'do the next best thing, and to use those hostilities to secure advantages for themselves'.[91]

Angell did not hesitate to draw the conclusion that democratic control would be of no benefit. It the masses were as susceptible to manipulation as Brailsford himself held them to be, no good could come of placing them in control of foreign policy. Angell's advice to Brailsford was that he should pursue his thought on the mass mind and rid himself of the illusion that foreign policy was the result of 'somebody's plot'.[92] Here Angell missed Brailsford's point, which was not that foreign policy was a plot, but that it was the inevitable outcome of contemporary capitalism.

(III) UNITED AGAINST WAR

The obvious differences between Angell and Brailsford did not prevent their collaboration. Within weeks of the outbreak of the First World War, Brailsford, Angell, Hobson, and Morel were all members of the Union of Democratic Control.[93] From its inception the UDC was in every way typical of the pre-war progressive milieu. Its founding triumvirate of Trevelyan, MacDonald, and Morel[94] had earlier worked together in the Congo Reform Association, an equally typical progressive body, and MacDonald and Trevelyan, despite their different party affiliations, had been close acquaintances as far back as 1895.

Many other leading members of the UDC had similar records of involvement in a variety of progressive causes and cross-party organisations. Helena Swanwick, who was a pacifist, had worked with Brailsford on the (Suffrage) Conciliation Committee. The Rev'd John Clifford, another CRA veteran, was a Christian Socialist and a member of the Fabian Society who had been in the SACC, as had Kate Courtney (Beatrice Webb's sister), Isabella O. Ford (a Quaker veteran of the Fellowship of the New Life and a long-time member of the ILP, who as a member of the National Union of Women's Suffrage Societies had played a leading role in promoting the Conciliation Bill), and Sophia Sturge, the daughter of Joseph Sturge, Cobden's Quaker friend and colleague in the Anti-Corn Law League and leader in a profusion of nineteenth-century radical organisations including the London Peace Society.[95] Seymour Cocks had been active in the CRA. Alex Gossip, a militant ILP trade unionist had been a fervent campaigner against the Boer War. For these people nothing could be more usual than to work together, across the lines of party, 'ideology', gender, and class to fight the evil they saw before them on the basis of those values and political ideas they held in common. The UDC was not a novelty.

The UDC's ability to acquire and retain this eclectic membership was due in part to another feature it shared with pre-war progressive organisations, a failure to impose or even to seek to impose an orthodoxy upon its members. Members were not even required to oppose Britain's participation in the war. One serving soldier was elected to its General Council, and another wrote one of its pamphlets.[96] The UDC was proud to proclaim its heterodoxy: 'Many men and women have already joined us holding varying shades of opinion as to the origins of the war. Some think it was inevitable, some that it could and should have been avoided.'[97]

The members of the UDC committed themselves only to four 'Cardinal Points', all of which were concerned with the nature of the peace to come rather than the war itself. They stated that there should be no annexations of territory without the consent of the populations concerned; that the British Government should commit itself to no treaties or understandings with foreign powers without the consent of parliament; that the 'Balance of Power' in international relations should be abandoned in favour of an 'International Council' to resolve disputes between nations; and that there should be all-round disarmament after the war, accompanied by the nationalisation of the manufacture of arms.[98]

These points represented something slightly more than the maximum agreement between the thinkers whose views were discussed earlier. Interestingly, however, the possible source of discord lay not in any difference between the socialistic perspectives of Hobson and Brailsford and the clearly non-socialist views of Morel and Angell, but rather between Angell and the other three, most especially Morel; for while Angell was sceptical about the benefits of open diplomacy, it was Morel's all-consuming passion.

Angell was thus something of an odd man out in the UDC, which, with the organising genius of Morel at the helm, laid heavy emphasis in its propaganda on the evils of secret diplomacy. For Angell, as Taylor has succinctly said, 'it was not necessary to carry through a democratic revolution in order to change foreign policy; it was only necessary to explain the real situation to those in power'.[99] It is not surprising then that Angell did little active work for the UDC after the first few months of the war. It was not merely – as Swartz has suggested – that Angell 'preferred educational work to political involvement'.[100] Rather it was that Angell's was an apolitical creed, at least within the terms in which progressives understood politics. Angell appealed for a change of mind rather than a change of institutional structures. Progressivism was always an appeal for both.

Secret diplomacy aside, the Cardinal Points could all be justified, at least implicitly, on the basis of the works of Morel, Angell, Hobson, and Brailsford. From their different perspectives, all had condemned Balance of Power diplomacy, the pernicious influence of arms manufacturers, annexations (at least of 'advanced' peoples), and the forcible suppression of international trade. The Cardinal Points thus provided an adequate basis for a coherent campaign of propaganda that was nevertheless broad enough to allow their authors to pursue their own particular concerns and inclinations; thus Angell wrote on British 'Prussianism', Hobson on the financial costs of the war, Morel on its effects on Africa as well as on secret diplomacy.[101] Among other members Swanwick wrote on its effects on women, and MacDonald on its effects on the working class.[102] Some of the pamphlets, however, expressed views which could not possibly have commanded the assent of all members – another clear indication of the UDC's roots in pre-war progressivism. Brailsford's suggestion that the war was being prolonged for the sake of the economic interests of British Imperialists who wished to annex Mesopotamia was clearly at odds with the whole thrust of Angell's thinking;[103] on the other side of the coin, Hobson and Brailsford could hardly have subscribed to the complaint in an unsigned pamphlet that 'Our vast commercial interests . . . are regarded [by the Foreign Office] as lying outside the orbit of diplomatic consider-ations.'[104] It is, therefore, impossible to speak of a UDC view of the war. There were a number of differing views which coalesced around a broad agreement on how its recurrence was to be prevented.

The UDC resembled the SACC in its disregard for the party affiliations, philosophical convictions, and ideological commitments of its members. There was, however, one absolutely crucial differ-ence: whereas the SACC had members and supporters drawn from every level in the Liberal Party, the UDC's Liberal members were, by virtue of their stance on the war, thoroughly estranged from the mainstream of their Party. The UDC's ILP members, by contrast, were their Party's leading spokesmen, supported, with a very few dissentients, by their entire membership. As Helena Swanwick put it, 'The ILP from the first needed no conversion. It had the root of the matter.'[105] The consequences of this seem quite natural; by the end of 1916 all of the UDC Liberals had left the Liberal Party, and by the end of 1919 all of them, after varying degrees of hesitation, had joined the ILP.

There is no simple interpretation of the causes or consequences of this process. It took place in a context of great political confusion, and had many different effects on the structure of progressive politics, some of them highly paradoxical. It seems reasonably clear that it was caused by the behaviour of the Liberal Party during the war, but it cannot be attributed merely to the Party's support for the war effort; many Liberals who had shared that support also joined the ILP at the end of the war. Moreover, by the time the war ended the leaders of the Liberal Party were beginning to advocate a peace along the lines proposed by the UDC. That the process brought into the Labour Party a body of people with a special interest and expertise in foreign policy is incontestable, but we cannot conclude thereby that it gave the Party a single distinctive analysis of foreign policy; no such thing existed within the UDC, as we have seen, and, in so far as there were points of agreement, many of these were shared by people who stayed in the Liberal Party. Moreover, as Dowse has shown, the range of opinions on foreign policy within the ILP at the beginning of the war, although less well articulated, was virtually identical to that in the UDC.[106]

Nor can the process be seen as a final splitting of progressivism into Liberal and Labour camps. While the two parties spent the inter-war years at each other's throats, and while the ex-Liberals showed very little sympathy with their former Party, the personal friendships and intellectual intercourse among progressives of both parties survived, and many progressives – in the Liberal Party at least – continued to hope for close, formal co-operation between the two parties. Still less, without the most severe qualifications, can the process be seen as signifying the 'liberalisation' of the Labour Party. Sections of the Labour Party were thoroughly 'liberalised' before the war, and while it is true that many of the ex-Liberals assumed positions of prominence in the most cautiously gradualist section of the Party, others, while not repudiating their Liberal heritage, left an indelible imprint on the outlook of the Labour left.

This is merely to outline the complexities of the processes that unfolded in the immediate post-war years. We must now attempt to unravel them, for unless we do our understanding of inter-war progressivism will be inadequate to the ultimate task of understanding the shifts and contradictions in the attitudes and behaviour of the most important advocates of progressive unity in the 1930s.

CHAPTER 4

The pilgrims' progress

> What had to be considered in 1920 by any one who was looking
> for colleagues with whom he could carry on such work as he had
> set his hand to, was whether to reassociate himself with the
> Liberals was the most promising way of progress towards the
> realisation of his ideals.
>
> Lord Haldane[1]

During and immediately after the First World War the question of
party affiliation assumed an importance unprecedented in the
history of the progressive tradition. We have seen the beginnings of
the process whereby the bulk of progressive intellectuals changed
their party allegiance from Liberal to Labour, or, more precisely, to
the ILP. The process, which did not merely continue but accelerated
in the years immediately after the war,[2] was both cause and effect of
the larger process of Labour replacing the Liberal Party as the
leading anti-Conservative force. The disgust which led many Liberal
progressives to leave the Liberal Party stayed with them afterwards
and was powerfully reinforced by the hostility which necessarily
prevailed between two parties competing for one position. The
decade following the war is soaked in inter-party spleen to which
former Liberals contributed at least their fair share.

Given that pre-war progressivism was characterised by the lack of
importance its adherents placed on organisational affiliation, it
would be easy to conclude that progressivism itself did not survive
the war. This chapter will show that such a conclusion would be
mistaken. Progressives who joined the Labour Party were hostile to
the Liberal Party, but they did not regard those progressives who
stayed in the Liberal Party as beyond the political pale, and the
patterns of cross-party collaboration of the pre-war period continued
after the war. Moreover, the philosophical eclecticism and ideo-

logical heterodoxy which was another of progressivism's defining characteristics survived and even prospered just as well within the post-war Labour Party as it had in the pre-war Liberal Party.

The sudden shift in the progressive centre of political gravity must necessarily mark a shift in the focus of this study. In subsequent chapters most of our attention will be given to the Labour Party, and especially to those progressives within it who attempted during the 1930s to prompt united action between the Labour, Liberal and Communist Parties. Our gaze cannot shift completely just yet, however, for in order to establish that progressivism did survive the war, it is necessary to consider the views and activities not only of those progressives who left the Liberal Party, but also of those who chose to remain within it. But first we must consider the ways in which the intellectual content of progressivism was effected by the war and its aftermath.

(I) THE BOUNDARIES OF PROGRESSIVISM

The First World War reinforced the intellectual and ethical boundaries of progressivism which had been established during the Boer War. Then, it will be recalled, progressivism was defined by instinctive ethical opposition to militarism and imperialism. In the First World War and immediately after, not only the definition but the individuals contained within it were virtually identical.

This claim may appear surprising. Many of those who opposed the Boer War supported the First World War wholeheartedly, Hobhouse, Massingham, and Hammond being conspicuous examples. But opposition to imperialism and militarism during the First World War did not necessarily result in opposition to the war effort. Rather, it resulted in a desire – to use the phrase of the day – for a 'clean peace'. In this all of those who had opposed the Boer War (with the conspicuous exception of Lloyd George and the conspicuous addition of Trevelyan) were united.

On this basis, the progressive milieu continued to function throughout the war. It thereby showed more cohesion and tolerance of differing opinions than either the Liberal Party or the Labour Party, both of which treated the members of the UDC harshly. Trevelyan and Ponsonby, for example, lost the parliamentary endorsement of their local Liberal associations, and, although they remained in parliament for the duration of the war, the electors

signalled their views on the matter by sweeping them both out when
the opportunity presented itself at the election of December 1918.
The Labour Party was somewhat less aggressive in its treatment of
UDC members. MacDonald, it is true, was obliged to relinquish his
chairmanship of the Parliamentary Labour Party, but this was more
a matter of logic than vindictiveness. The Party could hardly be led
by a man whose opinions differed sharply from its own policy on an
issue as big as the war. A better indication of the Labour Party's
attitude is the fact that it did not simply disaffiliate the ILP, despite
the forceful urgings of some patriotic trade union leaders.[3]

The clearest evidence of progressivism's survival during the war is
to be found in the pages of the *Nation*, a liberal weekly owned by the
Quaker Rowntree family. It superseded the *Speaker* in 1907, at which
time H. W. Massingham became its editor. Like most Liberals,
Massingham accepted the government's claim that Britain had no
choice but to declare war after the German invasion of Belgium. His
staff, however, were more or less evenly divided on the question.
Brailsford was the *Nation*'s chief leader writer on foreign affairs, and
remained so throughout the war. Hobson too continued to work
regularly on the paper. On the other hand Hobhouse, who believed
passionately in the necessity to defeat Germany and its Hegelian
philosophy, was on the staff, as were Hammond, who enlisted, and
Henry Nevinson, who also supported the war. All of them had
opposed the Boer War.

Massingham's tolerance of dissenting views cannot be credited
merely to a sense of professional fair dealing towards long-time staff
– although even that would be a remarkable thing considering the
appalling treatment dissenters were given by employers, clubs, and
even friends, not to mention mobs and the law during the war years.
Massingham also published occasional contributions from opponents of his own position to whom he owed nothing, including
Morel, Trevelyan, Angell, MacDonald, and other members of the
UDC.

Still more remarkable were the weekly *Nation* lunches held at the
National Liberal Club. The official purpose of these lunches was to
work out the contents of the next issue. They also served as a weekly
forum for general political discussion – an informal version of the
Rainbow Circle, with whose membership the participants largely
overlapped.[4] There was usually an invited guest, and many people
who were not on the staff attended fairly regularly. The lunches

continued throughout the war, although not without some difficulty. There were a number of heated exchanges between Hobhouse on the one side and Hobson and Brailsford on the other, culminating eventually in Hobhouse storming out never to return, although he did continue to write for the paper.[5]

Such divisions as there were among the progressives over the war revolved principally around the questions of whether Germany was solely responsible and whether it was necessary to defeat her in order to achieve a reasonable peace. While these differences could be serious they did not lead to a permanent rupture. Even within the UDC, as we have seen, there were differing views on these questions, from Swanwick's and Ponsonby's pacifism to MacDonald's belief in the need for victory, from Brailsford's belief that Russia was primarily at fault, to Angell's belief that Germany was to blame.

That the progressives were held together by their common desire for a 'clean peace' is demonstrated by their enthusiastic response to President Wilson's 'Fourteen Points'. Although not Wilson's first declaration of his desire for a reasonable peace, the Fourteen Points were his most comprehensive, and, appearing shortly after American soldiers fought their first battles in France, by far the most influential among British supporters of the war. The similarities between the Fourteen Points and the principles advocated by the UDC were remarkable.[6] Like the UDC, Wilson proposed the abolition of secret diplomacy, consideration of the interests of the populations concerned prior to any transfers of territories, all-round disarmament, the restoration of free trade and the establishment of an association of nations.[7] The 'crankish' proposals of the 'pro-German' UDC were now the declared objectives of a responsible statesman who had led his country to decisive economic and military support of the allied cause.

When Wilson proclaimed the Fourteen Points, Lloyd George had been in power at the head of a Conservative-dominated coalition for more than a year, having deposed Asquith in December 1916. This event had transformed the politics of the war for many Liberal progressives. The new government was a fitting object for their attack in a way that Asquith's had not been. Its worst offence, apart from a belligerent tone of which Asquith was temperamentally incapable, was its proposals for a post-war economic boycott of Germany and a system of imperial preference. Perhaps even more offensive was the fact that it was led by an apostate. Lloyd George had been a 'pro-Boer', and in the pre-war Liberal Governments had been the prime mover in the introduction of welfare measures and a land tax – schemes dear to the progressive heart. His alignment with the Conservatives to attain the premiership appeared to the progressives to be nothing but opportunistic chicanery, and may be said from a progressive point of view to have finished him.

Massingham nursed a particular hatred for Lloyd George, but his comment on America's role in the war neatly encapsulates general progressive attitudes of admiration for Wilson and distrust of the British Government: 'The Never-Endians, the Tariff-mongers, the Imperialists of Europe will salute her arriving legions with resounding fanfares. But they will pigeon-hole her President's peace speeches. These men are not out for a new world or a democratic one; they are out against the form of autocratic Imperialism which threatened to overshadow their own.'[8]

Asquith's leadership of the Liberal Party gave his relationship to progressivism particular importance. In its own way, that relationship was as problematic as Lloyd George's. As a leading light among the Liberal Imperialists he is clearly to be placed beyond the progressive pale after 1899. On the other hand, he earned great esteem as leader of the reforming pre-war government. For many members of the UDC his decision to go to war in 1914 was the end of any claim he may have earned to a place in progressive ranks; for progressive supporters of the war that was irrelevant given that Germany had provoked the war. Asquith's stocks were boosted by his removal from power, for it freed him to join the progressives in supporting a 'clean peace', which he did with obvious enthusiasm.[9] Together with Grey (who had lost the Foreign Secretaryship after Lloyd George's coup) he threw himself with special gusto into the campaign for a League of Nations, which he regarded as 'the most urgent constructive problem of international statesmanship'.[10]

This was another scheme particularly dear to the progressive heart. Since the first year of the war many progressives – inside and outside the UDC – had involved themselves in the attempts of the Bryce Group to work out a viable scheme for a League of Nations. The group, which evolved into the League of Nations Society, was founded by Goldsworthy Lowes Dickinson, who had moved on the fringe of progressive circles before the war without being actively involved in politics.[11] Like most progressive organisations, the Bryce Group operated on the basis of commitment to a general principle rather than an elaborate orthodoxy. The schemes generated by its members were varied, and even incompatible, as a brief outline will show.

Brailsford's and Hobson's ideas about the League of Nations demonstrate both the comprehensiveness of Brailsford's socialist thought, and the increasing convergence of Hobson's ideas with his. Brailsford was convinced that a truly effective League was itself impossible under capitalism, and had no faith in the idea of the League as a mere arbitration court or international police force. The only way forward was for the League to play an active role in the running of the world's day to day affairs, in particular its economic affairs.

> If, by the creation of a League of Nations, we mean merely that the external bond of a treaty of arbitration is to link States, which retain their old individualism and their traditions of nationalist morals and nationalist economics, it would be folly to suppose that we can abolish war. Theoretically, the only security seems to lie in some organic international association, which, by the creation of intimate and pervasive relationships of interdependence within itself, is at least in process of evolution towards the ideal of international solidarity.[12]

This implied an enormous concession of sovereignty on the part of existing national states, and it was here Brailsford believed that capitalism must of necessity prove a sticking point.

Hobson's views on the League of Nations were almost identical, although he perhaps expressed himself more radically. Brailsford's major work on the subject was entitled, modestly enough, *A League of Nations*; Hobson's title, *Towards International Government*, got more directly to their common point. Hobson's argument may be seen as a working out of an idea he had argued in 1900 in his attack on the socialist imperialists. Then he had suggested that in the absence of any international equivalent of the state, there could be no grounds to assess the justice of one state's claim against another; now he argued that such an equivalent could be brought into existence.[13]

These arguments placed Hobson and Brailsford at some distance from other advocates of the League. Much of the academic discussions of the views of the proponents of the League of Nations revolves around the question of whether the League should have had the right to apply economic sanctions or use military force to ensure the right conduct of its members. This indeed was a question which greatly exercised the minds of contemporaries, many of whom were absolute pacifists on religious or ethical grounds.[14] Hobson's and Brailsford's schemes, however, side-stepped this issue somewhat by proposing an 'organic' League in which sanctions would be unnecessary.

The most important proposal for a League of Nations to come from Labour ranks was the scheme drafted by Leonard Woolf for the Fabian Society in 1915. The scheme was, as Woolf freely admitted, modest: 'our aim is not to compass the impossibility of war but merely to increase its improbability'.[15] Woolf rejected the idea of an 'International State' as utopian.[16] He also rejected the proposal for an international body of elected representatives on the grounds that the peoples of the world were insufficiently homogeneous to work it.[17] Instead, Woolf proposed an international high court of government representatives, weighted somewhat in favour of the Great Powers, whose essential task would be the resolution of disputes on the basis of existing international law. Such law at present was embodied in the complex system of international treaties and congresses which grew up in the nineteenth century.[18] To this would be added an International Council to resolve those disputes not amenable to legal decision, and to secure, 'by common agreement such international legislation as may be practicable'.[19]

Woolf's was an eminently practical scheme. As one historian has observed, 'In characteristic fashion, the Fabians accepted the world as it was, then cast about for practical methods of transforming it.'[20] In Woolf's scheme the mechanisms of the proposed League were thoroughly outlined, and each of the organs and procedures described in the second part of the report was based on some well-reasoned argument in the first. Its most striking feature, however, from the point of view of the present discussion, is its utter lack of any reference, explicit or implicit, to socialism, and its complete lack of any recognisably socialist analysis of the causes of international disputes.

These were clearly very important departures from Hobson's and Brailsford's ideas. The same may be said for the similar ideas advanced by Lowes Dickinson – the other leading Labour advocate of a League of Nations – who also dismissed Hobson's and Brailsford's proposals as utopian.[21] Nevertheless, all four had points in common which in the context of wartime and post-war politics placed them equally in the camp of the opposition and which set their proposals well apart from the League of Nations that came into being in 1919: all of them stipulated the inclusion of Germany. Their arguments, which were essentially identical, were neatly summed up by Lowes Dickinson: 'If Great Britain and her allies, while entering into the proposed agreement among themselves, should deliberately exclude the Central Powers, they would be perpetuating the armed peace that preceded the war and preparing the way for a new war.'[22]

This argument, however, and a general enthusiasm for a League of Nations were by no means confined to the Labour Party. By the end of the war the League of Nations was a part of the common stock of all parties in British politics, and the suggestion that Germany's inclusion was a prerequisite to a just and lasting peace was espoused by almost every Liberal politician outside the government. The exclusivist League that eventually came into being was only one feature of a peace that was hardly any less offensive to Asquith and Grey, who had led Britain into the war, than it was to the members of the UDC, who had bitterly denounced them for doing so.

The peace, however, revealed the full weakness of Asquith's position, and the impossibility of his leading any rally of progressives to the Liberal Party. For all that the post-war settlement was at odds with the progressive principles he had espoused in the last year of the war, he could not effectively denounce it. He was a prisoner of his own imperialist past.

(II) FROM LIBERALISM TO LABOUR

In the last year of the war Asquith issued this warning to Liberals: 'Do not let us, while welcoming every whole-hearted ally, abandon the primacy which has always been ours in the army of progress, or, in a fit of timorousness or lethargy, hand over to others the torch which we have received from those who went before us.'[23] There is a double irony here. Not only did the Liberal Party lose its primacy; but the fact that it did so is in very large measure attributable to Asquith himself. Asquith's failure at the crucial moment to articulate the disgust felt by progressives over the peace settlement and the Lloyd George Government's post-war foreign policy was probably the most important single contributing factor to the continuation of the movement of Liberals into the Labour Party after the war. For on these matters – the Treaty of Versailles with its fantastic reparations; the armed intervention in Russia; the apparently permanent exclusion of Germany and Russia from the League of

Nations – progressive opinion was united across a broader band of opinion than at any time since before the Boer War or until the Munich settlement.

Asquith's failure added a great deal of spice to Labour's criticisms of the Liberal Party. His eventual return to full voice hardly helped matters, for it enabled Labour propagandists to argue that the Liberal Party was now only capable of following their lead. Phrases like MacDonald's 'only when the sorry tale [of intervention in Russia] was told and could not be untold, did he join us in deploring it', or, with reference to foreign policy generally, 'the Liberals drift nearer and nearer to us', were deadly because essentially accurate.[24] But there was a good deal more to Labour's criticism than this kind of 'told you so' one-upmanship. Asquith's temporary silence gave credence to the important argument that the Treaty of Versailles was, 'based on the very political principles or premises which were the ultimate cause of the war'.[25] As these principles were those of the Liberal Imperialists, it followed naturally enough that, 'every time [Asquith] hits [the Government] he hits himself'.[26]

The concrete proof of this argument was provided by the Russian Bolsheviks. At the end of 1917 the Bolsheviks published the 'Secret Treaties' which they had found in the archives of the former Tsarist Government. These were transmitted to England by the *Manchester Guardian*'s correspondent Morgan Philips Price, Trevelyan's cousin and a former prospective Liberal candidate who was converted to socialism in 1915 by the realisation that the Liberal Party was 'nothing more than a tool of capitalist camarillas'.[27] The publication of the treaties in the *Manchester Guardian* and the *Daily Herald* lent enormous credence to the UDC's arguments concerning secret diplomacy. Every sinister design that UDC publicists had claimed to be concealed behind the veil of secrecy was now revealed in the agreements bearing the signatures of all the allied foreign ministers, including Grey. France was to have the west bank of the Rhine; Russia was to have the Straits of Constantinople; Britain Mesopotamia. The effects of the revelation on public opinion are incalculable. As Trevelyan described it later, UDC speakers never again 'failed of a sympathetic hearing from a working-class audience'.[28]

It is not surprising that it was the single-minded Morel who most relentlessly vilified Asquith and Grey over the treaties and the Entente. His argument was based on a doctrine of original sin: 'The leaders of the Liberal Party no longer represent Liberalism in foreign policy. They cannot. They abandoned it when they began that long course of deception, betrayal of popular rights, confessed, at last, but in part only, on August 3rd, 1914 . . . Falsehood begets falsehood. It is the first step that counts.'[29]

This line of reasoning was the basis upon which many progressives changed their party allegiance during and shortly after the war. Of the approximately two thousand[30] who did so, the only one to publish a thorough account of his reasons was Trevelyan. His book, *From Liberalism to Labour*, is especially valuable because of the obvious reluctance with which he made his decision; although repudiated and execrated by his constituency Liberal Association as soon as his stance on the war became clear, Trevelyan did not finally burn his bridges until after the 1918 election, at which he, like Ponsonby, stood as an independent. Even leaving aside Brailsford's interestingly phrased assessment that Trevelyan was 'the most naturally Liberal and least naturally Socialist person of our way of thinking',[31] his reluctance is not difficult to understand and was probably fairly typical. He was, as he said, a Liberal 'by inheritance' as well as by 'deliberate choice'.[32] For Trevelyan, Asquith's and Grey's failure to denounce the peace was clearly the final proof of the Liberal Party's fall from grace, and is one of the most prominent themes of his book. 'Neither before, nor during, nor after the peace', he complained, 'did they offer one bleat of opposition to the forces of reaction.'[33]

Trevelyan's explanation of Asquith's and Grey's silence was very similar to MacDonald's and Morel's. Their inability to make any complaint 'that anyone could hear beyond their drawing rooms' was not, in his view, due to malice: 'It appears that in so far as the Liberal leaders had volition they were on the side of Wilson. Their utterances were very meagre and incomplete. The fact was they dared not be emphatic . . . Men who had consented to the annexations of the Secret Treaties could not oppose the settlement which divided the spoils according to their signatures.'[34] The fundamental flaw in Asquith's and Grey's position, however, lay still further back in the commitment to France that had committed Britain to war. Again, Trevelyan did not question their good intentions. Grey and Asquith, he thought,

sincerely believed that they were reserving the fateful decision for the House of Commons . . . [T]o interpret democratic consultation as meaning a twelfth hour acquiesence in the decisions of eight years . . . is to exhibit a complete blindness to the real meaning of popular control. Leaders who have held such a view and acted upon it can never lead the British democracy into new regions of diplomacy and secure self-government.[35]

To accept these arguments was to abandon the Liberal Party, although it did not necessarily imply that one should join the Labour Party, even if one also accepted Morel's other claim that Liberalism in foreign policy had 'passed to Labour'.[36] Lord Loreburn, for example, was a supporter of 'advanced Liberalism' and agreed with most of Trevelyan's opinions on foreign policy, but although he thought the Liberal Party was 'fit only to be burnt out of existence' and that Labour was 'in the main sound on foreign policy', he remained an independent on the grounds that the Labour Party's domestic policy was 'idiotic' and 'merely a copy of the old nihilist and Bolshevik creed.'[37]

Few progressives imagined that Labour's programme had much in common with Bolshevism, and, as Dowse had pointed out, 'in changing their allegiance the ex-Liberals did not change their opinions . . . Not one of the new ILP members gave, as a reason for joining, his conversion to socialism.'[38] As Dowse suggests, however, this needs to be placed in the context of pre-war progressivism. Quite simply, many Liberals did not need converting; as we have seen in earlier chapters, many of them had held views at least as socialistic as their friends in the ILP since before the war.

It is, of course, dangerous to generalise about this. Angell, despite some of his rhetoric,[39] can hardly be described as a socialist at all. Although 'greatly drawn' to the Guild Socialism of G. D. H. Cole,[40] Angell feared that socialism would reverse the 'economic inter-dependence' which capitalism, and especially finance-capitalism, had done so much to stimulate.[41] Morel's socialism consisted of only as much of Brailsford's small change as was required to give something of a rational account of the evils of the foreign office conspiracy which for him was the real cause of the war.

Hobson's socialism strengthened steadily while he was a member of the Liberal Party, and continued to do so after he joined the Labour Party in 1918. Brailsford had demonstrated that Hobson's thought on underconsumption and on capitalist imperialism could provide the basis for an explicitly socialist critique of contemporary capitalism. Hobson's own intellectual development may be seen as a journey down the leftward path which his own theories thus implied. But it was not this which drove him out of the Liberal Party. Rather, it was his disgust at the Party's abandonment of the liberal principle of free trade, a principle which Hobson himself was later to abandon on socialist grounds. Hobson's resignation from the Liberal Party was the act of a Cobdenite; by the time he died in 1940, he was as much a Hobsonian as Brailsford.

Trevelyan's evolution was slightly different again. At the turn of the century he took the common New Liberal position that Liberals should not 'bow the knee' to socialism but should 'Try to understand the reasons of it; try to understand the weaknesses of it, but above all try to get suggestions from it that we can use.'[42] By the early 1930s Trevelyan was, as we shall see, an ardent advocate of nationalisation, and progressivism's most uncritical admirer of Stalin. In 1920 he was somewhere between these positions, arguing that the first Labour Government's programme should include a capital levy, the nationalisation of mines and railways, and a stiff land tax as a step toward nationalisation.[43]

Trevelyan believed that these measures would 'mean the opening of a new order of society', but even this does not signify a 'conversion', as he explained:

I still believe that until the days of the war it was a reasonable judgement on my part that more could be accomplished to prepare the way for a complete democracy and new economic society through the powerful organisation of the Liberal Party, imbued with a deep democratic conviction from its greatest leaders, supported by the largest mass vote of the working-class given to any Party, and closely responsive to articulate demands for economic change. Party to me has never been more than an instrument.[44]

In 1920, after Asquith's failure and the transfer of much of the Liberal Party's working-class vote to Labour, it was clear to Trevelyan that the Liberal Party could no longer be considered the instrument he wanted. But because this was a judgement about practical politics rather than a stand on a point of principle, Trevelyan was quite prepared to concede, in typical progressive manner, that others could reasonably dissent. 'Many men and women who feel on fundamental questions much as I do will remain in the Liberal Party. They may be correct in believing that what is best in democratic thought can revive again and find fruition in action through the Liberal Party.'[45] It is to those people, and the reasons for their decision, that we will now turn.

(III) THE TRUE LINE OF CLEAVAGE?

Loreburn was an exception; just as it was not a conversion to socialism that pushed many Liberal progressives into the ILP, it was not, on the whole, hostility to socialism that kept some others out. Nor can it be said that all of those who remained in the Liberal Party were any less disappointed by Asquith's and Grey's stance on the peace than were those who left. Massingham undoubtedly spoke for many Liberals when he argued in 1919 that

Liberalism had its first great chance of renewing its influence when the true character of the treaty was revealed. Many then saw that the hopes of a durable instrument had been disappointed or betrayed and that every one of Mr Asquith's or Lord Grey's appeals for such a settlement had gone astray. Not one word was said ... The Liberal Party does not live on its ideals. It is afraid of them.[46]

This was as good an argument against the Liberal Party as Trevelyan was to mount more than a year later, yet Massingham was not to follow him into the Labour Party until 1923. In the intervening period his ideas did not so much progress, as swither between a number of political choices. He advocated at various times that the two parties should co-operate, that they should fuse, or, as he himself finally did, that progressives should simply abandon the Liberal Party and join the Labour Party. His views are for that reason all the more valuable, for they are truly indicative of the doubts and uncertainties in the minds both of those who left the Liberal Party and those who did not.

As early as November 1918 – even before Asquith's and Grey's decisive failure – Massingham seemed on the verge of joining the Labour Party. At this stage he attributed the Liberal Party's impending collapse not to any shortcomings of its official leadership, but to Lloyd George's action in splitting the Party, and his peculiar brand of opportunism. Not the least of Lloyd George's crimes was the form and timing of the pending election, which Massingham declared 'a fraud on the electorate', and 'a warning to the thinkers and workers to escape from this confusion, to unite, to consolidate, to MAKE A PARTY OF THE FUTURE'.[47] His own move to this end, he announced, would be to vote Labour.

Two other comments in the same issue of the *Nation* provide some clue to Massingham's reluctance to take the plunge. The most obvious is his criticism of the Labour Party for refusing to endorse

John Burns, whom Massingham regarded highly, as its candidate in the election in consequence of his service as a minister in the pre-war Liberal Government.[48] In Massingham's view this discipline smacked of 'the spirit of the shorter catechism [which] ill suits the hour when the Labour Party makes its catholic appeal to the nation'.[49] This, together with Massingham's wish that the Labour Party should be called the 'Democratic Party', indicates an important reservation that many Liberals felt about Labour, even including those who heartily endorsed its foreign policy, and whose political distance from the cautious brand of 'Socialism' advanced by leaders like MacDonald was certainly no greater than that of Ponsonby, Angell, or many others who did join the Labour Party either during the war or immediately after the 1918 election.

For those who remained loyal to the Liberal Party the problem was precisely that Labour's appeal was not 'catholic'. As Massingham had himself asserted only two months earlier when arguing for co-operation rather than fusion, 'Liberalism speaks, or ought to speak, for all classes; while the Labor party, as it is at present constituted speaks for one.'[50] This refrain was at least as old as the ILP itself. In 1893 it had been the basis of Massingham's angry departure from the Fabian Society.[51] In the post-war years it became central to all Liberal criticism of the Labour Party, and one of the Liberal Party's principal justifications for its own continued existence. Such justification was becoming increasingly difficult to find for those who had been associated with the New Liberalism before the war, for as Charles Masterman admitted in 1920, 'In practical policy there is no . . . difference between Radicalism on the one hand and the Labour leaders, who in practice preach a moderate Radical policy, on the other.'[52] Given this concession Masterman's recycling of the standard liberal argument that socialism destroys liberty had little bearing on the matter at hand, which was whether there was any case for the continuation of a separate Liberal Party. His most important argument was that Labour was at that moment, 'struggling between formation as a Party of Class and a Party of Ideas, and the Party of Class is obviously today triumphant'.[53] His evidence for this assertion was the composition of the Labour Party's parliamentary representation, which after the election of 1918 had forty-nine trade union sponsored MPs in a total of fifty-seven.

Masterman's charge that the trade unionists were mediocrities who had reduced Labour to 'Parliamentary futility' was indisputable from the progressive point of view. These were men, after all, who had with only one exception voted in favour of the Treaty of Versailles, and whose deputy leader, J. R. Clynes, thought the framers of the Treaty had 'acted with motives of the highest patriotism and with the highest and noblest considerations for human government'.[54] MacDonald, writing in reply to Masterman, made no attempt to defend them, but rather side-stepped the charge by claiming that 'the life of the Labour Party is in the constituencies rather than the Parliament'.[55]

It is possible that Masterman gave some weight to these arguments, for in his book of the following year he considered the evils of the 'class party' in its extra-parliamentary workings. Here he argued that the nexus between the Labour Party and the trade unions was such that any trade unionist with even limited aspirations to advancement in the hierarchy had no choice but to become an active supporter of the Labour Party. In its extreme form, this tendency led to 'a repetition of the old feudal and landlord system ... Members of Trades Unions, in meetings where Trades Unionists are present in bulk, are sometimes as afraid to lift up their hands in support of the Liberal candidates as once they were in country villages under the eyes of the representatives of the landlords.'[56]

Many Liberals shared these views. Hobhouse for example felt that, 'The constitution of the Labour Party binds it tight to the Trade Unions and their sectional selfishness, a most serious defect.'[57] Gilbert Murray deplored the tendency of Labour propagandists, 'if not to preach class war, at least to appeal constantly to class feeling'.[58] He imagined 'two possible contingencies' that might even drive Liberals into co-operation with the Conservatives; both were based on his fears of the class Labour represented. One was that 'the Labour Party might fall under the sway of that mass of reactionary, low-minded ignorance that in the old days we called "the Tory mob"'; the other, more likely possibility was that the trade unions 'may possibly become an anti-social influence'.[59] J. M. Robertson, who with Hobson and Herbert Burrows had been a travelling lecturer for the South Place Ethical Society, set out similar arguments in more forcible terms, reasserting one of classical liberalism's favourite dogmas:

The old typical aristocrat ... claimed to be above his fellow-creatures in respect of his birth and status. The zealots of 'Labour' do the same. They too hold by caste, merely turning the scale upside down ... Alike, they obliterate in their professed politics the moral grounds of a sane human valuation. Alike, they take for granted that to be born in their 'class' is a certificate of merit. Alike, they refuse to ask whether the man of their class is good, kind, truthful, wise, or public-spirited as distinct from being merely class-spirited ... Before the Liberal Party bore that name, its forerunners saved Britain from civil war and revolution by refusing to let class ideals prevail against the healthy human aspiration for political equality.[60]

Some of those who joined Labour had similar reservations about the party's link with the trade unions, a fact which may help to account for the many conflicts between the union leaders and the progressive intellectuals. Hobson, for example, claimed in 1938 that he had 'never felt quite at home in a body governed by the trade union members and their finance'.[61] When Massingham publicly announced his allegiance to the Labour Party in 1923 in consequence of the return to Liberal ranks of Lloyd George, whom he detested passionately, he still continued to express private doubts about the unions' role within the party.[62] In any case, the Labour Party's leading spokesmen – themselves veterans of pre-war progressivism – were often at pains to deny the charge and return it with interest:

the Labour Party is working for all men and women of every class who live by honest and useful work ... The means of production are to be owned in common, not by a class, not by the Labour Party, not by the Trade Unions, not by the manual workers, *but by the community* ... The Labour Party is the very opposite of a Class Party. It has come into politics to abolish class government and class control. Liberals defend the private ownership of land and the means of production. That is to say, that Liberals believe in class ownership and control ... But not only the programme but the personnel of the Labour Party show how ridiculous is the statement that the Labour Party is a 'Class Party'. Its membership is drawn from every class – bishops, ministers, lawyers, doctors, professors, authors, artists, employers, managers, skilled craftsmen, manual workers of all sorts ... What unites the Labour Party is not class, but agreement on principles and aim.[63]

The Liberal progressives who joined the Labour Party did not do so because they supported the idea of a 'class party'. To the extent to which they did think Labour was a class party they had qualms; on the other hand, Snowden's argument was powerful, and became more powerful with every middle class progressive who joined. Labour's alleged class basis may have been an important obstacle to some Liberal progressives' joining the Labour Party; it was not, however, an obstacle to co-operation between them and those who did join.

Massingham's public declaration of his change of allegiance provides a powerful illustration of both the central themes of my argument and the essential features of progressivism.

You reject the materialism of the age, and believe that it is time to have done with what is base or merely fugitive in the capitalist system? Then you must quit the leadership of old men and break the attachment of dead or fulfilled issues. In effect you have no choice. So far as Mr Asquith has lifted the responsibility for the Treaty of Versailles and all its load of misery from Mr George's shoulders and transferred it to his own, he has left Liberalism as resourceless in foreign affairs as it is empty of spiritual appeal. And in the field of home policies Liberal dependence on Capitalism fixes the Party more and more in an attitude of scepticism and despair. The Party ... [now has] nothing in common with Gladstonian idealism or with John Bright's pacifist faith ... JOIN THEN, THE LABOUR PARTY, AS I HAVE JOINED IT. IT IS YOUR PROPER PLACE. You will gain with it a repository for the faith that many of you have lost as members of an almost exclusively middle-class Party, in detachment from the mass of your countrymen and countrywomen.[64]

The only detectable change from Massingham's earlier position is on the 'class party' question, but even here it is not his fundamental belief that has changed, but only his assessment of the nature of the two parties. The essence of his advice to Liberals, in fact, is not that they should change their views, but that they must join the Labour Party in order to be consistent with their views. This reminds us again of the small place that party loyalty occupied in progressives' minds: parties commanded their loyalty only for as long as they were effective instruments for the expression and realisation of progressive ideas and values. It reminds us too that the decision to remain in the Liberal Party or to join the Labour Party did not turn on differing ideals, but rather on differing judgements about the ability and willingness of each party to advance the ideals that progressives held in common.

(IV) PROGRESSIVE CO-OPERATION: ECHOES OF PAST
AND FUTURE

With so little of substance between their position and that of their former colleagues now in the ILP, it is hardly surprising that the thoughts of some Liberal progressives turned to the idea of co-operation between the two parties. It is no less surprising that Massingham was among the first to do so. As early as August 1918 he proposed co-operation between the parties as the only way of preventing a peace dictated by jingoes such as the press barons Beaverbrook and Northcliffe and the Australian Prime Minister W. M. Hughes. Massingham despaired that Asquith and Henderson, who together could change 'the evils of our State', were each too busy 'roofing in their own particular tabernacle'.[65]

The other Liberals we have considered were also interested in co-operation with Labour, despite their objections to its class base. Gilbert Murray outlined most clearly the arguments and sentiments in favour of co-operation. Unsurprisingly, the first of these was that 'On the whole vast problem of war and peace we and Labour think instinctively the same.'[66] Typically for progressives, Murray pitched all his arguments on this level of 'instinct' and belief rather than the level of concrete programmes. Discussing his first-hand observations of the Workers' Educational Association and the Workers' Travel Association he declared, 'the thing I saw before me was true Liberality, though it happened, of course, to call itself Labour. We belong on the side of those people, not on the side of those who wish to economise on schools and to stir up feeling against foreigners'.[67] More generally, Murray pointed to the progressive faith that he believed was at the core of both parties: 'Labour ... believes in the rule of the good elements of life. It believes in making life a better thing. It believes in progress, enlightenment, self-mastery, "plain living and high thinking", and all the other ideals which we Liberals secretly cherish.'[68] Hobhouse echoed these sentiments, but was able to list more specific areas of agreement between the parties; again, the order in which he placed them is telling: 'Labour in office has on the whole represented essential Liberalism ... *better* than the organised party since C[ampbell]-B[annerman]'s death ... Liberals may be full of fight but as against the main body of Labour what have they to fight for? Internationalism? Free Trade? Ireland, India, any particular kind of Social Reform? No, on all these there is agreement.'[69]

The forms of co-operation advocated by Liberal progressives varied. Hobhouse, who as the above quotation implies sometimes seemed to doubt the need for a separate Liberal Party, suggested that Liberals ought to take up the educational task of teaching Labour that 'true Socialism is the point of view of the community as a whole'.[70] In other words, Liberals could wean Labour away from the evils of a class party. J. M. Robertson, who was the most frankly partisan of the Liberals we have considered, had an ideal of co-operation based on a vision of the Labour Party that bore little resemblance to contemporary realities: 'To a Labour Party as such, Liberalism has never been hostile ... It is eminently desirable that where both of the old Parties claim to stand by labour votes, there should be accredited representatives of labour who can speak with a measure of special authority on questions directly affecting the workers.'[71] This was to consign Labour forever to the role of a class party. It was also patently little more than nostalgia for the days when Labour knew its place, a nostalgia which gave an uncomfortably patronising tone to Robertson's judgement that, 'No better Liberals ever sat in Parliament than the series of "Liberal – Labour" members.'[72]

Masterman and Gilbert Murray, by contrast, fully recognised that the days when such comments could fill a Labour activist's heart with comradely affection or deferential gratitude were long past. Murray nominated a 'Labour Government with a Liberal wing' as his second preference after 'a Liberal Government with a Labour wing'.[73] Masterman, writing four years earlier with Labour's rise to government still in the future, may be credited with more insight than Murray. Even in 1921, Masterman's political calculations were based on the assumption that Labour was and would remain a major party. He firmly rejected the idea 'that Labour can be reduced to the subordinate conditon of an "advanced" wing, patronised by the Liberals, but not substantially a competitor'.[74] Instead he advocated an understanding based on a presumption of equality between the two parties. 'Without such an understanding', he believed, 'progress dies.'[75] His fleshing out of this proposal, especially in its apprach to the problems of the organisational and ideological integrity of the two parties bears some resemblance to the arguments advanced by the advocates of the Popular Front fifteen years later.

A programme of specific reform for some specific Government to undertake, found common alike in the Labour and the Liberal programme, could be one for the fulfilment of which both parties would be honourably committed. Such programme of a two-party majority would involve legitimate political compromise. It would not involve greater political compromise than that formerly needed in the programme of one political party;

when (for example) extreme Whiggism and extreme Radicalism would unite to terminate Tory rule . . . Under such conditions Liberalism would be prepared to take office again, with the general support of Labour members. It would be prepared to welcome a Labour Party in office, with the general support of Liberal members. It would be prepared for a combination of the two parties . . . being content that the future should decide what questions of honest divergence of opinion should create a separation.[76]

Massingham had arrived at a rather similar position in October 1920, apparently having lost faith in his argument of the previous winter that Liberals should rally to the Labour Party in order to rescue it from its single-class basis. Such a fusion of 'the Radical Left and the Labor mass', he had then maintained, was the only way to 'work out the salvation of progressive England'.[77] By October, however, he had opted again for co-operation between the Parties, hoping that the 'class party' problem could be temporarily banished with a flick of the wrist:

If only [Labour] had a man who could say to them: 'For the present I will lead no more strikes, no more bread-and-butter movements. I am going to lead you against the rabble that calls itself a Government. I am out for 350 seats in the next Parliament. I am for turning Lloyd George out of it, and for setting up in his place a ministry of honest men. Allies? I'll take any helper that comes along if he will agree, politically, on a few points that I am going to put to him. Radicals? Certainly! Decent democratic Tories like Lord Henry Bentinck? Of course! Come on, and we'll map out the seats together.' Will Labour say this? Has it the pluck? It's the way to win, and there is no other.[78]

Such proposals for co-operation had not the slightest chance of success for the simple reason that nobody in the Labour Party was interested in them. It was hardly likely that working-class men and women who had struggled to create a party specifically to represent themselves politically would be tempted into co-operation with a party which unanimously declared this to be its greatest evil, nor was it likely that people who had recently given up on the Liberal Party as a vehicle of progress should accept the idea that the Party was an essential component of an effective progressive strategy. The one published Labour response to Massingham's plea was a long letter from Ponsonby, one of the most recent recruits from the Liberal Party. Ponsonby conceded that the political situation was grave, and that 'The temptation to unite in order to overthrow is great'; but, he argued, the Liberal–Labour coalition government to emerge from the overthrow would exhibit the same 'infirmity of purpose, and divided counsels, the fatal results of which we are feeling now'. What was required was 'a Government solidly and wholeheartedly united in principle', and the only way to get it was simply to wait until the Labour Party had acquired sufficient strength and experience to govern in its own right.[79]

The replies to this line of argument reveal the urgency that many Liberals saw in the existing political situation. One writer urged that Massingham's scheme 'would have only one merit. It would probably save the country.'[80] Masterman wrote angrily,

Ireland may perish, Russia may perish, Europe and the whole of European civilisation may perish, so long as the Labour Party maintains its independence of entangling alliances, and that in some few years or decades it may be called to assume the government of this country. How long before this call comes will this country itself be in a condition when it does not much matter what kind of Government it possesses?[81]

Either of these comments – if we substitute 'Spain' for 'Ireland' – could easily have been written eighteen years later by an outraged Popular Fronter, and Ponsonby's rejection of Massingham's idea is very similar to the arguments the Labour Party leadership advanced against the Popular Front. This is where the parallel ends. In the 1930s the idea of co-operation between the two parties had considerable minority support within the Labour Party, of which a significant component came from veterans of pre-war progressivism. In the 1920s it had no support within the Labour Party whatsoever. The appeal for co-operation could hardly have found a less favourable political climate. Despite or rather because of the large common ground between them, the two parties spent the decade in mortal combat; the British electoral system entailed that one must destroy the other if it was to be a serious contender for power. The formation of two minority Labour Governments dependent on Liberal parliamentary support – the inevitable (given the parties' common commitment to free trade) but unwelcome outcome of a parliamentary situation for which only the voters were responsible – only added fuel to the fires of recrimination, as the parties' propaganda of the period shows.

The most vocally anti-Liberal component of the Labour Party was the ILP, the component to which almost all of the former Liberals actually belonged. They, it seems, were no less eager than their new comrades to finish off their old Party, and Ponsonby's rebuff of Massingham shows that they were certainly in no mood to co-operate with it. Strategically this was sensible. As Trevelyan had suggested to Ponsonby before either of them had actually joined the ILP, 'it may be good to have [the Liberal Party] utterly discredited so that all youth and intellect may flock to Labour and make a party for the future'.[82]

Given these attitudes, and given the ILP and Labour Party's official hostility to the Liberals, expressed in a steady stream of pamphlets and speeches, it is surprising that some Liberal progressives continued to hope for close and cordial co-operation between the two parties. To some extent this may be explained in terms of tactics: before 1922, by the massive hegemony of the Coalition Government, whose foreign policy was seen by many progressives as an evil to be stopped at all costs; after 1922, by the Liberal Party's decline, which indicated that co-operation with Labour was its only route to influence. It is a major claim of this book, however, that progressives' tactical decisions – whether wise or unwise – cannot be properly understood without reference to the principal features of the progressive tradition. The Liberal progressives' appeals for co-operation between the two parties had a broader context than the tactical considerations of the day. That context was the progressive tradition itself, which, as we know, was characterised by concerted action and open discourse that transcended the boundaries of party.

The bitter hostility between the Liberal and Labour Parties was not reflected in the dealings between those who had been active in the progressive milieu before the war. Indeed, that milieu continued to operate after the war largely unaffected by the fact that a large number of its participants had changed their party allegiance. It is this that accounts for the continued hopes of Liberal progressives for cross-party collaboration; it was the norm of their daily lives and work.

Progressive co-operation across the demarcations of party continued most conspicuously in journalism, the field in which a great number of the leaders of progressive opinion gained at least a part of their daily bread. The reader will have observed already that the *Nation* continued to draw on a pool of talent from both parties; among its staff and contributors until 1923 were Masterman and Gilbert Murray of the Liberal Party as well as Brailsford, MacDonald, Henry Nevinson, Leonard Woolf, and Harold Laski of the Labour Party, and Hammond, who may or may not have been a member of the Labour Party.[83] In 1923, a new regime was established when the Rowntree family trust gave up the proprietorship to the Liberal Summer School movement. John Maynard Keynes became chairman of the board with Hubert Henderson as editor.[84] This was preceded by a dispute – only partly political – between Massingham and the old proprietors, in which Massingham resigned the editorship.[85] The whole staff, with the exception of Labour's Leonard Woolf, resigned in protest against what they saw as unfair treatment of Massingham.[86] The *Manchester Guardian* also recruited staff and solicited contributions from people of both parties. These included the Liberals Hobhouse and Robertson, and Labour's Laski, R. H. Tawney, and G. D. H. Cole, as well as virtually all of the *Nation* contributors.

This diversity cannot be explained merely by pointing to the dearth of available Liberal journalists resulting from the mass defections of 1915-20. The UDC, whose leadership in the 1920s consisted entirely of ILP members, nevertheless opened the columns of *Foreign Affairs*, its monthly organ, to a number of Liberal writers; and the ILP's weekly *New Leader*, under Brailsford's editorship in 1922–6, 'celebrated the diversity of progressive thought'[87] by placing contributions from Hammond alongside those of long-time ILP stalwarts like MacDonald, Fenner Brockway, and Clifford Allen, and new recruits such as Hobson, Ponsonby, Morel, Angell, Nevinson, and Bertrand Russell. That Liberal thought – or at least a section of it – was still considered an essential component of progressivism is most explicitly illustrated in Leonard Woolf's informal invitation to Hammond, in 1928, to join Harold Laski as co-editor of the soon to be launched *Political Quarterly*: 'the Quarterly is to be progressive, i.e. it must include the general outlook of both "Liberals" and "Labour"; the combination of the two colourations in a joint editorship would therefore have obvious advantages'.[88] In the event, the *Political Quarterly* was launched with an editorial board of nine, including Hammond, Laski, Keynes, Woolf, and Kingsley Martin, who later became editor of the amalgamated *New Statesman and Nation*. In its first issue, the *Political Quarterly* announced that its function would be 'to discuss social and political questions from a progressive point of view ... [I]t has been planned by a group of writers who hold certain general political ideas in common.'[89] The *Quarterly*'s contributors in the thirties included Cole, Shaw, Hobson, Brailsford, Hugh Dalton, Hugh Gaitskell, Leonard Barnes (a prominent Hobsonian writer on imperialism), and D. N. Pritt whose fame was achieved as an apologist for Stalin's purge trials.

The participation of men like Cole and Laski in these journalistic activities is important, for it shows that the continuation of easy relations among progressives of both parties was not due merely to the reluctance of ageing men to change their habits. The people who have had any significant part in this discussion so far were all old enough to have been prominent in the pre-war progressive milieu; with the exception of Leonard Woolf, who was thirty-four, all were in or past their forties when the war began. Cole and Laski, who at that time were twenty-five and twenty-one respectively, were of the next generation. Their natural home was the Labour Party, and within the Labour Party their place was on the left, with Brailsford and Trevelyan, and only slightly less clearly, Hobson. They were often uncomfortable with its relatively strict organisational norms, and when they partook of its tendency to ideological dogmatism, as they did in the mid 1930s, they thereby sacrificed much of their political heritage. The Labour left was thus in some respects a peculiar place for heirs to the progressive tradition to be. In other respects, which we shall discover, it was the only place for them to be. In any case, as this book argues, it is there that they are found.

CHAPTER 5

Inside the left

J. A. Hobson, Harold Laski, Brailsford, G. D. H. Cole, R. H. Tawney – we did not lack brilliant theoreticians pointing the way we ought to go.

Jennie Lee.[1]

The topic of the 1932 Conway Memorial Lecture was 'Nationalism and the Future of Civilisation'. The lecture was delivered, as always, at Conway Hall, the home of the South Place Ethical Society, and still, as the advertisements in the progressive press tell us, an important venue of London progressive life.

The lecture contained few if any arguments that its audience would not have heard before. The speaker told them first that nationalism had a definite positive role: 'The suppression of the [national] yearning to be free always poisons the well-springs of the body politic ... Whatever the loss of administrative efficiency, a nation that is deprived of the right to determine its own way of life suffers an abridgment of personality which, sooner or later, issues in violence.' Some of those phrases doubtless warmed the hearts of the very oldest members of the audience, and they, along with those a decade or two their juniors, would certainly have felt a glow of nostalgic indignation as the speaker continued: 'The arts of propaganda are exhausted in the effort to persuade us that some particular search for profits is a holy war ... We did that in the South African War. We surrounded a mean search for gold with every sort of noble motive – progress, the rights of British subjects, and the rest.'

But the speaker was not there merely to kindle the fires of nostalgia. His purpose was to present a progressive case relevant to contemporary problems. Old and young heads could nod in equal proportion when he told them of the importance of educating the masses in 'social and international relations', lamented the tendency of modern education to foster only nationalism, told them that they were 'members of nation-states in which, even though there sometimes be the formal aspect of democracy, its reality remains unachieved'. It is possible though that some of the older members of the audience shifted uncomfortably in their seats at the slightly Bolshevik tone of the moral the speaker drew: 'The bias of state-action is always in favour of those who possess the levers of economic power ... The will of the state means, in daily action, the will of those who possess the economic power of the community ... Capitalism becomes imperialism by the very nature of its being.'

Still, the argument was older than the Bolsheviks, and in any case the speaker soon returned to safer ground when he noted the significance of the fact that the 'two legal members of the Viceroy's Council in India, Sir Henry Maine and Fitzjames Stephen, were both, after their experiences of autocracy abroad, the passionate critics of democracy at home'. Any lingering doubts about the speaker's Bolshevik inclinations were decisively put to rest as he reached his conclusion:

I am not so foolish as to suppose that we can destroy the dangers of nationalism merely by creating an equal society. Such a state would still need markets and raw materials ... The erosion of inequality would give to the claims of the state a title to allegiance it does not now possess. Its citizens might easily come to feel a patriotism almost religious in its intensity. There is some interesting evidence that this is the case in Soviet Russia.[2]

The speaker was not the seventy-four-year-old Hobson, although as a regular at South Place he was almost certainly in the audience. Nor was it the fifty-nine-year-old Brailsford; he was in the chair. The speaker was Harold Laski, who by 1932, at the age of thirty-nine, was one of the most important intellectual leaders of the Labour left. Laski's honoured presence at Conway Hall shows us something of the continuities in the life of the progressive milieu, and perhaps also something of the shift in its focus from the Liberal Party to the Labour Party in the inter-war years. More clearly still, the content of his speech shows us the continuing importance of Hobson's and Brailsford's arguments. There is not one sentence in it which could not have been paraphrased from *Imperialism* or *The War of Steel and Gold*.

Laski's personal and intellectual biography place him firmly in the British progressive tradition. He grew up in a prominent Jewish Liberal family in Edwardian Manchester, where he daily digested the *Manchester Guardian*.[3] A prodigy, Laski became interested in eugenics at the age of sixteen and had an article published in the *Westminster Review* when only seventeen. At Oxford he joined the Fabian Society and with his wife, Frida, was active first in the militant and then the moderate wing of the Women's Suffrage movement, through which he became a close friend of Henry Nevinson. Immediately on his graduation in 1914 he was invited by George Lansbury to write for the quasi-syndicalist cum Guild Socialist *Daily Herald*, a position he held until he took up an academic post in Canada in September of the same year, having been rejected as a volunteer for the army in August. Within eighteen months he was invited to teach at Harvard, where he remained until 1920. Laski thus spent the crucial war years away from England, although his volunteering, considered together with his disgust at the 'war fever'[4] that later gripped the United States, suggests that his position would not have been unlike Massingham's, or perhaps even like that of the few uniformed members of the UDC.

Laski returned to England in 1920 to take up a post at the London School of Economics that had been arranged for him by Graham Wallas, Sidney Webb, and Lord Haldane.[5] The life he entered immediately on his return is itself testimony to the continued vitality of the progressive milieu in the post-war years. In October he began a series of articles for the *Nation* on the violence Lloyd George had done to constitutional freedoms.[6] He soon became a regular attender at the *Nation* lunches, where he became friendly with Hobson, Brailsford, and the rest.[7] He also began to contribute to the *Manchester Guardian*. Other friends in the 1920s included Lowes Dickinson, Gilbert Murray, J.M. Robertson,[8] and Hobhouse, whom Laski regarded as 'the one English thinker who has made the search, practical and academic, for justice his life work'.[9]

Laski's political thought was complex and fluid, and cannot readily be summarised. Indeed, the only full-scale study of his work consists largely of a discussion of its many contradictions.[10] These 'contradictions' are indicative of the milieu in which he lived and worked. As one student of inter-war Liberalism has observed,

A 'horizontal' consideration of [Laski's] idea-environment rather than a misconceived 'vertical' location of Laski in a 'socialist' tradition reinforces the claim that the boundaries of liberal ideology were not institutional, and that previous delimitations of liberalism within party political confines have ignored the impact of left-liberalism between the wars. On questions of social policy, workers' participation, and state regulation of the interests of workers, consumers, and investors, there was complete accord between Laski and progressive liberals.[11]

Another way of approaching Laski which will lead to substantially the same results is to view him 'vertically' as a part of the *progressive* tradition – a tradition broad enough to require at all times a 'horizontal' treatment.

Laski's philosophy returns us briefly to the themes of the first chapter, for his ideas and influences provide one of the best possible illustrations of the unhelpfulness of a hard and fast distinction between 'individualism' and 'collectivism' in understanding progressive thinkers. Laski never accepted the superogatory claims of the state advanced by the Idealist philosophers. For him, the state's claim to our obedience was conditional; nevertheless, his way of formulating the conditions was, as he acknowledged, very reminiscent of Green.

I have as a citizen, a claim upon society to realise my best self in common with others. That claim involves that I be secured those things without which I cannot, in Green's phrase, realise myself as a moral being ... I am given rights that I may enrich the common life. But if these rights fail of realisation I am entitled to examine the State upon the hypothesis that its will is directed to ends other than the common good. I regard its power as force exercised in order to secure those rights. Its moral character is known to me by the rights that it maintains.[12]

This passage shows clearly that even at the level of formal philosophical discourse Laski can be contained by neither of the categories 'individualist' or 'collectivist', for while he employs the notion of the common good, he denies that the state has any automatic claim to be the incarnation of the common good. Moreover, he denies the reality of the general will.

The root of Laski's socialism was his belief that the modern capitalist state failed the test he proposed, for, under the existing system of property relations,

[T]he basis of the State is envy ... A State so divided is compelled to use its instruments to protect the property of the rich from invasion by the poor. It comes to think of order as the final virtue. It neglects its larger aims. It perverts the equal aid it owes to all in the effort to afford the special advantage required by some.[13]

To the complex mixture of liberal thinkers who influenced his thought Laski had little difficulty in adding the influence of Karl Marx. His attraction to Marx grew considerably after 1931, as we shall see, but it was already evident in the 1920s. Commenting on the materialist conception of history in 1927, for example, he wrote: 'There is no department of human life in which the governing ideas and institutions will not be found, upon examination, to be largely a reflection of a given set of economic conditions.'[14] His acceptance and use of Marx, however, was as critical as his use of liberal thinkers. Given the close attention he had given the works of his friend Graham Wallas on social psychology, he could not help but regard the materialist conception of history as 'too exclusively preoccupied with a rational theory of human action to remember how much of a man's effort is non-rational in character'.[15] Many actions and beliefs, for example religious sectarianism, were not amenable to materialist explanations.

The eclecticism of pre-war progressivism is thus exemplified in the thought of one of the most important leaders of Labour's intellectual left in the inter-war years. Laski was a true successor to the progressive tradition not only in his friendships, which knew no bounds of party, but also in his intellectual influences, which knew no bounds of orthodoxy. Paramount among those friends and influences were many of the leading pre-war progressives themselves – most of them many years his senior: Wallas, Hobhouse, Hobson, and Brailsford.[16]

The early career of G.D.H. Cole was only slightly less typical of pre-war progressivism than Laski's. Four years older than Laski, he had already established himself as something of an *enfant terrible* by the outbreak of war. He was converted to socialism while in his teens, 'quite simply, by reading William Morris's *News from Nowhere* . . . on grounds of morality and decency and aesthetic sensibility'.[17] In 1908, at the age of nineteen, he joined both the Oxford University Fabian Society and the ILP. Within the Fabian Society, Cole, together with his friend William Mellor (of whom more later), soon became well known as a theorist and advocate of Guild Socialism – an Anglicised, intellectualised adaptation of the syndicalist ideas that briefly captured the imagination of many British workers before the First World War.[18] Cole, who appears when young to have had a somewhat prickly temperament, left the Fabian Society in 1915 after attempting unsuccessfully to 'capture' it for Guild Socialism in a 'dispute that was characterised by much rudeness on the part of the insurgents'.[19]

If this episode was atypical of progressivism, the sequel was not, for Cole, while continuing to proclaim his lack of 'any feeling of obligation or friendship toward the Fabian Society', [20] continued with his Guild Socialist friends to work for the Fabian Research Committee, a form of co-operation which Beatrice Webb did her best to facilitate.[21]

Cole opposed the war and was active in the organisation of the Amalgamated Society of Engineers, one of the most militant unions of the war years. He was also an active participant in some of the various progressive discussion groups on post-war problems. Cole's distinctively left-wing views evolved earlier than Laski's, and he had a more difficult temperament; his relationship with the broad progressive milieu was therefore more problematic. He contributed only a few articles to the *Nation* before angrily ending his association when Massingham rejected one as 'too extreme'.[22] None of this, however, prevented his enjoying the 'great honour' of contributing to the *Manchester Guardian*, to which he was first recommended by A. D. Lindsay, the Idealist philosopher who was later to be 'Independent Progressive' candidate for Oxford City at the height of the Popular Front campaign.[23] In the same year as his dispute with Massingham he negotiated with Scott to write a daily letter on labour issues. When Scott terminated this arrangement in 1921 for financial and administrative reasons, Cole cheerfully offered to write casual articles, declaring, 'There are few other papers I should feel any pleasure in serving.'[24]

Cole was not a philosopher, and his philosophical position was far more straightforward than Laski's. It nevertheless provides an equally firm demonstration of the uselessness of a dichotomy between 'individualism' and 'collectivism' as an analytical tool in the history of progressive ideas. Cole's Guild Socialism, which he never abandoned even though the National Guilds League collapsed in 1923, implied a rejection of state socialism, which he regarded as largely 'a bureaucratic and Prussianising movement'.[25] His early statements of his views, it is true, appear at first to be thoroughly 'individualist'. 'The crowning indictment of Capitalism', he wrote, 'is that it destroys freedom and individuality in the workers.'[26] His rejection of the notion of state sovereignty, however, did not stem from philosophical individualism, but from the view that

the person of the community cannot truly be sustained by any single form of association . . . States exist for the execution of that very important class of collective actions which affect all the members of the communities in which they exist equally and in the same way. For other classes of action, in respect of which men fall into different groups, other forms of association are needed, and these forms of association are no less sovereign in their sphere than the State in its sphere.[27].

The concrete political structures Cole deduced from this insistence on the reality of the functional group remained vague, but broadly he proposed that 'The State should own the means of production: the Guild should control the work of production.'[28] To this proposal of what we would now call workers' self-management, Cole wished to add a small state apparatus with authority residing in two legislative chambers: one elected by geographical units, the other consisting of the delegates of the Guilds. Mere territorial representation he rejected as resting on 'essentially individualistic assumptions'.[29] The arrangement he proposed would reflect the duality of collective and individual existence which he insisted characterised each person's life: 'A man may be a 'detail-labourer' in a factory, with no isolable individual product of his own, without losing his individuality as a person, however much he thinks as a member of a group.'[30]

These were the considerations that made Cole a Guild Socialist rather than any other kind of socialist. In describing why he was a socialist at all, however, he could do no better than fall back on the Benthamite formula: 'I want socialism because I believe it will make for the greatest happiness of the greatest number.'[31]

The post-Boer War Fabian Society may seem an odd place for a man to form views like Cole's. So it would have been if it had consisted of nothing more than acolytes of the Fabian Junta. Even after the Boer War, however, it consisted of something more than that – at least outside London. The Oxford University Fabian Society had a distinct character, redolent of the parent body's earlier years. It was presided over by Sydney Ball, a long-time Fabian who was simultaneously 'a leading member of the liberal club'.[32] Ball's tendency to proclaim alternatively Mill and Green as his most important influences may perhaps help to account for some of Cole's later views,[33] as might Ball's early conversion to Hobsonian under-consumption and his active opposition to the Boer War.

Cole explained Hobson's influence on his own thought in an obituary:

I myself can well remember, from my undergraduate days, the vindictive-ness with which I heard Hobson's subversive notions assailed – with the natural consequence that I began reading his books with a strong disposi-tion in their favour . . . His ways of stating his criticism of [orthodox] theory were often open to serious objection; but who will deny today that there was substance in the alternative theory which he consistently maintained?[34]

Underconsumptionist theory permeates Cole's writings on eco-nomics, and his views on economic imperialism were, equally clearly, based on Hobson's thought, as the following outline shows:

During the past half-century, the advanced States of Europe, followed later by Japan and in some degree by the United States, have reached a stage of capitalist development at which it has become economically necessary for them to find outside their own territories and one another's not only markets for surplus goods, but also outlets for the investment of capital on an ever-increasing scale.[35]

It should be clear from the preceding discussion that Laski and Cole had quite different philosophical views and political interests. On underconsumption and capitalist imperialism, however, they subscribed to very similar ideas. This is hardly surprising. These two theories, both derived ultimately from Hobson, were the most cohesive strands of thought in the post-war Labour left to which Laski and Cole belonged.

(II) A ROOM OF ONE'S OWN?

By 1925 the ILP was roughly synonymous with the Labour left. To some extent it had always been so. Before 1918, when one could only become a member of the Labour Party by joining one of its affiliated bodies – such as a trade union, the Fabian Society, or the ILP – the ILP had stood well to the left of almost all of the trade unions that made up the bulk of the Party. The new Labour Party constitution of 1918, by establishing constituency Labour Parties open to indivi-dual membership, deprived the ILP of its institutional role as the natural avenue of individual membership, and left it with only its political and intellectual role of 'advance guard of Socialist thought'.[36]

This process was obviously gradual and partial. MacDonald and Snowden for example, who in the post-war years could never be counted as a part of the left, nevertheless continued to play an important although decreasing role in the ILP throughout the 1920s. The point remains, however, that after the First World War, and particularly after the first Labour Government, of which the ILP MPs were bitter critics,[37] the ILP was the left of the Labour Party. That being so, a number of the Liberal recruits, who had joined the ILP largely on account of its position on foreign policy, and perhaps also because it was already the home of their former Liberal colleagues, took less and less active parts in the ILP and began to focus their attention on the broader and less radical Labour Party.[38] Those progressives who did remain active in the ILP, however, did so because they were committed to socialism, and because the ILP, far more thoroughly than the Labour Party, had accepted their distinctive analyses of foreign policy and other issues.

This claim must be qualified. The Labour Party certainly did not formally reject the Hobsonian theory of capitalist imperialism, and other perspectives are easily discernible within the ranks of the ILP. In the latter's 1921 resolution on imperialism and socialism, for example, there is an apparently deliberate equivocation on the question:

on its economic and industrial side imperialism is either the product of an attempt of financiers and speculators to exploit the natural wealth of foreign countries, or an idea of the British manufacturer that he needs military intervention in the capture of foreign markets for trade, and is therefore an excuse for the want of his business enterprise. Imperialism therefore tends to perpetuate the reign of capitalism, not only by increasing the power of wealth, but by neglecting the needs of the home market and leaving the natural resources of our own country undeveloped.[39]

The ILP moved an abridged version of its resolution at the Labour Party conference later the same year. This motion, which was accepted unanimously, did not contain any explicit statement of the origins of imperialism, although it did include the argument that imperialism 'tends to perpetuate the reign of capitalism, not only by increasing the power of wealth, but by neglecting the needs of the home market'.[40]

The idea that imperialism was due to the inadequacies of British manufacturers was advanced by MacDonald as early as 1907. In his opinion this was the root cause of imperialist ventures, and although he maintained that 'the financier is the most dangerous man for implicating us in foreign trouble' and that 'high finance and politics cannot be separated', he was convinced that these were but incidents of imperialism. 'Finance' did not create imperialism, but imperialism 'encourage[d] the mere financier and the parasite'.[41]

MacDonald's text exemplifies the theoretical mushiness that sometimes followed from pre-war progressivism's instinctive eclecticism. It also foreshadows the tendency, which became very pronounced around the end of the war, for members of the UDC and ILP to borrow phrases from each other's arguments without actually adopting, or perhaps even understanding, their theoretical basis. Lowes Dickinson furnishes a good illustration:

Competition of the capital of the different nations . . . does not affect . . . the total national interest. It should not therefore affect the policy nor the political relations of States. But in fact it does . . . Everyone knows that the effort of this or that nation to get some monopoly of the *resources and markets* of such areas constitutes a great part of the international tension. But, once more, why? Because policy interferes with the natural economic mechanism.[42]

The distance between this position and Brailsford's is obvious. Brailsford, as we have seen, did not regard the participation of diplomacy in financial matters as an interference in the 'natural economic mechanism', but as the 'inevitable accompaniment of the capitalist system', that is, as part and parcel of the existing economic mechanism. Dickinson's distance from Hobson, although less obvious, is equally important. By suggesting that the search for 'resources and markets', rather than outlets for surplus capital was the engine of the process, Dickinson divorced the problem from any fault, curable or incurable, in the existing economic order; every society needs resources and markets. From this position Dickinson was able to reach a conclusion which Hobson could never allow. Hitherto, he argued, only small groups had benefited from the increase in resources and markets, but, 'Socialise your wealth . . . and the temptation to which minorities succumb becomes a temptation of a whole people.'[43]

By 1920, even Norman Angell was sounding a little like Brailsford. He couched his condemnation of the allied intervention in Russia thus: 'Shall the people acquiesce in the creation of an international junta or cabal of military and capitalist concession mongers, carrying on . . . vast military campaigns aiming at the destruction of any form of democracy other than the political bourgeois form which has made militarism and capitalism such prosperous institutions in the past.'[44]

This, at least, was what Angell *thought* Brailsford was saying; it was precisely the conspiracy theory that he had condemned in 1914.[45] Despite the rhetoric, however, Angell made no attempt here or anywhere else to establish any precise connection between the workings of capitalism and militarism. The intervention against Russia was the work of a 'camarilla'.[46]

By 1925 Angell had reverted to his earlier position, if indeed he ever really abandoned it. The opportunity to create an economically unified and stable Europe after the war, he believed, had not been taken 'because the political thinking of the generation responsible for the Versailles Treaty was obviously still dominated by the fallacies which *The Great Illusion* had attempted to refute'.[47]

The Labour Party's post-war propaganda tended to denounce the evils of reparations – Angell's special concern – and secret diplomacy – Morel's special concern – and although it also frequently denounced 'finance', only rarely did it link this to the problem of surplus capital – what Hobson called the 'Economic Taproot of Imperialism'. The fact that Hobson and Brailsford also condemned secret diplomacy and reparations gives a superficial, but misleading, appearance of unanimity on international questions within Labour circles. In the first years of peace, as in the war, concrete, immediate prescriptions put forward by all sections of Labour opinion resembled each other so closely that important theoretical differences remained obscured and temporarily irrelevant. This is not really surprising given the composition of the Labour Party's Advisory Committee on International Questions in the period: Brailsford, Hobson, Angell, Morel, Lowes Dickinson, Trevelyan, Ponsonby, Leonard Woolf, G. D. H. Cole, Hammond – in other words the leadership of the UDC and a few others.

The ILP too denounced secret diplomacy and reparations, and Angell, who never became a socialist and who never subscribed to Hobson's theory of capitalist imperialism, remained an active member of the ILP throughout the 1920s, a fact which might be read as testimony to the continuation within the ILP of the heterodoxy of pre-war progressivism. Nevertheless, despite the many qualifications and equivocations we have been bound to consider, it is plain enough that Hobson's and Brailsford's ideas on capitalist imperialism exerted enormous influence within the ILP. The evidence from the grass roots, where ILP speakers frequently kept a copy of *The War of Steel and Gold* handy on the rostrum,[48] and where *Imperialism* and *The War of Steel and Gold* were favourite books of Aneurin Bevan while he was still establishing his local reputation in Ebbw Vale,[49] certainly suggests that this was so. So too does the evidence from the pinnacle of the Party, where R. C. Wallhead in his chairman's address to the 1921 conference declared, 'It is not industrial progress that demands the opening up of new markets and access of investment, but maldistribution of consuming power which prevents the absorption of commodities and capital within the country.'[50]

The ILP's definitive pamphlet on international affairs in the early twenties was in essence an up to date summary of *The War of Steel and Gold*:

The French support of Turkey in the recent crisis in the Near East can be explained by the fact that French bondholders hold the greater part of the Turkish national debt ... The constant quarrels between the little States of Central Europe are almost entirely directed to the control of mineral and oil resources, and the pressure of the bigger Powers, on one side or the other, can generally be traced to the possession of invested capital. The world over, the ownership of rich natural resources and the interests of investors constitute the bone of contention which sets the States at each other's throats.[51]

Everything about this pamphlet but its style suggests that Brailsford was its author. It hardly matters; by 1922 Brailsford was, directly or indirectly, the source of most ILP thinking on foreign policy issues. When he became editor of the ILP's weekly paper, the *New Leader*, an editorial 'introduced' him to the readers with these words: 'Brailsford's books ... became at once, and will remain, the library from which our speeches come and where our thought is moulded. These books are the best interpretation of recent events and the most powerful vindication of internationalism that have anywhere appeared.'[52] Even allowing for the hyperbole usual on such occasions, this account of Brailsford's influence was probably not far wide of the mark. After his four-year tenure as editor it was probably still closer, for Brailsford wrote a large proportion of the copy himself, and his distinctive analysis stands out from almost every page.

Brailsford and Hobson exerted an influence on the ILP which extended well beyond questions of foreign policy, for, unlike Morel's and Angell's, their views on foreign policy were clearly based on a socialist or quasi-socialist analysis of the existing economic order. Indeed, the scope and limits of their influence on domestic policy is far easier to isolate than their influence on the ILP's foreign policy, for in 1926 the ILP – now firmly established as the Labour left – formally adopted a programme for the transition to socialism that was explicitly based on Hobsonian economics, and which was effectively rejected by the Labour Party. *The Living Wage*, as the fullest elaboration of the programme was called, was drafted by Hobson, Brailsford, Arthur Creech-Jones, and E. F. Wise. Brailsford appears to have played the leading role in formulating the programme, and as editor of the *New Leader* was its most active populariser.[53]

Creech-Jones and Wise had strong and varied progressive credentials. Both grew up in modest circumstances and educated themselves for the Civil Service by means of scholarships. Both were active in workers' education; Creech-Jones through the WEA, Wise as a University Extension lecturer. Creech-Jones, who was born in 1891, achieved most of his fame after the Second World War as a minister at the Colonial Office active in the work of dissolving the British Empire. He began his political life by joining the Liberal Christian League in 1910, and by 1913 he was in the ILP. Imprisoned as a conscientious objector during the First World War, he used his spare time to read leaders of progressive thought such as Mill, Hobson, Brailsford, Hobhouse, the Webbs, Morris, and Angell.[54]

Wise rose rapidly in the Civil Service and by 1912, at the age of twenty-seven, he was a friend and economic adviser to Lloyd George.[55] He advised the British government on economic questions during and after the war, but appears to have had as low an opinion of the post-war settlement as did his fellow-adviser, Keynes, whose *The Economic Consequences of the Peace* was the richest single source of arguments for Labour's anti-Versailles propagandists. It was at an anti-Versailles meeting that Wise became convinced of the urgent need for normal trade links between Britain and the USSR. He specialised in this field, and in 1924 resigned his Civil Service post to become an adviser to the Soviet Government's international trade agency. He joined the ILP shortly after the First World War and sat in parliament during the life of each of the inter-war Labour governments. In 1931 he became founding chairman of the Socialist League, a position he held until his premature death two years later.

The Living Wage began with an underconsumptionist analysis of contemporary economic problems, and directed its readers to Hobson's books for further elucidation. Its basic prescription was simple: 'There must be an increase in the total real income of the nation, while a larger proportion of it must go to mass-consumption, and a smaller proportion to rent, profit, interest and banking.'[56] The document's political-strategic and economic arguments were intended to dovetail. Economically, the achievement of a living wage would require the nationalisation of the Bank of England and government direction, if not nationalisation, of other financial institutions in order to establish the 'national credit policy' necessary to ensure the correct level and distribution of investment and to stabilise the trade cycle and thereby guarantee both the value of money wages and levels of employment.[57] Likewise, those other industries that 'govern the pace and direction of the nation's industrial growth' – coal, electricity, and railways – should also be nationalised.[58] Merely to nationalise the odd industry, however, without also acting on wages and taking the other measures necessary to guarantee those wages, would serve no useful purpose, for while the economy remained prone to slumps, nationalised industries would periodically be compelled to do what no Labour Government dare do – shed labour.[59] The programme was thus intended as 'a logical whole'.[60] This, the authors felt, was its greatest strength:

In the process of raising the general standard of life we should attain much more than we set out to win. The measures necessary to attain our object would go far to transform society itself . . . [T]his policy has the merit of making a simple and concrete appeal to the average worker and his wife . . . Once their attention is concentrated on these things the rest of the scheme will enlist their defensive instincts. They can be led to understand that their Living Income would soon be dissipated, unless means were taken to deal with the predatory legions which lie in wait to lower the purchasing power of wages.[61]

The criticisms directed against the living wage programme indicates something of the distinctive position the left-wing progressives occupied within the Labour movement and something of the difficulties inherent to it. I shall consider them in turn.

Possibly the most severe criticism of the policy from within the ILP itself came from a member of its 'utopian' wing, W. T. Symons, who was sufficiently enraged to set out his objections in a pamphlet. Symons did not doubt the good faith of the authors, but he was convinced that 'The attempt to extract a Living Wage from modern industrial employment is an attempt to draw a quart of liquor from a pint pot.[62] While Symons made some rather clumsy attempts to flaw the programme's logic, the real burden of his criticism was that the authors had 'forgotten that socialism came into being to supersede the wage system'.[63] The programme, he believed, was born out of 'pity' for the poor and 'impatience' for the day when socialism would arrive. Barring a paragraph proposing that capital costs be deducted from prices, however, he offered no alternative proposal for hastening that day forward.

This was a slightly ridiculous version of a school of thought common in the Labour Party: nothing could be achieved under capitalism, therefore any concrete proposals of reform were useless. The only thing to do was wait until a Labour government was given the opportunity to nationalise industry, although precisely how this was to be done was not to be discussed either; that was a matter for the future government to decide. This was the essence of Emmanuel Shinwell's argument against the policy at the ILP's 1926 conference. It was also the line taken by MacDonald, who opposed the programme on the grounds that it was an attempt to force the leadership's pace. The dispute was not over any fundamental difference in theoretical analysis; MacDonald himself frequently employed underconsumptionist arguments. It was, at bottom, a confrontation between the 'inevitability of gradualism' and the notion that the transition to socialism, even if pursued by democratic methods, must at some point involve bold initiatives deeply offensive to the propertied classes.

The living wage programme was also criticised by trade union leaders. Commenting on the early version of the programme, Ernest Bevin proclaimed, 'I stand four-square against political interference with wages.'[64] More generally, trade unionists feared that the declaration of a living wage would jeopardise the ability of workers above that level to improve their position. *The Living Wage* tried to circumvent these criticisms by protesting that 'any process is objectionable which might weaken Trade Unionism', and by affirming the important role unions must play in the achievement of the living wage.[65] The whole tendency of the document, however, was in another direction: 'If the rule that wages are the concern of Trade Unions exclusively, is rigidly followed, it is difficult to feel confident that any general improvement in the level of wages can be secured. It is still more difficult to look forward to the removal of the gross inequalities which obtain at present in the wages of various trades.'[66]

These differences between the perspectives of the trade union leaders and the progressive intellectuals of the ILP recall the objections that some Liberals had raised against the Labour Party. The living wage policy was based on ethical and economic objections to inequality. It was directed to the common good, and its authors saw no reason to assume that individual trade unions which were able for one reason or another to advance their members' wages more than other workers were necessarily contributing to that common good. *The Living Wage*, to take Hobhouse's phrase from its more general context, implicitly struck a blow against 'the Trade Unions and their sectional selfishness', and could perhaps even be seen as an attempt to 'teach Labour [that] true Socialism is the point of view of the community as a whole'.[67]

The trade unionists and the 'utopian gradualists' were unfriendly critics who between them made up the vast bulk of Labour Party opinion. There were, however, friendlier critics, who objected less to the political spirit of the programme than to its economic plausibility. Keynes, whose ideas on the use of credit to counteract the vagaries of the trade cycle had actually been borrowed by the authors of *The Living Wage*, found it 'flimsy', and doubted whether its 'concrete proposals ... would provide enough resources to pay the bill'. Its faults, he thought, sprang from the fact that it fell 'between the two stools of popular propaganda and scientific programme building'.[68]

The similarities between Keynes's and Hobson's views are well known and often perhaps even overstated.[69] Keynes himself told Hobson that his own position was an attempt to create a 'satisfactory synthesis of orthodox economics with your own unorthodoxy'.[70] However important the theoretical differences, there were many points of attraction between the Liberals grouped around Keynes's ideas and the ILP members grouped around Hobson's. The Liberal 'Yellow Book' of 1928 – the work of the milieu of the post-Massingham *Nation* – incorporated the essential Hobsonian argument for an increase in domestic demand, although its proposals for achieving it revolved around increasing employment by means of

government expenditure on infrastructure projects funded by bor-
rowing, rather than on the redistribution of wealth demanded by
Hobson.[71]

The common ground was enough to turn Brailsford's mind to the
idea of close co-operation. In the first issue of the *New Leader* after the
1929 election, which had again failed to give any party a clear
majority, he wrote:

> I know our party too well to advocate any formal treaty or conference with
> the Liberals, though I hold to my opinion that something of value might be
> won in this way. If we are to believe their Yellow Book, they are no longer
> opposed on principle to every step towards Socialisation ... We might
> avoid many a mistake by listening to Mr. Keynes on questions of currency
> and credit. From Mr. E. D. Simon we might derive some useful hints on
> housing. Would it not be worthwhile to talk to Sir Herbert Samuel before
> we finally fix our immediate policy over coal?[72]

A few readers were sympathetic to Brailsford's idea, pointing out,
as he had in effect, that there were 'Liberals and Liberals'.[73] This
however was against the grain of opinion within the ILP, which was
so hostile that its National Administrative Committee adopted a
resolution dissociating itself from Brailsford's views.[74] Another
reader, more representative of the majority, wanted to know, 'What
has happened to H. N. Brailsford? Surely he does not expect the
vested interests of the Liberal Party to support the socialisation
measures in our programme?'[75] The truth was, of course, that
nothing had happened to H. N. Brailsford; he was merely reasserting, as he was to do again in 1936, the old progressive habit of
seeking unity around common ideas, and acting on the equally old
progressive assumption that he could find it.

(III) COMRADES AND CITIZENS

The lengthiest and most ferocious criticism of *The Living Wage* came
from the Communist Party of Great Britain, whose leading theoretician, Rajani Palme Dutt, devoted an entire book to the task. Dutt's
main criticism of the programme's underconsumptionist theoretical
basis was that 'The problems of distribution cannot be separated
from the ownership of the means of production, which determines
the character of distribution.'[76] The essence of the capitalist mode of
production was the extraction of the surplus value of labour.
Perpetually to increase this surplus value was 'the whole be-all and

end-all, the whole inevitable driving force, the whole competitive mainspring of capitalism'.[77] As, according to Marx's labour theory of value, the value of commodities originated in labour, the total amount paid as wages for this labour could, by definition, only be sufficient to purchase that part of the value of goods and services that was not surplus value. It followed, therefore, that once extracted, surplus value must find some outlet other than wages. According to Dutt there were three such possible outlets: luxury goods for the consumption of the capitalists, investment in capital goods, or foreign investment. As there were natural limits to the scope of luxury consumption, and as an industrialised country provided ever diminishing possibilities for new capital investment, it followed that the only alternative for British capitalists was foreign investment. The underconsumptionist idea that the home market was capable of expansion was therefore just another of 'the liberal myths of harmony and progress' in which the ILP specialised.[78]

This point takes us closer to Dutt's more general purpose. His 238 page response to a not very complex 54 page programme was bound to stray somewhat from its immediate subject. *The Living Wage* was the peg from which Dutt hung a general critique of the ILP and the Labour Party. This it had in common with most British Communist critiques of underconsumption theory. As Stuart Macintyre has pointed out, while British Marxists condemned the theory, 'they frequently employed similar arguments in their own writings . . . [T]heir hostility seems to have been directed primarily towards the reformist political perspective of the popularisers of the underconsumption theory rather than against the economic doctrine itself.'[79]

Dutt's task then was to extrapolate from *The Living Wage* – or from other sources where it was unsuitable for the purpose – proofs of his general propositions concerning the Labour left. The most important of these was that there was no real distinction to be made between 'left' and 'right' in the Labour Party. The ILP, 'by its policy of sham "leftward" phrases and practical support of reformist bureaucracy in all real issues . . . constitutes the principal safety-valve of the existing bureaucracy against the real leftward drive of the workers, and therefore the principal obstacle to the advance of the working class'.[80] With this criticism Dutt was merely following the general line of the CPGB on the ILP, and indeed of the Communist International on all leftist versions of democratic socialism throughout the world.

Among the identities Dutt discovered between the ILP and the Labour right was their allegedly common view of imperialism. From *The Living Wage*'s support for 'a policy of international agreement' to regulate exports, and with the aid of a few quotations from Snowden, Maxton, and the *New Leader*, Dutt deduced that the ILP subscribed to the theory of 'ultra-imperialism'. This theory, which was first developed by the German Marxist Karl Kautsky, Dutt defined as 'the belief that capitalism can overcome and is overcoming its internal conflicts, and is developing to a single internationally unified, harmonised, pacific whole'.[81] Dutt then proceeded to attack the theory with quotations from Lenin's *Imperialism, the Highest Stage of Capitalism*, in which it was roundly condemned: ' "Compare the ideas of Kautsky about 'peaceful' ultra-imperialism with this stern reality, with the vast diversity of economic and political conditions, with the extreme disproportion of the rate of development of different countries, with the violent struggles of the imperialist states." '[82]

This was dangerous ground for Dutt to tread, for as is well known, and as Lenin himself repeatedly acknowledged, Lenin's work was profoundly influenced by Hobson's *Imperialism*. Lenin's work on imperialism was to a large extent a polemic against Kautsky, and one of Lenin's most frequently employed polemical touches was to compare the 'Marxist' Kautsky unfavourably with the 'social-Liberal' Hobson. Lenin made great play of this when discussing ultra-imperialism. Had Dutt's reader cared to glance at Lenin's text (first published in English in 1926)[83] his eye might have been caught by this passage: 'Kautsky, while claiming that he continues to advocate Marxism, as a matter of fact takes a step backward compared with the *social-liberal* Hobson, who *more correctly* takes into account two "historically concrete" (Kautsky's definition is a mockery of historical concreteness!) features of modern imperialism: (1) the competition between *several* imperialisms, and (2) the predominance of the financier over the merchant.'[84] Further on the reader might have come across a lengthy comparison of Kautsky's and Hobson's views on ultra-imperialism and Lenin's conclusion that 'the only progress Kautsky has made in the sphere of "scientific" thought is that he gave out as Marxism what Hobson, in effect, described as the cant of English parsons'.[85]

The similarities between Lenin's and Hobson's theories were striking.[86] The differences between them can be reduced to two.

First, Lenin did not share Hobson's belief that underconsumption could be remedied within capitalism.

It goes without saying that if capitalism ... could raise the standard of living of the masses ... there could be no talk of a superabundance of capital. This 'argument' is very often advanced by the petty-bourgeois critics of capitalism. But if capitalism did these things it would not be capitalism; for both uneven development and a semistarvation level of existence of the masses are fundamental and inevitable conditions and premises of this mode of production.[87]

Secondly, it was axiomatic to Lenin, as a Marxist, that the capitalist state was not and could not be made 'neutral'. On these points, therefore, Lenin was closer to Brailsford's position than to Hobson's.

Important and fundamental as the differences were, they had little effect on the practical application of the theory for as long as underconsumption persisted. Hobson, no less than Brailsford or Lenin, believed that *the then existing conditions of capitalism* entailed imperialism and that imperialism entailed international rivalry.

In the 1920s the lines of political division were not drawn along these axes. On the issues of imperialism and foreign policy the only practical difference between Labour's mainstream and its left was the latter's more radical criticisms of the existing League of Nations, and even here the left welcomed the Party's attempts to use the League to attain goals like disarmament. On the other hand, it is doubtful that anyone on the Labour left had even read Lenin's *Imperialism* before 1926; throughout the decade Hobson's *Imperialism* and Brailsford's *The War of Steel and Gold* remained, as we have seen, the left's standard works on the subject.

In any case, the similarities between the Communist and Labour left analyses of imperialism were only partial. Against the issues which divided the two groups they were rather trivial. The Labour left's commitment to the parliamentary road to socialism, its reservation of the right to criticise the Soviet Union, and its willingness to accept ameliorative measures while capitalism endured were the things that mattered, the things that separated the left from the CPGB and which kept it in the Labour Party.

On the last point, we have seen that all sections of Labour opinion, in common with many Liberals, objected vehemently to the British Government's armed intervention in revolutionary Russia, and stoutly maintained the right of Russians to determine their own form of government. On the other hand, there was widespread although not universal agreement within the Labour Party that the Bolsheviks' revolutionary strategy was entirely inappropriate in Great Britain. These were the outward bounds of ILP discourse on the matter: to deny one was to be a Conservative, to deny the other was to be a Communist.[88]

There was clearly scope here for a wide range of views, as the ILP's debates on the question of affiliation to the Communist International show. At one end stood MacDonald, who denounced the Bolsheviks for their anti-democratic theories and their suppression of non-Bolshevik socialists.[89] At the other end stood people like C. H. Norman, who held that 'Russia was the only State that would be able to organise an International armed against the international financiers'.[90] Many arguments revolved around the question of force. The substantial body of absolute pacifists in the ILP rejected any association with the Bolsheviks purely because of the Bolsheviks' use of violence; others argued that nothing could be achieved without force, while still others held merely that to advocate the use of force was unnecessary and dangerous given the existence of parliamentary democracy. Clifford Allen raised still another argument. While he recognised that 'it might be necessary to defend the majority against a minority', he declared that 'he would not take up arms until they had educated the majority of the country in the principles for which they stood'.[91]

Nothing in these debates captures the excitement that the Bolshevik Revolution created among rank and file members of the ILP. Jennie Lee, who was fourteen at the time, recalled the feeling vividly.

I knew that something of extraordinary importance had happened when I saw my father, James Lee, chairman of the local ILP, meeting Will Gray, treasurer of the local ILP, under the railway bridge across Cowdenbeath High Street, on a rainy Sunday afternoon. They were shaking hands as if they would never stop and there was the light of Heaven in my father's eyes. The first news of the Russian Revolution had reached them.[92]

This excitement does not appear to have been shared by the progressive intellectuals, who, with a very few exceptions, had little to say about the Revolution after their initial euphoria at the overthrow of the Tsar had subsided. In stark contrast with the 1930s, there is only a tiny handful of texts about Russia by British progressive writers in the 1920s. Those texts are generally cautious in their judgements and insistent on the theme that Bolshevik strategy was irrelevant to Britain. Unlike the young literati of the 1930s who have attracted so much historical attention, the established leaders of progressivism had thought about and rejected Bolshevism even before it took its Stalinist form.

Laski's *Communism* (first published in 1927) was primarily an analysis of Marxist theory. Bolshevik-style revolution he considered possible only in the near unique conditions of Russia in 1917.[93] The Bolshevik regime he regarded as a 'new and more powerful tyranny' than Tsarism, 'but at least a tyranny conceived in the interests of the masses'.[94] This was a theme that was to recur in the comments of progressives on Russia in the 1930s, as was Laski's claim that there was 'a new hope of achievement' there.[95]

Bertrand Russell, who had made the transition from the Liberal Party to the Labour Party via the UDC and Guild Socialism, after an earlier brief foray into the Fabian Society, set out his views after visiting Russia for five weeks in 1920. He liked Lenin, with whom he had an hour's chat, and exonerated the Bolsheviks from responsibility for many, although not all, of the social and economic problems Russia faced. He was nevertheless critical of Bolshevik theory and methods. The revolutionary dictatorship, he thought, was bound to be permanent: 'The system created by violence and the forcible rule of a minority must necessarily allow of tyranny and exploitation; and if human nature is what Marxians assert it to be, why should the rulers neglect such opportunities of selfish advantage?'[96] In the true spirit of progressivism, Russell reserved his strongest criticism for the Bolsheviks' insistence on orthodoxy: 'Bolshevism is not merely a political doctrine; it is also a religion, with elaborate dogmas and inspired scriptures.[97] Despite these important criticisms Russell valued the Revolution as an inspiration, for which 'Bolshevism deserve[d] the gratitude and admiration of all mankind'.[98]

Cole appears to have attached no such value to the Revolution. In an article in 1920 on the formation of the CPGB, which he considered 'not important', Cole offered no comment whatsoever on the internal affairs of Russia. He was convinced, however, that the Bolsheviks' talk of world revolution was empty rhetoric, and that their real concern was to consolidate their power in Russia. The whole thrust of the article was that Russia and Communism were completely irrelevant to the British Labour movement.[99]

Judging by their silence, this view was common among progressives. Within the ILP the progressives had very little to say on the question of the relationship between the ILP and the Labour Party and the CPGB. Not one of them spoke in any of the Labour Party's four conference debates on the Communists' application for affiliation in 1921–4, and in the ILP's two debates on affiliation to the Communist International only Allen and C. R. Buxton spoke. Buxton's point is interesting and perhaps indicative of the progressives' approach to the problem. Advocating that the ILP affiliate to the Vienna Union – the so-called two-and-a-half International – he stated his belief that,

Vienna was the place for the ILP. It was not the main business of the ILP to declare its disagreement with Moscow. That was not Vienna's position. Vienna stood midway between the Second and the Third, equally, not less, dissociated from the one as the other ... [But] the whole policy of Moscow was alien to the circumstances and the temper of the ILP and it would be deceiving Moscow to go to it ... [T]he Second['s] ... policy was too much a mere anti-Bolshevism.[100]

This was substantially Brailsford's position. Unlike most on the left Brailsford had by 1921 actually travelled widely in the Soviet Union. He came back a critical admirer – a position he was to maintain, although his criticisms became sharper in the 1930s. His judicious approach was indicated in the preface to the book he wrote on his return: 'I have never felt so little confidence in my own conclusions. I may also add that I have never been so anxious to arrive at the objective truth.'[101]

Brailsford was obviously excited by Russia's economic progress against tremendous odds, by the *élan* of the workers and peasants, and by the experiments with Soviet democracy in the villages and workshops, although he clearly recognised that the power of the Soviets was in decline. Even during the Civil War, however, Brailsford did not hesitate to name and condemn the terror.

One must strive to understand the conditions which made the Terror, but nothing can excuse its cruelty. To save the revolution, it is ruining Russia ... Almost worse than the bloodshed is the demoralization caused by this irresponsible tyranny. Its directors have developed the casuistry of all fanatics. All means for them are good which seem to their narrow minds to serve the end, and humanity and truth are consciously disregarded ... Communists have a trick of laughing at 'bourgeois morality', and though it may be fairly argued that our current ethics have been formed to suit the capitalist system, this argument in the mouths of half-educated men becomes a pretext for disregarding all morality.[102]

Brailsford, then, did not manage to persuade himself that his revulsion at the Bolsheviks' methods was merely a product of residual liberalism. Rather, their methods were alien to his conception of socialism:

We differ from Communists not merely because we believe and they deny that Socialism can be won under democratic conditions. We differ because we conceive of democracy as something much more than a form. It penetrates and shapes our ideal of a Socialist society, and, indeed, we demand the Socialist solution largely because we believe that democracy can be fully developed only under its economic arrangements.[103]

While this was a radical difference it was not ultimately as important as the difference between capitalism and socialism. Writing in reply to a full-page attack on the Communists by J. R. Clynes in the *New Leader*, Brailsford, while supporting the Labour Party's rejection of the CPGB's application for affiliation on the grounds that the Communists were a 'distracting nuisance' impossible to work with, still held that 'we should insist on regarding them, however much we differ from them, as men who are on the same side of the dividing trenches as we are'.[104]

Only five years after this dispute, Brailsford, without any major change in outlook, was to incur the wrath of the ILP leadership by advocating co-operation with the 'left-wing' of the Liberal Party. The tension this implies was inherent in the position of the progressive intellectuals of the Labour left. They placed themselves on one side of a line between capitalism and anti-capitalism, while simultaneously working with and sharing the outlook of others who either placed themselves on the other side of the line or denied the line's existence altogether.

On that point this chapter may end where it began – at Conway Hall in April 1932. Brailsford, as chairman, is introducing Laski, who is to speak.

The academic student who is half of Laski is most himself, I feel, among the individualistic rationalists of the eighteenth century and the French Revolution; their passion for liberty burns in him. The man of experience who is the other half of him is the contemporary of the Russian Revolution: he understands its imperious call to order and planning, its grasp of the significance of the machine, its passion for social equality, its sense that the whole is greater than the part. But I cannot imagine him at home in Soviet Russia, and, indeed, it is probable that either revolution would have made away with him, because of his sympathy in retrospect or anticipation with the other effort. His work is to attempt a synthesis of these two tendencies, which are shaping the world of to-day and to-morrow. On that, indeed, we are all engaged, though few are conscious of it, and most of us are content with slovenly patchwork that tears with every movement.[105]

It could well have been a prophecy. In the decade dominated by Hitler, Franco, and Chamberlain, the patchwork was torn in every direction. The remainder of this book is a study of how, and how well, the progressive intellectuals struggled to keep intact what stitching they could.

CHAPTER 6

Fascism, unity and loyalty: 1932–1937

The 1932 Conway Memorial Lecture, with which the previous chapter began and ended, fell neatly between two much more momentous events which upset the precarious balance of which Brailsford spoke: the formation of the 'National Government' in August 1931, and Hitler's accession to the Chancellorship of Germany in January 1933. It is only in the context of these two events that the Labour left's support for the United Front can be understood, for between them they served to strengthen every argument that leftists had ever put for uncompromising socialist solutions, while seriously undermining their belief that any such solutions could be found via the institutions of British democracy. Ramsay MacDonald and Adolf Hitler make an odd couple, but the British left tended to see their actions as proof of the same truth: capitalism and democracy were radically incompatible, and only by the swift destruction of capitalism, or at the very least of large-scale capitalism, could democracy be achieved. In this context co-operation with Liberals, who, no matter how well intentioned, continued to support both capitalism and the orderly processes of parliamentary democracy, could have no place. This point is vital to our understanding of the United Front, which, it will be remembered, was intended in part as an anti-Liberal tactic. The Labour left, by proposing unity between the Labour Party, the ILP, and the Communists hoped thereby to place continuing pressure on those in the Labour leadership whom they suspected of seeking an understanding with the Liberal Party.

With a few important exceptions, it was not until 1938 that the left began to advocate a Popular Front, that is, an alliance that would include Liberals as well as socialists. That episode, distinct from and in many ways contradictory to the United Front, will be the subject of the next chapter. For the present I shall concentrate solely on the theoretical bases and the practical political consequences of the Labour left's support for the United Front, giving particular attention to those leading members of the Labour left whom I have identified as having deep roots in the progressive tradition.

The period under discussion coincides almost exactly with the life of the Socialist League, which in 1932 replaced the ILP as the organised body of the left within the Labour Party. During its existence the Socialist League was virtually synonymous with the Labour left. Very few Labour leftists – Aneurin Bevan is the most conspicuous exception – never joined the League. Any study of the Labour left during the years 1932–7 is thus in some measure inevitably a history of the Socialist League. It is convenient that this should be so, for the dissolution of the League not only marks a fairly clear break in the Labour left's anti-fascist strategy, it also neatly encapsulates the left's central difficulty during the period, for the Socialist League destroyed itself in a quixotic attempt to create unity between the Labour Party and the Communist Party. There is a further irony in the birth and death of the League. While its death was a direct consequence of flagrant breaches of Labour Party discipline, its formation was a decisive reaffirmation of its members' desire to work within the framework of the Labour Party.

(I) BETRAYAL AND LOYALTY: THE BIRTH OF THE
SOCIALIST LEAGUE

The Socialist League was formed principally out of a large remnant of the ILP.[1] In 1932 the ILP seceded from the Labour Party. Despite its timing the secession had little to do with MacDonald's 'great betrayal' of the previous year.[2] The ILP MPs had been vociferous critics of both Labour Governments and had had numerous scrapes with the Labour whips.[3] In 1930 the ILP had proclaimed its MPs to be free of Labour Party discipline in the House of Commons. Its departure was the final act in the dispute that this action precipitated.

The crisis itself may be briefly outlined. Faced with an international fiscal crisis, Snowden, as Chancellor of the Exchequer, proposed a series of austerity measures including drastic cuts in unemployment assistance. The cabinet split, at which point MacDonald resigned the Prime Ministership and was immediately recommissioned to form a 'National' Government, which apart from

MacDonald, Snowden, and a few Liberals, consisted almost entirely of Conservatives. Its policies reflected its composition. The establishment was ecstatic, and at the ensuing General Election, Labour, which had repudiated MacDonald, saw its representation in the Commons fall from 288 seats to 52.

Those members of the ILP who supported disaffiliation from the Labour Party saw the collapse of the second Labour Government merely as a demonstration of the Party's serious political inadequacies. Whereas official Labour Party propaganda stressed MacDonald's treachery and the so-called 'bankers' ramp' – the idea that the whole crisis had been engineered specifically in order to remove the government – the ILP was convinced on the one hand that Labour's faults extended well beyond MacDonald and his few friends, and on the other that the crisis had far deeper causes than the Labour Party would admit. As the ILP MP William Brown put it when explaining his resignation from the Parliamentary Labour Party:

Let there be no mistake about it – all talk about the crisis being artificial is bunkum; it is a real and desperate crisis for the British Capitalist system . . . The Labour Opposition, the leaders of which were committed in the late Cabinet to nine-tenths of the Capitalist programme and some to the whole of it, now poses as the defenders of the country against the National Government's programme. So far as a large section of the Party is concerned, this is frankly dishonest, and the calculation behind it is clear. It is that at one stroke they can free themselves of responsibility for the last two years, free themselves from all responsibility for handling the present situation, and gain electoral advantage from being in a position of opposing cuts in wages, cuts in Unemployment Insurance, and so on.[4]

Brown analysed the crisis in terms of the ILP's theoretical position, although it is interesting to note that he did not cite as his authority his comrades Hobson or Brailsford, who had both written much pertinent matter, but rather the Liberal Keynes. Brown argued that the government's attempt to return to the Gold Standard was merely a means of redistributing wealth from the masses of the people to 'the bondholders'. Moreover, the attempt to enforce a reduction in living standards, by contracting the home market, could only exacerbate the crisis.[5] Brailsford and Fenner Brockway[6] advanced virtually identical analyses of the economic aspects of the crisis, but both of them went a step further in explaining the power of 'finance'. According to Brockway, the crisis showed clearly that 'The real Prime Minister is Mr. Montagu Norman ... This Government is the most brazen servant of Capitalism that ever ruled in this country.'[7] Brailsford too laid the blame squarely with the financiers, arguing that since the war power had 'passed unquestionably from the industrialist to the financier'. His conclusion, which was as militant as Brown's, neatly encapsulates the reasons behind the Labour left's shift to a type of ideological exclusivity unprecedented in the history of British progressivism. The crisis, Brailsford believed, made inevitable 'a break with reformist traditions', because it showed that the City would 'not tolerate even the mild quasi-Liberal reformism for which the late Government stood'.[8]

The dispute within the ILP over whether to disaffiliate from the Labour Party turned not on any fundamental ideological division, but on differing interpretations of the Labour Party's response to the crisis, and differing assessments of the effectiveness of a party split from the main body.[9] Brockway and Brailsford, for example, although their analyses of the crisis were so similar, took opposing views. Nevertheless, the special conference of the ILP that decided (by 241 votes to 142) to disaffiliate from the Labour Party was bitterly divided. The minority took the obvious course of foregoing their ILP membership in order to remain within the mass organisation. Two of the most prominent opponents of secession, Brailsford and Frank Wise, immediately formed a National ILP Affiliation Committee with the aim of obtaining the anti-secessionists' affiliation as a body. Wise, in an article entitled 'Why We Remain Loyal to Labour', made it clear that the affiliation would benefit the Labour Party as a whole, as well as the left. He pilloried the leaders of the ILP secessionists, accusing them of seeking 'the fun of being in an irresponsible minority able to hurl brickbats and epithets at any-thing and everybody'.[10] He predicted, accurately, that 'what little is left of I.L.P. branches in most cities will be reduced to complete and fatuous futility'. Arguing that 'the moral claims of Socialism are [generally] conceded', he maintained that the Party's new need was for concrete and detailed plans to present to the voters, for only then would a parliamentary majority be attainable. To assist the Party in the formulation of such plans was 'the essential task for which we need a Socialist organisation inside the more comprehensive apparatus of the National Labour Party'.[11]

Many leftists in the ILP were in one sense unaffected by the disaffiliation. Cole, Hobson, Trevelyan, and William Mellor[12] were all members of either their Constituency Labour Party or the Fabian

Society. The disaffiliation of the ILP did not affect their membership of the Labour Party. All of these people were also members of the Socialist Society for Inquiry and Propaganda, as were Sir Stafford Cripps, Clement Attlee, R. H. Tawney, and Ernest Bevin.[13] The SSIP was a young, loosely formed discussion and propaganda circle whose main purpose was to provide the Labour Party with precisely those concrete and detailed plans mentioned by Wise. It held that 'loyalty to the Labour Party was . . . a fundamental condition' of its existence.[14]

The SSIP took the initiative in finding a means to keep the ILP affiliationists in the Labour Party as a body. Even before the ILP's secession, Cole circulated for endorsement a draft letter to the SSIP's executive and other prominent members inviting members of the ILP to join the SSIP *en bloc*. Trevelyan and Hobson supported the idea enthusiastically.[15] Others were not so sure; another *Nation* veteran, Henry Nevinson, while prepared to sign, expressed the fear that the resulting organisation would 'imply another division in the Labour Party',[16] a fear echoed by others in the SSIP as the situation developed. With the formation of the ILP Affiliation Committee, Cole's proposal was superseded by a proposal to dissolve the SSIP and merge it with the former body to form a new organisation to be named the Socialist League 'in reminiscence of William Morris'.[17]

This development caused considerable disquiet among some members of the SSIP, to some of whom Cole felt obliged to write reporting that the ILP affiliationists had offered 'a perfectly explicit safeguard of their allegiance to the Labour Party and its standing orders', and had agreed that the main activity of the League should be research rather than electioneering.[18] Cripps was 'specially concerned about the possibility of Wise and his friends wanting to make the Socialist League the nucleus for a political party with the possibility of a row with the Labour Party at a later stage'.[19] Cole reassured him by pointing out that the SSIP's view had been strongly supported by 'some of Wise's leading supporters, notably Brailsford and [J. F.] Horrabin'.[20] This did not entirely satisfy Cripps, who, in the light of the affiliationists' insistence that Wise rather than Bevin should be chairman, was still concerned that the League 'may be liable to come under the sole domination of Wise'.[21] While Cripps swallowed his doubts and joined the League at its inception, not everyone felt able to do so. Ernest Bevin stayed out because he could not be convinced that the League would 'change very much from the old ILP attitude',[22] and Aneurin Bevan, who unlike Bevin had been a member of the ILP and was sympathetic to the leftist views of the Socialist League, also stayed out, wishing to remain free of 'those obligations arising out of associations which tend to obscure one's vision and limit one's freedom of decision'.[23] In other words, Bevan feared that the League would become a caucus.

Neither Bevin nor Bevan, however, prophesied that the Socialist League would come into mortal conflict with the Labour leadership. Nor could they have, for as the above account shows, not only was the League founded on a clear choice by the ILP affiliationists to remain within the Labour Party, but many of its prominent members were determined that the League should remain, as the SSIP had liked to describe itself, a 'society of loyal grousers'.[24] None had been more determined on this than Cripps – the man who was later to lead the League onto its collision course with the Party leaders. Still, an ominous sign can perhaps be detected in the *New Clarion*'s report of the League's inaugural meeting. While Brailsford was reported as stressing the League's wish 'to make itself indispensable to the three wings of the Labour Movement by zealous and loyal co-operation', Frank Horrabin, who chaired the meeting, had a more ambiguous approach: 'The Affiliationists, Mr. Horrabin said, had been described in the Press as "the loyalists". They were loyal, not to a particular group of leaders or a particular set of ideas existing at the moment, but to Socialism and the working-class movement in the widest sense.'[25]

Horrabin's emphasis on 'Socialism and the working-class movement' represented a departure from the usual rhetoric of progressivism, and alerts us again to the severely ideological terms in which progressives of the Labour left were prone to define their position in the 1930s; but Horrabin's conception of loyalty as something owed to ideas and principles was entirely consistent with the attitudes which had permeated the pre-war progressive milieu, and had led to the post-war migration of Liberals into the Labour Party. It was the conception of loyalty that dominated in the later years of the Socialist League's existence, and which was to lead it into conflict with the Labour leadership.

In the first year of its life, the League seemed set to settle down into the familiar role of the radical wing of a party of reform. Indeed, in its first weeks it seemed destined for more success than such groups usually enjoy, for at the 1932 Labour Party conference many of the

League's proposals were accepted as the Party sought to complete its break with MacDonald and all his works by adopting unambiguously framed commitments to specific socialist measures such as the nationalisation of banking. This mood was deceptive, however, for while the League had some limited success at Labour's 1933 conference, the more comprehensive and more coherent proposals which it presented at the 1934 conference, and every motion it put at conferences thereafter, were heavily defeated.[26]

Shortly after the 1932 conference the League's leaders found themselves in a dispute with the leaders of the Labour Party which was to set the tone of much of their subsequent relationship. It began when Cripps delivered a public lecture for the League in which he argued that it would be necessary for an incoming socialist government to revise parliamentary procedure by, among other things, passing an Emergency Powers Act to give itself enormous freedom of rapid action. Cripps envisaged the possibility of resistance or even sabotage from the capitalist class and proposed that a socialist government should be prepared to act ruthlessly to prevent it.[27]

The idea was by no means new. Brailsford and Laski had been arguing along these lines since 1925. They, however, were not in the leadership of the Parliamentary Labour Party. Predictably, the press represented Cripps as seeking to impose a socialist dictatorship. The speech caused considerable embarrassment to the leaders of the Labour Party, the more so as it became clear that this was no isolated 'indiscretion', but the considered opinion of other leaders of the Socialist League, most notably Cole and Laski. Speaking at the TUC annual congress, Sir Walter Citrine repudiated Cripps's ideas. In January 1934, after the Socialist League's conference had adopted a resolution embodying them,[28] the NEC issued a more explicit repudiation stating its opposition to 'individual or group dictatorship whether from Right or Left', and concluding 'In so far as any statements which are at variance have been, or may be, made by individuals, these are hereby definitely repudiated by the national executive.'[29]

At the core of this dispute lay conflicting ideas not just about tactics, but about the nature of British political institutions and the British ruling class. On one side the Socialist League was convinced that the ruling class had no inherent respect or sympathy for democratic institutions, and, being 'just as anxious as any other capitalism to preserve its privileges ... [would] fight just as tenaciously on their behalf'.[30] On the other side the Labour leadership assumed that, barring a few extremists, all classes, interests, and parties had a common desire and duty to defend existing liberties and democratic institutions. These important differences in outlook underlay the Labour leaders' and the Socialist League's widely divergent interpretations of fascism and their opposed strategies for combating it.

(II) FASCISM, THE HIGHEST STAGE OF IMPERIALISM?

A comparison of the Labour Party's official literature on fascism and that produced by the Socialist League and its members reveals a striking difference not merely in tone but in subject-matter. The Labour Party's propaganda focussed clearly and consistently on the existing fascist regimes and on the British Union of Fascists. It was based on the assumption that the greatest, if not the only threat of fascism in Britain came from Sir Oswald Mosley. The purpose of Labour's propaganda was therefore to prevent people from being seduced by Mosley. The method was to show that each of the fascist regimes was 'a slave state'[31] by virtue of its brutal suppression of democratic liberties and its tendency to worsen rather than improve the economic position of workers. It then remained only to show that the BUF's occasional attempts at soft-soaping were 'mere smoke screens', and that 'Fascism is Fascism the world over.'[32]

The Socialist League's focus was entirely different. It held that fascism 'is growing rapidly in our midst not in the number of people wearing Black Shirts, but in the minds and actions of the ruling classes and of the Government itself'.[33] On the face of it this is a rather startling claim, but Labour leftists believed that both the empirical evidence and the theoretical arguments for it were overpowering.

Theoretically, the Labour left understood fascism as a development of capitalism. There was nothing especially novel about it, as the Socialist League's official declaration made clear: 'Fascism is Reaction writ large. It is capitalism grown desperate. It is a forcible attempt to stabilise the existing system of class relationships.'[34] The very formation of the National Government was an attempt to do exactly the same thing; different in method to the Hitler regime, but identical in purpose, as Cripps argued:

If the workers attempt to insist upon keeping their gains, every constitutional method is used to overcome them – if these methods fail, others, less pleasant, are utilised as has been witnessed in Germany and other countries. The easiest method for the Capitalist to adopt, within a Capitalist democracy such as our own, is to deceive and delude the electors into a belief that it is necessary to withdraw the concessions to 'save the country', or to invent some lie which will frighten them into opposing their own leaders.[35]

So far British capitalism had attempted to 'stabilise existing class relationships' only by constitutional methods. But in the eyes of the left a number of measures indicated that the attempt was beginning to falter, and that the government was turning to methods which, although legal, were incompatible with traditional democratic practices. One of these was Lord Trenchard's introduction of a Police College in London, which was seen as a 'deliberate' attempt to introduce an 'officer class' within the force.[36] Traditionally, promotion through the ranks had permitted even the most proletarian constable to aspire to high authority. Trenchard's reforms were universally condemned by the left as an attempt to make the force a more reliable instrument in the class struggle. Another measure which enraged the left was the 'Sedition Bill' introduced in 1934. The Bill in its original form attempted to make it an offence to print or to possess any literature which might incite a member of the armed forces to disaffection. Critics of the Bill argued that in practice this would mean that anyone in possession of radical literature of any description would be liable to prosecution, and although the Bill was amended so as to prevent such a possibility, the left still saw the resulting Incitement to Disaffection Act as a dangerous and deliberate attack on freedom of expression. Earlier, the government had revived a statute of Edward III to imprison political agitators who, although they had committed no offence, refused to give undertakings that nothing unlawful would happen at their meetings. This heavy-handed action was taken exclusively against Communist organisers of demonstrations by the unemployed.

The arrests of Communists were very frequently mentioned in passing in leftist literature, but it was Laski, as a student of constitutional law, who dwelt on them at greatest length. The development of his ideas on the topic is instructive. In January 1933 – a few days before Hitler became Chancellor of Germany – the front page of the *New Clarion* was devoted to an article in which Laski questioned the legality of the arrests and predicted, accurately, that 'the Government proposes to confine its actions to men and women of whose views it disapproves'. It was, he argued, 'the typical method of Tory reaction', and a clear sign of 'the beginning of a Sidmouth regime'.[37] The only way to prevent this was a 'militant temper' on the part of the Labour movement, for 'unless we make it plain to the Government that we will not have it such a regime will come upon us like a thief in the night'.[38] In September – with Hitler's dictatorship firmly established – Laski, writing in reply to Citrine's attack on Cripps, referred again to the same case, this time seeing it as a sign of something rather more sinister. Together with the undermining of the second Labour Government, the National Government's 'remarkably benevolent indifference to Fascist propaganda', the Trades Disputes Act of 1927, and various suggestions by Conservatives that the House of Lords and the monarchy should be used to combat socialist legislation, Laski now saw the arrests and 'the growing persecution of opinion' they represented as clear indications of the possibility of fascism in Britain.[39]

In common with the rest of the left, Laski had little patience with the notion that Britain's 'long-rooted democratic tradition . . . makes a decisive difference'. He was prepared to accept only that it made 'some difference'.[40] Although Laski did not elaborate, it is probable that he was thinking along the same lines as Brailsford, who thought that British traditions would do little to prevent the coming of fascism, but would merely give it a somewhat different form from the continental versions: 'We shall wear our coloured shirts with a difference – if we ever put them on. We shall not tamper with music, or make bonfires with books: they do not matter in England. And when our labour leaders are interned, our Storm Troopers will not beat them: they will play cricket with them on Saturday afternoons.'[41]

Not only did British democratic traditions offer no safeguard against fascism, but the British Empire demonstrated daily that the 'imperially-entrenched master-class'[42] would adopt any methods necessary to maintain the 'dictatorship of property'.[43]

On the whole, however, members of the Labour left wrote surprisingly little during the 1930s about the actual methods of rule in Britain's imperial possessions. With the exception of Brailsford and a few others, they were not much interested in those empirical details. What they did write about was 'Imperialism', for it was imperialism, considered as a world system of relations between classes and nations, that furnished the theoretical basis of many of their arguments about fascism, including their argument that Britain was in danger of becoming a fascist state. Labour leftists understood facism as a form of imperialism. Brailsford, who had done so much to shape the left's views on imperialism, was naturally among the most explicit writers on this theme. His observation that 'Imperialism, in its Nazi variety ... as in its older manifestations is an outgrowth of large-scale capitalism and concentrated finance',[44] did not and could not meet any dissent on the left. Indeed, so well had Hobson and Brailsford done their job, that the terms 'imperialism' and 'capitalism' were, in Labour left writings, virtually interchangeable. Thus the Socialist League's claim that fascism is 'capitalism grown desperate', could equally well have read, 'imperialism grown desperate'.

More specifically, imperialism accounted for the economic policies and military postures of the fascist states, which were, respectively, autarchy and aggressive expansionism. Military aggression the left regarded as the normal and inevitable policy of imperialist states, which had been rendered temporarily superfluous to British requirements only by the Treaty of Versailles.[45] Autarchy was simply a rather extreme form of the policies of economic nationalism adopted by all imperialist states since the crash of 1929, and in some cases before. As Wise argued, 'Economic nationalism is the first cousin of Fascism ... The economic policy of our own National Government differs little in principle from that of Hitler, except that, as usual, the Germans are more ruthless, more blatant, and less subtle.'[46] The distinctively British form of economic nationalism was the scheme of 'Imperial Preference' devised at Ottawa in July 1932. This was but a pale echo of the scheme of 'Empire Free Trade', which the imperialist Joseph Chamberlain had proposed at the beginning of the century, and although the formal grounds of their opposition were rather different, Labour leftists opposed the Ottawa Agreement as vehemently as Edwardian progressives had opposed Chamberlain. Brailsford made the link between this scheme and imperialism's roots in finance-capitalism. Illustrating his aphorism, 'Empire is Debt', he explained, 'The reason why I must buy Australian rather than Californian fruit is that Australia is the mortgaged estate of the City of London, while California is the debtor of Chicago and New York ... Property has an interest, therefore, in fostering Australian exports, and Property in this context means especially banking and the *rentier* class.'47

According to Laski, fascism was a threat in Britain because 'the causes of Fascism [were] world-wide'.48 This accounted also for the many similarities the left detected in the behaviour of the fascist and democratic nations. Ultimately the causes could be reduced to two; underconsumption (the fundamental cause of imperialism) and the Treaty of Versailles (imperialism's rottenest fruit). The Labour left's views on underconsumption, which recurred frequently in their literature, had changed little since Hobson's elaboration of the doctrine in the 1890s, and not at all since Brailsford had argued that it was an essential feature of capitalism.49 Thus the Socialist League's major policy statement of 1934 maintained that 'Capitalism, however much its defenders may claim, cannot distribute the goods it can produce.'50 All capitalist societies were therefore victims of underconsumption's inexorable logic. All too were in some measure victims of the Treaty of Versailles, which had, as Angell and Keynes had predicted, and as was now axiomatic to the left, wrecked the world economy and precipitated the general rush to economic nationalism.51 Versailles, however, had clearly borne most heavily on Germany. It was this that accounted for Germany's peculiarly violent response to the general crisis. The left saw the emergence of German Nazism as a dramatic vindication of every criticism they, in common with other progressives, had ever made of the post-war settlement.

It is hardly surprising that Hobson's views on the international crisis of the 1930s in general, and fascism in particular, closely resembled those of his intellectual descendants on the Labour left, although Hobson himself is not generally reckoned among their number. In 1937 Hobson again set out the arguments he had elaborated at the turn of the century. Imperialism, rooted in underconsumption, was bad business for the nation as a whole but served the interests of a powerful elite of property owners admirably. A redistribution of income remained Hobson's *theoretical* solution, but significantly he left the question of whether it was *politically* feasible open for dispute 'between Marxists and radical reformists'.52 Like other progressives, Hobson believed that the 'main purpose' of the fascist regimes was 'the defence of landed and industrial property and of capitalism' against the German and Italian workers' efforts to improve their economic position by constitutional means.53 But the danger went much further than those countries, for the 'passionate sympathy for the [Spanish] military rebellion among large sections of the possessing classes in France and Britain' showed that class sympathy had become international. The struggle between democracy and capitalism was going on 'even in Britain, though, in accordance with our traditions, [it was] less direct and less openly avowed'.[54] In tones reminiscent of the Socialist League, Hobson concluded that progressives 'need not look to the possibility of a definite fascist organisation under some bigger Mosley to indicate the danger to democracy which might arrive' in the event of an attack on the 'sacred rights of property'.[55]

The similarities between the Socialist League's analysis of fascism and that advanced by the Communist International are almost too obvious to require discussion. The Comintern too held that fascism was the result of capitalism's 'profound, insoluble contradictions',[56] and was 'the dictatorship of the most reactionary, most chauvinistic and most imperialist elements of finance capital'.[57]

Striking as these similarities are, they should be no cause for wonder, and they certainly do not need to be explained by elaborate theories about Communist 'penetration' of the Labour left, or even in terms of Communist intellectual and ideological 'leadership' of the left. As we have already seen, Brailsford's reworking and development of Hobson's thought, which had made the theory of capitalist imperialism a keystone of leftist thought, had also taught that imperialism was inherently unstable. Fascism, with its worship of militarism, its oppression, and its naked territorial ambitions, seemed simply to embody to an extreme degree all of imperialism's worst characteristics. Through Lenin's work and thus, ultimately, also through Hobson's, imperialism held very similar meanings for Communists and occupied an equally important place in their thought. It was inevitable that the two groups should analyse fascism in broadly similar terms.

From the similarities of their respective analyses of fascism, there followed also a broadly similar strategy. According to the CPGB's leading theoretician, fascism could only 'be finally overcome ... by the working-class revolution and the establishment of the working-class dictatorship'.[58] In the slightly less assertive phraseology of the Labour left, it could be defeated 'only by challenging the dictatorship of capitalism'.[59]

(III) THE UNITED FRONT – FORWARD FROM LIBERALISM?

This broad theoretical and strategic agreement, together with the obvious and undisputed fact that Hitler's rise to power had been greatly facilitated by the bitter enmity between the German Communists and Social-Democrats, was the basis on which the Socialist League eventually came to support the proposal for a 'United Front' against fascism. Before this could happen, however, there were significant points of difference that had to be removed – or at least glossed over. The most obvious was the attitude of the Communists to the Labour Party itself. Between 1929 and 1933, the Comintern had characterised Social-Democracy as 'Social-Fascism' and had urged its constituent parties to engage in the 'sharpest struggle' against it and, in particular, against its 'left' variety.[60] This task the British Party had performed punctiliously.[61] In March 1933, however, after Hitler had attained power, the Comintern instructed its parties to approach the Social-Democratic leaders with offers of joint activity against fascism, and, if this were accepted, 'to refrain, for the period of the common struggle against capital and Fascism, from attacks on Social-Democratic organisations'.[62]

The Labour Party's official response to the Communists' overtures starkly reveals the distance between the Labour leadership and the Communist Party on the issue of fascism. While the Labour leadership agreed with the Communist Party and the Labour left that the chief victims of fascism were the political and industrial organisations of the working class, and agreed also that fascism received active support from among the capitalists, they did not believe that it was the outcome of the contradictions of capitalism. Rather, they believed it to be a consequence of a general move towards anti-democratic extremism of all kinds. In a pamphlet entitled *Democracy v. Dictatorship*, the leadership argued, 'The reaction of the upper classes throughout Europe has strengthened the demand for Dictatorship of the Working-class. The fear of the Dictatorship of the Working-class in turn has evoked the iron dictatorship of Capitalism and Nationalism.'[63] The leadership therefore warned, 'If the British Working-class ... toy with the idea of Dictatorship, Fascist or Communist, they will go down to servitude such as they have never suffered.'[64]

In the eyes of the Communists, this was precisely the attitude which had led the German Social-Democrats to their fate, as the

CPGB's reply to Labour's pamphlet made clear: 'The line of the Labour Party is the line of German Social-Democracy, the line of bidding the workers to trust in capitalist "democracy" which has led to the disaster of the working class in Germany and the victory of Fascism.'[65] Few in the Socialist League would have questioned this line of thought. Indeed, most of their own writings on the subject echoed the argument that the SPD's legalistic caution had been a prime cause of its defeat, and drew the lesson that an aggressive socialist policy was the only way to avoid a similar outcome in Britain.

The Socialist League, however, differed sharply from the CPGB both in its explanations of the leadership's attitude and in its apportionment of blame for the divisions between the German parties. The CPGB, in accordance with its 'Social-Fascist' thesis, attributed the leaders' attitude to simple treachery, and laid all blame for the events in Germany at the Social-Democrats' door. Socialist Leaguers could accept neither of these claims, as one of them made clear in his response to the Communist Party's 'united front' proposals.

The tactics of the Third International have been vigorously disruptive. It is this that has made the cry of the 'United Front' not quite honest when it has come from Communists ... The bureaucratic conservatism of the Social Democratic leaders in Germany has been driving the keen younger men to the Communists. Yet the Communists have put the interests of their own Party organisation before the interests of general working-class action.[66]

Despite these reservations, the writer concluded in favour of the United Front (provided only that the Communists keep their pledge not to attack the Social-Democrats), maintaining that 'if we would not prefer any kind of Socialist government to Fascism then we are merely frivolous in our politics'.[67]

The Socialist League, however, rejected the United Front proposals at its conference in May 1933, in the interests of party loyalty. Relations between the League and the Communist Party remained tense for more than two years afterwards, principally because the Communists, after Labour's rejection of the United Front proposals, persisted with its abuse of Social-Democrats only very slightly abated. As late as 1935, Dutt could publicly revile the German Social-Democrats for their repeated rejections of 'the united front, for which the Communist International has consistently striven since 1921',[68] and could argue that both Social-Democracy and fascism 'are instruments of the rule of monopoly capital. Both fight the working-class revolution. Both weaken and disrupt the class organisations of the workers.'[69] This was a disingenuous reference to the Communists' tactic of the 'United Front from below', whose main object had been to drive a wedge between the Labour movement's leaders and rank and file trade unionists by involving the latter in unofficial political and industrial movements under Communist direction. The Labour left, no less than the right, had always considered it – to use Laski's phrase – a 'Machiavellian manoeuvre'.[70]

Dutt's comment drew an angry response from J. T. Murphy – a member of the Socialist League and a founding member of the CPGP – in the Socialist League's official journal. Although he agreed with Dutt's general analysis of fascism so strongly that he described Dutt's work as 'the best ... so far published on Fascism', Murphy nevertheless demanded indignantly,

Why the silence concerning the Communist Parties of [Germany and Italy]? Have the Communist Parties committed no blunders? Are we to regard them as the custodians of infallibility? ... Their attitude to the working-class movement itself ... is non-historical and fundamentalist. It neither allows for new differentiations to grow within the Labour Movement nor will it consider the possibility of any Labour leader being honest or honestly changing his views. So much is this the case that the more to the left he moves the more he is to be denounced as 'the greatest enemy'.[71]

There was more to the dispute between the Socialist League and the Communist Party than the historical rights and wrongs of the old feud between the Second and Third Internationals. The Labour left, after all, were democratic socialists with a genuine commitment to democracy, even if they did have little faith in British democratic institutions. They explicitly rejected revolutionary violence. As Cripps put it:

The violent revolutionary alternative I am convinced is hopeless. With modern mechanised armed forces, armed revolution has not the ghost of a chance, even if it were desirable. I should in any èvent oppose it with all my power, but in present circumstances I look upon the suggestion as sheer lunacy. Our only alternative then is to attempt to rid ourselves of capitalism by the machinery of democracy.[72]

Brailsford took this argument still further with a line of reasoning whose implicit condemnation of the Russian Bolsheviks would have disgusted any Communist:

A movement that starts with violence must continue by terrorism. It must be prepared, that is to say, not merely to repress a rebellious minority, but to intimidate a majority. That means a ruthlessness which would corrupt and disfigure its own ideal. The socialism that emerged from a reign of fear might bring order and even wealth, but it would be, morally, an ugly and distorted creation. There are in life higher values than order and wealth.[73]

This was consistent with the position Brailsford had taken thirteen years earlier in *How the Soviets Work*. In his consistency he was rather unusual on the left, for in the 1930s most leftists, including the progressive intellectuals, looked to the USSR with renewed interest and sympathy. It is important to observe, however, that this did not lead all of them to a slavish, uncritical acceptance of every aspect of the Soviet regime, as a brief survey of some leading leftists' attitudes will show.

George Orwell has attributed the left intellectuals' interest in the USSR to a sinister motive: 'These people look towards the USSR and see in it, or think they see, a system which eliminates the upper class, keeps the working class in its place, and hands unlimited power to people like themselves. It was only *after* the Soviet regime became unmistakably totalitarian that English intellectuals, in large numbers, began to show an interest in it.'[74] This is a plausible, although extremely ungenerous explanation of the Webbs' interest in the USSR, which culminated in 1935 in their mammoth eulogy, *Soviet Russia: a New Civilisation?* (later republished without the question mark). In general, however, the left's growing warmth towards the Soviet regime may be attributed to less sinister causes. Simply, the USSR appeared to be the only place on earth – with the partial exception of the USA, which I shall also consider – where anything recognisable as 'progress' was taking place. In Britain progress appeared to have stopped dead in its tracks in 1931, if not before. From this the left had learned the lesson that progress and capitalism were incompatible. Only in a socialist country could progress reasonably be hoped for.

This idea appears clearly in the comments of Trevelyan, who of those leftists with deep roots in the progressive tradition was the most sympathetic and the least critical of the USSR. He first travelled there in 1935, and on his return published *Soviet Russia: a Description for British Workers*. This work was typical of many accounts of the USSR produced in the 1930s in its descriptions of the flourishing industries and cities with neither rich, poor, nor prostitutes; the holiday resorts full of happy, laughing workers; the model penal colonies where inmates often voluntarily overstayed their sentences. Aside from his observation that the exile of Trotsky was a 'grave misfortune' Trevelyan offered no criticism.[75] This was quite deliberate, as he explained:

> I could have spent my time in finding fault, in explaining the crudity of Russian life, the utter absence of tidiness, the bad roads, the crowded trams, the present poorness of living, and the over-crowding in the towns. But what are the faults of a people or their deficiencies, which they know as well as we know our own, but unlike us are confidently dealing with. What concerns us is their accomplishment ... When the vast resources of Russia have made her population the most prosperous in the world the bad past and the hard living of the present won't matter at all.[76]

It almost seems that Trevelyan knew, and did not care, that the rest of his description was fictional in the sense that it lacked a single jarring note. What really mattered was that Russia was 'The one country in the world ... steadily marching to greater prosperity.'[77]

In the climate of despair which progressives faced in Britain, with its unemployment (15·5 per cent of insured workers in 1935 – higher in Trevelyan's native north-east)[78] and other apparently permanent social problems, it was desperately important to Trevelyan that such a society should exist. As Jennie Lee wrote to him on reading his *Description*, 'I would have felt it a very great tragedy if you had written otherwise about Russia. You hoped and believed in it so intensely before going that I suppose you would have felt like giving up belief in everything except the Devil, if the reality at close quarters had appeared feeble or a cheat.'[79] Russia appeared to be a progressive community on the criterion enunciated by T. H. Green six decades earlier. It bestowed 'power on the part of the citizens as a body to make the most and best of themselves.'[80]

Others among the progressive left shared Trevelyan's admiration for Russia's achievements. As Cole put it,

> we Socialists are watching with intense sympathy and anxiety what is happening in Soviet Russia. For the Russians ... are struggling in face of the bitter hostility of world Capitalism to build up their Communist society on radically new foundations, putting their trust not in the incentives of personal profit, but in the solid will of the Russian workers. Almost shut off from the rest of the world they are straining themselves almost to breaking point to turn a desperately poor land of half-barbarous peasants into a Socialist community fully equipped with the means of happy and healthy

living. They are spending on the children, on health and education and other social services a far higher proportion of their national income than any other country in the world . . . More than anything else in the world, I hope they will succeed. For elsewhere the outlook seems black enough to threaten universal disaster.[81]

This still left the problem of the compatibility of Russian methods with democratic liberty, which, as we have seen, was the factor which more than any other distinguished the Labour left from the Communists. On this problem all of the progressives, including Trevelyan, were agreed that Russian methods were inappropriate to British conditions, but on the question of whether the Russian approach was acceptable in the USSR, there was a wide disparity of views. Trevelyan simply denied that the problem existed. Russia was at least as democratic as Britain. On the evidence of the workings of the local Soviets he concluded that 'the workers have a much more effective control over their everyday life [than British workers] and just as much influence on the higher policy of the country'.[82] Moreover, Stalin was no more a dictator than Stanley Baldwin. Both men, were powerful because 'an enormous part of the community trusts their character and judgements, and because the predominant political party gives them its confidence'. Trevelyan did recognise that Stalin was more powerful than Baldwin, but only 'because the influence of the Communist Party in Russia is greater than that of the Conservative Party in Britain'.[83] He did not think it worthwhile to speculate that this might have been due to the fact that the Conservative Party had not forcibly liquidated its rivals.

None of the other progressives swallowed Trevelyan's line. Cole, while he thought that the USSR was 'run from below' more than any other country, nevertheless pointed out that the factory com-mittees, which Trevelyan admired, were often not elected by any recognisable democratic process, and offered 'no provision' for any challenge to their decisions.[84] More significantly still, Cole discussed the GPU, the Soviet regime's notorious secret police, and although he made some attempt to play down its significance, he did not attempt in any way to justify its activities. Instead he pointed out the obvious fact that 'A body which is even partly engaged in espionage and terrorism is not one which lovers of freedom can contemplate with pleasure.'[85]

Laski took a slightly different view. Like Cole he acknowledged that political freedom in the USSR was severely limited, and even that 'Russian policy in relation to freedom has been full of grave errors of judgement.'[86] But on the dictatorship itself he merely repeated – without criticism or approval – the Leninist argument that the classless society which would eventually result would bring 'a freedom far more profound and effective' than the freedom of capitalist states.[87] There is no evidence that Laski ever accepted this logic, although he did regard it as a proof that the Communists' hearts were in the right place.

Laski, in fact, was profoundly ambivalent about the USSR. The full extent of his ambivalence is amply illustrated in a letter to Beatrice Webb on the publication of *Soviet Russia: a New Civilisation?*. Laski admired the glowing descriptive part of the book, but suggested that the Webbs could have laid more stress on positive features such as the role of non-communist members of the Soviets, and on the 'liberating effect of equality of opportunity', which, he believed, gave to the people 'the sense of an elbow room they have never had before' and which accounted for their 'willingness to make sacrifices on so gigantic a scale'. This comment, once again, is redolent of a Greenian conception of an ideal state in which all are free to contribute to the common good. But this was by no means the only aspect of Laski's response. The negative aspect is worth quoting at length, for, better than any published work could do, these private reflections reveal the full complexity of his attitude:

I regret the attempt on your part to evade the question of dictatorship by what seem to me verbalisms. I agree, of course, that both the volume and the intensity of autocratic power can be immensely exaggerated. But I think you enormously underrate it. My own view is that the average man, not interested in basic ideas, is rarely disturbed by it; but the person interested (as you or I would be) in the fundamental contours of the regime pays a heavy price, above all in sincerity of criticism. I see no evidence to support your view that Stalin was a 'necessary' hero; and the degree to which he has built up a personal 'machine' in the American sense goes far beyond anything you indicate ... The people finds [*sic*] equality a compensation for the very real autocracy.[88]

With the exception of Trevelyan, none of these progressives accepted the Soviet myth. Cripps actually wrote nothing on the character of Soviet society or the regime, but, for all that he may have been prone to Communist manipulation on tactical matters, it is fairly clear that he was not a slavish follower of the Moscow line. This is indicated in an exchange of letters with Trevelyan in 1935 over the question of the application of economic sanctions against Italy after its invasion of Abyssinia. The Socialist League opposed sanctions on the grounds that they were merely an imperialist manoeuvre. This line was consistent with the Socialist League's general view – axiomatic to progressive leftists since 1919 – that the League of Nations was simply an alliance of the imperialist victors of the First World War. Until 1935 this view was shared by the Soviet Government and CPGB. In 1935, however, both changed their minds in consequence of a shift in Soviet foreign policy towards the goal of creating alliances with capitalist states in order to contain fascist expansionism. Trevelyan's response to this was to claim that 'If Russia supports sanctions then [the argument that sanctions are imperialist] becomes a frankly ridiculous attitude.'[89] Cripps responded crisply to this piece of casuistry, informing Trevelyan that he had 'always taken the view that Russia's foreign policy at the present time was extremely dangerous to the working classes in other countries'.[90]

This brief survey of attitudes to the USSR is enough to illustrate the important point that, with one exception, the prominent Labour leftists who had roots in the progressive tradition did not lose their capacity for independent thought. They did not accept the fundamental Communist postulate that the Soviet Union was beyond criticism. Their views coincided with those of the Communists on many points, most importantly on the nature of fascism. Where they did not coincide, however, as on Abyssinia, and for a time (as we shall see) on the Popular Front, the Labour left marched to the beat of its own drum.

Another important question on which the left progressives differed from the Communists was the policy adopted by Roosevelt in the United States. In the eyes of the Communist Party Roosevelt's administration was proto-fascist in much the same way as the National Government. Trevelyan, Brailsford, and Laski were far more ambivalent in their approach. Charles Trevelyan's views here were distinctly heretical: 'As I see it now [he wrote in 1934] Roosevelt voices the new spirit but is not yet or dares not to be a real Socialist.'[91] Brailsford took a similar view when he began 'to suspect that the United States may adopt Socialism because it has no Socialists ... Mr Roosevelt ... is obviously a man of unusual courage and resource who will not accept defeat easily. Secondly, he has no fixed ideas to hamper him.'[92] Brailsford admitted that

Roosevelt's regime was 'still only orderly capitalism, with the private owner still in command', but begged the reader to 'watch the logic of facts at work'. That logic, he argued, was leading Roosevelt to the conclusion that 'the only choice left ... was between private and public direction of the directors of industry'.[93] Laski too was favourably disposed towards 'the Roosevelt experiment'. In a Socialist League pamphlet with that title he claimed, 'President Roosevelt is the first statesman in a great capitalist society who has sought deliberately and systematically to use the power of the state to subordinate the primary assumptions of that society to certain vital social purposes. He is the first statesman deliberately to experiment on a wholesale scale with the limitation of the profit-making motive.'[94] Laski drew important lessons from the American experience for the Labour Party. Roosevelt had shown the necessity for boldness and urgency, the savageness with which capitalists would resist real change, and the absolute futility of attempting to achieve change within the orthodox mechanisms of government.

None of these writers was prepared to state categorically that Roosevelt was bound to institute socialism in the USA. None the less all clearly thought that it was possible for a well-intentioned and intelligent liberal to evolve towards socialism when confronted with the contemporary crisis of capitalist irrationality. While Brailsford, Trevelyan, and even Laski may have had excellent evidence for this in their own biographies, it was an important break from the official views of the Socialist League and, indeed, from the views that these writers themselves frequently expressed. Brailsford soon abandoned his optimistic attitude to Roosevelt, declaring in 1935 that there was 'no future along the paths of the "New Deals" and capitalist-minded Liberalism'.[95] This view was central to Socialist League thinking and flowed logically from their view that capitalism and democracy were incompatible. As Cripps told the Socialist League's 1934 conference, 'the nervous humanitarian ... will always finally come down on the side of capitalism and no change'.[96]

It was this rejection of liberalism, together with a dramatic shift in the Communist Party's position, that led the Socialist League to support the Communists' attempts to create a united front between itself, the ILP, and the Labour Party. On the one side, developments in the parliamentary lobbies had led the League to suspect that some members of the Labour Party leadership were attempting to create an alliance with Liberals and disaffected Conservatives.[97] As early as

September 1934, the League's official organ began to rumble against 'the danger of a progressive alliance', and the 'liberalisation of the Labour Party'.[98] The Socialist League's support for Communist affiliation was in part a tactical counter to these moves.

It was a new departure in the policy of the Communist Party, however, that was the major trigger of the Socialist League's action. Immediately after the election of 1935, the CPGB applied for affiliation to the Labour Party. Cripps, in an article explaining the Socialist League's decision to support the application, stressed the novelty and the significance of this step:

It was ... quite understandable and, I believe, right, that the Labour Party should reject unity so long as the Communist Party followed its objective of destroying the Labour Party and insisted on maintaining its separate existence as a political party. The position, however, has now altered. The Communist Party, by applying for affiliation is asking, not for a coalition of forces, but for a real unity within a single political party ... We in the Socialist League have always insisted that the proper place for Socialists was within the working-class movement ... Now that the Communists have adopted the same view we should welcome them wholeheartedly to assist us in a task that is as difficult as it is urgent.[99]

The Labour Party executive was clearly unimpressed by this argument. Instead, it argued that unity with the Communists was a risk not worth taking given that the Communists in the past had shown themselves completely untrustworthy and that they would almost certainly be an electoral liability. More importantly, the opponents of affiliation stressed yet again the irreconcilable difference that must exist between the Labour Party as a party dedicated to democratic methods and a party whose ultimate aim was violent revolution.[100]

To the Socialist League these differences were now less important than the theoretical common ground between the Labour left and the Communist Party. Cripps made this clear when he argued,

The circumstances of to-day are such that the risks entailed by accepting Communists as members of the Labour Party and so joining our forces, are as nothing compared with the risks entailed by continued disunion among the workers. If only we can be sure of the Socialist aim of our party and that its policy is based upon an appreciation of the issues arising nationally and internationally out of the class struggle, there is ample room within the party for such differences of opinion as are bound to exist.[101]

The Communist Party's application for affiliation to the Labour party was overwhelmingly rejected by the Party's 1936 conference, which took the opportunity to renew the Party's ban on all joint action with Communists. Within three months, the League decided, by a minority vote at a special conference, to join with the Communist Party and the ILP in a 'Unity Campaign' with the stated object of achieving 'Unity of all sections of the Working Class Movement ... to oppose Fascism in all its forms, to oppose the National Government as the agent of British Capitalism and Imperialism, to oppose all restrictions upon civil and trade union liberty, to oppose the militarisation of Great Britain.'[102] In the opinion of the NEC, the League, by co-signing the manifesto, had acted 'in clear defiance of repeated and emphatic decisions of the Annual Conferences of the Party'.[103] Accordingly, the NEC disaffiliated the League and shortly afterwards announced that it would be proscribed as from 1 June.

At the heart of the conflict lay rival conceptions of loyalty. For the NEC and its supporters loyalty was owed, above all, to the Party, a belief that was powerfully reinforced by MacDonald's defection. As the NEC proudly asserted: 'The Party has a more widespread and closer-linked organisation that has withstood the greatest strain that any Party has suffered in modern political history.'[104] To the supporters of the Unity Campaign, on the other hand, loyalty was owed first to their ideas. Ultimately, it was their loyalty to their conception of socialism, and to the analysis of the political situation that it implied, which led them not only to support the Unity Campaign, but also to dissolve their own organisation rather than forfeit their membership of the Labour Party. The decision was opposed by many members of the Socialist League, and could have easily gone the other way. Within two years the Party loyalty of many of the former members of the Socialist League was to be put to the test again. In many cases it did not survive.

That test had its origins in the deep tactical paradox that followed from the Socialist League's support for the Unity Campaign. The Communist Party's decision to apply for affiliation to the Labour Party was a part of a longer agenda in which the League could have no part. Acting in accordance with a Comintern directive, the Communist Party now blandly contradicted every previous statement it had made on the question, and decided to work for the formation of a Popular Front of all anti-fascist and anti-National Government forces.

The Popular Front was clearly inconsistent with the position that the Socialist League had expressed since its inception. Accordingly, the League's initial response to the Communist proposal was hostile. It was outlined by Barbara Betts[105] in an article on the decisions of the seventh world conference of the Communist International. Betts accepted that the USSR had little alternative but to seek alliances with non-socialist states, but she deplored the effects of this necessity on the political direction of the Comintern. She regarded the Comintern's attempts to include elements 'which are not consciously Socialist', and its claim that a war to defend Abyssinia would be 'progressive', as an opportunistic abandonment of Leninist principles, and asked, 'Has the Comintern forgotten Lenin's slogan: "Turn imperialist war into Civil War" in its concern for the fact that the capitalism of one side of the struggle is blacker than that of the other?'[106] Betts was right. The Socialist League's analysis of fascism – theoretically indistinguishable from that of the Comintern – precluded any possibility of an anti-fascist alliance with anybody but socialists. Opposition to the Popular Front remained the Socialist League's position until its dissolution in May 1937, and continued to be the view of most of its members for several months afterwards.

The tactical absurdity of the League's position is obvious. As soon as the CPGB took a significant step towards the League's own position that the Labour Party was the proper place for socialists, the League gave its support. Yet that was also the moment at which the Communist Party adopted the policy of the Popular Front, to which the League was opposed by virtue of its own analyses of capitalism and fascism. The League and the CPGB supported the United Front for diametrically opposed reasons: the former in order to prevent a Popular Front; the latter as a step towards its realisation. For the Communists, who had never recognised the Labour Party as a socialist organisation, the decisive change of attitude came with their decision to seek affiliation to the Labour Party. It was then a small matter to extend the proposed alliance to include those who did not even call themselves socialists. For the socialists of the Labour left, however, the dividing line between the Labour party and the capitalist parties was of vital importance. In 1937 few were willing to cross it.

By 1938 most people who had been in the Socialist League came to support the Popular Front, that is, to support the policy they had vehemently opposed for the last several years. Nothing could illustrate more strikingly Ben Pimlott's incontestable claim that 'in the 1930s the Labour Left was consistently wrong on tactics'.[107] Clearly, the change is barely comprehensible on this level. We must seek understanding elsewhere. As I shall argue in the following chapter, we must seek it in the ethical values, fundamental political assumptions, and enduring institutional norms of the British progressive tradition.

CHAPTER 7

The Popular Front

In the present crisis, men and women are to be judged rather by
their behaviour than by their professions of theoretical beliefs.
For us, democrat is as democrat does; and the democrats are all
those who are prepared to play their part in defending democratic institutions against Fascist attack.

G. D. H. Cole[1]

The Popular Front campaign differed from the United Front
campaign in tone, content, and context. The United Front campaign was largely concerned with British politics. Even when its
supporters spoke of fascism they frequently understood it as a
problem presented by British capitalism. The Popular Front campaign, by contrast, was concerned almost exclusively with foreign
policy. The United Front, for the Labour left at least, had its basis in
ideological considerations. Allies were to be sought among socialists
who shared their theoretical perspective on the nature of capitalism
and fascism. The Popular Front was largely ethical. Its supporters
were united in their desire to stop the evil of fascism by removing
from power in Britain a government which appeared to encourage it.

Both of these differences are clearly products of the campaigns'
differing contexts. The context of the United Front campaign was
the formation of the National Government in 1931 and its re-
election in 1935. In so far as the rise of fascism formed a part of that
context, it was, as we have seen, immediately subsumed within the
context of British political issues by the theory of capitalist imperialism. The context of the Popular Front campaign was a prolonged
crisis in the conduct of British foreign policy. Indeed, it is almost
possible to follow, step by step, the parallel development of the
Popular Front campaign with the worsening of the international
crisis.

The Popular Front campaign therefore requires a slightly different treatment from the United Front campaign. Rather than proceeding, as in the previous chapters, on the basis of analysis and comparison of theoretical positions, we are to a great extent obliged to follow the chronology of the international crisis of 1936 to 1939 and to observe the corresponding shift from ideological to ethical argument.

(I) FROM UNITED FRONT TO POPULAR FRONT

The crisis in European democracy began with the Italian invasion of Abyssinia in October 1935. This had no immediate effect on the Labour left, which regarded Britain's half-hearted support for the half-hearted sanctions imposed upon Italy by the League of Nations as signifying merely a falling out between rival imperialist powers. The Socialist League's newspaper warned workers against falling into the trap of trying 'to root out the Satan of Fascism by aiding the Devil of Imperialism'.[2] In December, however, the Abyssinian war became a major political issue in Britain, when a plan devised by the Foreign Secretary, Sir Samuel Hoare, and the French Prime Minister, Pierre Laval, partially to dismember Abyssinia in Italy's favour was leaked to the press. This revelation of hypocrisy created a furore which forced Hoare's resignation. Although the Socialist League did not concern itself with this controversy, it marks the first of a series of actions by the British Government which were interpreted by the left as proof either of its extreme cowardice or of its complicity in fascist aggression.

The Abyssinian crisis is important for another reason. Together with the election of Popular Front governments in Spain and France in February and May 1936 respectively, it provides the context of the formation of the earliest non-communist inspired Popular Front organisation. The driving force behind the first such effort was, ironically, the former Communist J. T. Murphy. Still more ironically, he made his first move at the very meeting of the Socialist League council in 1936 which decided to support the Communist Party's application for affiliation to the Labour Party. Murphy, the League's secretary, had only one supporter at this meeting.[3] Regarding the Socialist League's ultimate aim of a United Front as 'hopeless from the outset',[4] Murphy left the Socialist League before the end of June in order to form the People's Front Propaganda Committee.

The nucleus of this committee was Labour. Its most active member apart from Murphy was Jim Delahaye, who had contested unwinnable seats for the Party at the general elections of 1931 and 1935. Another active member was Allan Young, a chronic party-hopper who had left the Labour Party with Sir Oswald Mosley to form the New Party in 1931, and had left the New Party when Mosley took his turn towards fascism. In 1936 he was an adviser to Harold Macmillan MP on economic policy.

The Committee's supporters were drawn from a wide range. At a meeting in December, which Murphy claims drew more than 2,000 people,[5] Robert Boothby, the Conservative critic of the National Government's foreign policy, John Strachey, a 'fellow-traveller' and member of the Left Book Club committee, Richard Acland, a prominent Liberal, and G. D. H. Cole all spoke in support of a Popular Front.[6] Unfortunately for the Committee, however, the momentum was arrested by the issue of the Unity Manifesto the following month, which drew the energies of Labour leftists in a different direction.

The People's Front Propaganda Committee's first public announcement made clear that foreign policy was its central concern. It began: 'If British foreign policy continues to be one of wavering and unimaginative timidity the desire of the great masses of the people here and abroad for assured collective security will be frustrated and a new period of war will be thrust upon mankind.'[7] While it went on to decry the consequences of '19th century resistance to any real programme of economic and social reconstruction', the manifesto's conclusion showed again the primacy of foreign policy and the extent to which domestic economic policy was to be subordinated to it by emphasising 'the need for a campaign support-ing a Charter of immediate concrete demands dealing with the League, foreign affairs and the practical daily life of the people, in support of which many National bodies and persons from as far left as the Communist and as far right as the democratic Tory could be expected to co-operate'.[8]

With the loss of most of its active Labour support to the United Front campaign the Committee's days were numbered. After its death, Richard Acland was instrumental in establishing, in October 1937, a 'National Progressive Council' which included – as well as Murphy, Delahaye, and some others from the People's Front Propaganda Committee – Lord Layton and Arthur Salter, the renegade Conservative. Acland was aiming for a good deal more than the earlier body had tried to achieve: 'I am not putting forward the Popular Front as a short-term policy; as a mere election pact it is useless. I am putting it forward as a . . . stepping stone towards the re-creation of one party which shall be the channel through which all progressive opinion shall make itself felt.'9 This remark, which drew a rebuke from the Labour speaker, was nothing more than nostalgia for the days before the birth of the Labour Party. Such nostalgia, as well as nostalgia for the days of the progressive movement, did occasionally appear during the Popular Front campaign. Nevertheless, the campaign cannot simply be dismissed as some sort of reversion to earlier habits.

Some of the earliest proposals for the Popular Front thus came not from the Communists or their 'fellow travellers', but from Liberals and from people on the left of the Labour Party who were among the most critical of the Communist Party and the USSR. Indeed, the first time the Popular Front was proposed within the Labour Party at a national level, it was advanced explicitly as a counter-move against the Communist Party. At Labour's 1936 conference there was moved an amendment to the United Front motion, instructing the Executive 'to take all practicable steps to mobilise the support of all peace loving and democratic citizens in the struggle for peace and the fight against Fascism'.10 The mover made it clear that Communists were not included in this definition. He was convinced that a United Front with Communists would alienate large numbers of uncommitted voters. Rejecting the amendment as vague, C. E. G. Catlin then urged the Party to think seriously about 'the "Popular Front" – I would prefer to call it "national progressive front".'11 Catlin also took the view that association with the Communist Party would damage Labour's electoral prospects, maintaining even that the 'united front is exactly what [Mosley] wants'.12 Instead he advocated 'A co-operative federation of all workers' parties and progressive parties and groups, in which Communists will remain Communists and Liberals will remain Liberals, but in which you will get practical co-operation in Parliamentary action on a limited and immediate programme'.13 Catlin's reasons for a Popular Front strikingly fore-shadowed the rhetoric of 1938–9; but in 1936 it was a rhetoric that most of the later advocates of a Popular Front still eschewed.

The Labour Executive made no move against the early campaigners for a Popular Front. It had no grounds to do so. The

Popular Front had never been debated at a Party conference, so technically the Popular Front activists had committed no breach of party discipline, except by speaking from the same platform as Communists. But as speakers at the 1937 conference pointed out, this prohibition was applied very selectively by the leadership. On occasion some of the leaders had done it themselves. More importantly, the Popular Front agitation before 1938 was insignificant next to the United Front campaign which preoccupied the party leaders. No useful purpose could have been served by attempting to discipline such politically unimportant figures as Murphy and Delahaye. The effect could only have been to add credibility to the charge that the Executive was engaged in a witch-hunt.

(II) THE BASIS OF UNITY

One of the earliest converts to the Popular Front idea within the Socialist League was Brailsford. A fortnight after the outbreak of the Spanish Civil War, Brailsford wrote to Cripps to tell him of his decision and to seek his views.[14] For Brailsford too foreign policy considerations were uppermost: 'It's the international situation that moves me. I see no hope of avoiding war, or of saving Russia if it does come, unless we can soon create a firm, defensive alliance of England, France, and Russia, plus some smaller "Left" states. But only a Left government in this country would enter such an alliance with Russia.'[15]

The creation of such an international alliance – often with the addition of the USA – was one of the standard demands of Popular Front propagandists. It happened also to be the objective of Soviet foreign policy, and therefore of the CPGB, but this does not alter the fact – illustrated by the course of the Second World War – that it made sound strategic sense. Brailsford, however, was obviously convinced that any Conservative Government must rule out such an alliance on ideological grounds. This view was a product of his socialist analysis, but in the inter-war years there was a good deal of *prima facie* evidence to support it, beginning with the allied intervention in Russia. As the international crisis of the 1930s developed, the British Government supplied even more evidence for the left's general view that its foreign policy was determined ideologically.

The first such piece of evidence was coming into being as Brailsford sat down to compose his letter to Cripps. This was the policy of 'non-intervention' in the Spanish Civil War, which in practice allowed German and Italian arms and men to reach the rebels while banning British and French assistance to the Popular Front government. Like Hobson, whose views we have already considered, Brailsford and the left generally were in no doubt about the reasons behind the policy: 'It is property in this crisis that has shown its sense of solidarity, passively and hypocritically in Downing Street, actively and openly in Rome and Berlin.'[16]

It was not necessary to interpret the government's action this way. The Labour Party, for example, could not decide whether the government was 'the fool or the dupe of Franco'.[17] The Liberal Party had still another explanation of the government's failure to take any firm action against the dictators: simple cowardice. This view was sometimes aired in Labour circles. One thing, however, became clearer with each successive crisis: whatever the reason – class interest, stupidity, or cowardice – the government would not act. Its policy of appeasement was, it appeared, less a desire to redress the wrongs done to Germany at Versailles, than a firm commitment not to challenge her actions in any way.

Not all progressives were united in opposition to appeasement. Within the Labour Party there were many who believed that violence could not be justified under any circumstances. These people, among them Arthur Ponsonby and George Lansbury, became steadily more isolated within the Labour Party in the middle and late 1930s. In 1935, Lanbsury resigned the leadership of the Labour Party when it decided, against its previous practice, not to oppose the annual service estimates in parliament. In their opposition to this change, the pacifists had the support of the left, who were not prepared to entrust the National Government with arms. In 1936, however, with the outbreak of the Spanish Civil War and the left's militant support of the Spanish Republic's armed struggle, the long alliance between the pacifists and the left was over.[18]

This was the only division within progressive ranks to emerge during the immediate pre-war period. For all other progressives, their shared opposition to appeasement, although based on differing analyses, was a powerful force for unity. But for those who had supported the United Front campaign, there remained the equally obvious difficulty that if Liberals were supporters of capitalism, they could not be useful allies against fascism. For Brailsford, this difficulty could be overcome if the Liberals could demonstrate that they were not irrevocably wedded to capitalism: 'I should stipulate at home for some measures of socialisation covering coal, electricity, railways, armaments and perhaps land. Of these I think the Liberals would swallow easily all but coal, – but coal is indispensable.'[19]

Cripps's reply to Brailsford has unfortunately not survived, but it appears that Brailsford was persuaded to modify his views, or at least to refrain from stating them publicly. In a pamphlet he wrote for the Socialist League later in the same year he confined his demands for unity to 'the labour movement'.[20] Elsewhere at about the same time, however, he advanced a line that was indistinguishable from the Communists': 'The first step is to ... bring about unity within the Labour movement under virile leadership, yet with a limited and moderate programme. That done we may hope for a rally to this nucleus of other sections of the democratic forces.'[21] The rest of the article followed a line of reasoning identical to that contained in his letter to Cripps. Clearly, this two-stage proposal was the only compromise available that would allow him to remain in the Socialist League. Its resemblance to the Communist Party's agenda was coincidental.

G. D. H. Cole, who was not in the Socialist League, was freer to express his views. He did so in *The People's Front*, the Left Book Club's selection for June 1937. The book had two purposes: to protest against the Labour leadership's action against the Socialist League, and to put Cole's own case for a wider unity. His position was a very long-winded version of Brailsford's. Like him, Cole was moved by considerations of foreign policy, but was also determined that unity should be on the basis of something very like the Labour Party's socialist programme.

Cripps did not begin to campaign for a Popular Front until April 1938. Like the others, he was moved by considerations of foreign policy.[22] The first move in the campaign was the organisation by ten MPs of all parties of a National Emergency Conference on Spain. Promoting the conference in the *Tribune*, Cripps wrote that the conference could be said

to be constituted by all those to the Left of Neville Chamberlain. By 'Left' I here mean more inclined to support democracy, peace, and collective security. This is the sort of constitution for a Popular or Democratic Front that a good many people have been hankering after ... Clearly, any idea of real Socialism would have to be put aside for the present ... The real question to be decided is whether the chance of altering the foreign policy of this country and of calling a halt to Fascist aggression ... is worth the abandonment for the time being of the hope of real working-class control.[23]

The Emergency Conference itself was called in response to the rapidly worsening military position of the Spanish Government. Its objective was to bring an end to non-intervention. It was attended by just over 1,800 delegates representing trade union, Labour Party, Left Book Club, Communist, Liberal, and other branch organisations. It was chaired by Brailsford's old mentor Gilbert Murray, and the speakers included Ellen Wilkinson, Brailsford, and Cripps from the Labour Party, Harry Pollitt and Tom Mann of the CPGB, the Liberal MP Wilfred Roberts and a few Liberal parliamentary candidates, and a number of trade union officials. Conservative opinion was represented (or rather, misrepresented) by the eccentric Duchess of Atholl MP.

Various speakers stressed the necessity for united action on Spain and the irrelevance of party squabbles in the existing international situation, but it was left to Sir Charles Trevelyan, the thirteenth speaker on the list, to use the magic words, as the report of the conference graphically described: ' "What we need in this country, is a Popular Front —." The end of his speech was drowned in cheers.'[24]

The remaining speakers took up the theme, urging the need for unity not just to aid the Spanish Popular Front, but to remove the Chamberlain Government. Cripps wound up his speech and the meeting by urging delegates to 'make certain ... we do not look back to this great conference as nothing but another spate of words. Let us look back to it as the beginning of a great movement in our own country to rally the forces of British Democracy, to save not only Spain, but our own liberty and our own freedom.'[25]

The Labour Executive responded quickly to these developments by issuing a pamphlet (drafted by Laski, who had previously supported an unsuccessful motion for a Popular Front in an Executive meeting) which outlined its opposition to the Popular Front. It is worth summarising at some length as it is the most dispassionate outline of the anti-Popular Front case available.

Labour and the Popular Front argued first that in the absence of 'any evidence of an internal crisis in the Conservative Party', there was no reason to think that the formation of a Popular Front would lead to the fall of the National Government or to an early election. It questioned the assumption that the Front would be more successful electorally than the Labour Party alone. The Liberal voters themselves could not be relied upon to vote for a Labour candidate in the absence of a candidate of their own party: 'In many constituencies the absence of a Liberal candidate assists the Conservative rather than the Labour candidate.' The participation of Communists would make this outcome even more likely. As it had in 1936 and 1937, the Executive maintained that the Communists were an electoral liability: 'The presence of the Communists would bring some few thousand votes to the alliance; but it may well drive millions into Mr Chamberlain's camp.' The Executive did not believe that a Popular Front Government could govern. Neither the Communists nor the Liberals could be relied upon. The Communists were 'committed rather to manoeuvre than to principle. They could be capable of stabbing us in the back at any time.' The Liberals stood condemned by their record during Labour's two periods in office. More recently they had 'Officially participated in Mr Ramsay MacDonald's "National" Government. They supported the savage economies of that time. They helped to impose the "means test" on the unemployed. They were a party to the abandonment of China to Japanese aggression in 1931 – the first tragic blunder in the "National" Government's disastrous foreign policy.'

Although the Executive professed a 'high regard for what is best in the Liberal tradition' and did 'not deny that among Liberal Members of Parliament there are some sincere progressives and friends of peace', it held that the Party as a whole was 'uncertain and unreliable'. A government that included the Liberals would therefore be 'weak and indecisive', and could thereby provide fascism with its opening in Britain.[26]

The only way ahead, the Executive urged, was to continue to work for a Labour victory at the next election. The recent growth of the Party's membership, and its record in recent by-elections was evidence that this could be achieved.

Before concluding with an exhortation to the Party faithful to remain true to socialist principles, the Executive made a remarkable appeal for the allegiance of non-Labour supporters:

We shall go forward, however, in no spirit of Party exclusiveness. We invite all men and women who desire Great Britain to take the lead for democracy and peace – whatever their political attachment – to join us in our effort . . . We appeal to all that is best in the nation – to all men and women of goodwill – to make a victory for democracy and peace possible while there is still time.[27]

This amounted to a claim that the Labour leaders were to make repeatedly during the Popular Front campaign. There was no need for a Popular Front. It already existed within the Labour Party.

Cogent as it was, the Executive's argument did not meet the case for the Popular Front. On some crucial points there was no common basis on which to argue. To begin with the electoral calculations of both sides were merely hopeful guesses. The Executive guessed and hoped that Labour could win the next election. There was no convincing evidence for this, any more than there was for the Popular Fronters' claim that the Labour, Liberal, and Communist Parties combined would do better than the Labour Party alone. Most advocates of the Popular Front, however, disavowed mere arithmetical calculation. As Brailsford had put it in 1936: 'The formation of a People's Front would be a new event so startling that it would (1) interest the apathetic elector (2) win by-elections and (3) shake the government so severely that it might fall. I'm relying more on these psychological effects than the numerical weight of the Liberal + Communist + I.L.P. votes.'[28] Cole had put the matter more strongly when he spoke of the need for 'a crusade to arouse and to unite democratic opinion upon issues that have to be faced at once'.[29]

A similar faith in 'psychological effects' and crusading zeal underlay the Popular Front left's attitude to the question of the likely effectiveness of a Popular Front Government. Unlike the Executive, they did not base their calculations on the discouraging lessons of recent parliamentary history. Rather they hoped, as had some progressives in the aftermath of the First World War, that the parties involved would be prepared temporarily to give up those points in their programmes which divided them. A strong statement of the grounds for this belief was provided by Louis Fenn, who (perhaps not coincidentally) had been the only member of the Socialist League Council to support Murphy's original proposal for a Popular Front:

He who sincerely fights for liberty and peace fights also for Socialism, whether he will or no. Given resolute and resourceful leadership, the Party might today swing the great mass of the nation into line against the exploiting few, and in the next inevitable crisis break the power of entrenched wealth under the historic plea that "the will of the people must prevail".[30]

This was the same line of reasoning which had earlier led Brailsford, Trevelyan, and Laski to hope that President Roosevelt, as a well-intentioned liberal, could evolve towards socialism. Brailsford believed that he had concrete evidence for this. The Liberal Party, he argued, had been 'purged of its office-seekers and its plutocrats in a series of secessions', and would not shrink, 'if its abler, younger men fairly represent it, even from some measures of socialisation'.[31]

These arguments did not imply that Fenn or Brailsford had given up on their socialism, but rather that they no longer regarded a commitment to capitalism as a defining characteristic of the Liberal Party. Instead, they defined liberalism as a commitment to values which could and did lead their adherents to some form of socialism. This version of liberalism was identical to that which had flourished within the progressive milieu before 1931. Then it had not only made possible the close collaboration of Liberals and socialists, but had also led many Liberals – notably Hobson, Brailsford, and Trevelyan – to move steadily towards a powerful socialist commitment. It is not surprising in this context that the term 'progressive' returned to vogue during the Popular Front campaign and supplied it with much of its crusading zeal. Although the Popular Front campaign was triggered by, and fundamentally concerned with, foreign policy, it is important to keep in mind that it did assume some agreement on domestic policy. On one level this was political common sense; a Popular Front Government, like any other, would need an agreed domestic programme. On another level, as this argument suggests, it was essential as a means of defining progressivism, for only a true progressive could be moved towards socialism by the logic of events, and only socialism – so the Popular Front left still believed – could be an effective antidote to fascism.

What is remarkable is that the definition of a progressive programme in 1938 was in all essentials identical to the agreed common aims of progressives before the First World War. The parallels can be seen clearly in the minimalist programme contained in the Cripps memorandum. The programme proposed protection of democratic rights and liberties, a positive policy of peace, improved wages and conditions, improved standards of nutrition (especially for the unemployed), higher pensions, work towards equality of educational opportunity, a co-ordinated attack on unemployment, land reform, and 'national control' of transport, mining, and the Bank of England.[32] Philosophically, then, 'progressivism' was neither collectivist

nor individualist, but it did insist on the necessity for state intervention in order to alleviate distress, to ensure justice between employer
and employed, and to improve education. As we have seen, all of
these measures were advocated by Liberals of both individualist and
collectivist persuasion in the latter part of the nineteenth century
and beyond.[33] Cripps's proposed control over finance was a reitera-
tion of one of the earliest demands of the Fabian Society and the
ILP. Hobson's work at the turn of the century had introduced it to
Liberal progressives of the era, and Keynes acknowledged his debt to
Hobson's thought in making it one of his central proposals.

Preceding all of Cripps's other demands, however, was the
traditional liberal cry of liberty. Cole, writing in October 1938 of the
need for a 'People's Freedom Front' clarified the content of this
liberty in terms that would have won the hearty approval of Mill or
any of the progressive thinkers who later proclaimed their allegiance
to him: 'The condition of unity is that men should learn to set store
by freedoms which they do not themselves wish actively to use. If
each defends only such liberties as he desires for himself, the enemies
of liberty will easily defeat the divided forces of the opposition.' He
added, though, an argument strongly reminiscent of Green and his
successors when he insisted that the Front should work for 'a higher
standard of living for all, because nothing more enlarges freedom
than the possession of an income that allows some margin above
everyday needs'.[34] Trevelyan took up a similar viewpoint when he
described the traditional liberal freedoms destroyed in the fascist
countries as the freedoms 'which make life tolerable and out of which
you intend to evolve economic freedom as well'.[35]

For Cole and Trevelyan it was clear in 1938 that the traditional
liberal freedoms were prior and necessary conditions of the struggle
for economic justice, even though both saw economic justice as itself
a component of freedom. During the Popular Front campaign, it
was the left of the Labour Party rather than the right which seemed
willing to heed Keynes's plea to 'face the fact that they are not
sectaries of an outworn creed mumbling moss-grown demi-semi
Fabian Marxism, but the heirs of eternal liberalism'.[36]

The gulf between Liberals and socialists – especially those left-
wing socialists who constituted the Popular Front's strongest support
– was still considerable, as is shown by the observations of a Liberal
advocate of the Popular Front. He or she condemned 'the selfishness
of the merely acquisitive aim, whether individual or collective', and

claimed that, 'Socialism must be related to the welfare of the whole country, and should be sought in company with all progressive elements.'[37] This argument was no more relevant to the socialism of the Popular Front left than it had been to the position of the ILP progressives when Masterman, Hobhouse, and others had advanced it in the 1920s. The Popular Front left believed that socialism was essential to the common good. As Cripps stated in his 'Memorandum', 'the only ultimate solution of the National and International difficulties [is] along the lines of [the Labour Party's] fullest socialist programme'.[38]

This was an argument *within* progressivism, whose defining characteristics we have already considered. For the Popular Front left, however, there was another, more important way of defining the limits of the alliance than these domestic considerations. It was the same criterion as that which defined progressivism during the Boer War and at the end of the First World War: anti-imperialism.

For many on the Labour left the proposed Popular Front was necessarily confined to anti-imperialists. Men like Churchill and Eden, for all that they opposed appeasement, could have no place in the Popular Front. *A fortiori*, leftists vehemently opposed such tentative steps towards war preparation as the government actually took. If the government was prepared to fight Hitler, this was, 'in defence not of Democracy, or Collective Security, or the League of Nations Covenant, or Spanish Liberty, but of the interests of British Imperialism'.[39] From this point of view, the purpose of the Popular Front was to prevent the formation of the sort of coalition which eventually emerged in 1940:

The real alternatives are between Labour leading a coalition of the Left, including the Liberals, or Tories leading a coalition of the Right, including a handful of Right Wing Trade Union and Labour leaders. Labour's leaders are perfectly aware that these are the only real alternatives and have long ago consciously made their choice. They do not want to govern in these critical times.[40]

(III) IDEAL OR PARTY: THE PROGRESSIVE DILEMMA

As envisaged by the Labour left, the Popular Front campaign was not, as we have seen, a mere indiscriminate search for any ally against appeasement, but an attempt to rally around common political values, of which anti-imperialism was the most important.

Nevertheless, it was a marked reversal of the position that Cripps, and the Socialist League, had advanced until the eve of the campaign. As we have seen, the main source of friction between the leadership and the left in the period 1932–7 was the left's militant insistence that only through socialism could the international situation be saved, and that any attempts to compromise with non-socialist elements would lead to fascism. This was the line now taken by the Labour leadership, which gleefully ransacked its files for choice quotations from Cripps with which to condemn the Popular Front.

This was the greatest irony of the Popular Front campaign. As Keynes had observed, the Labour leadership was as much imbued with the political and ethical values of liberalism as were the advocates of the Popular Front. Indeed, the left had frequently in the past condemned the leadership for just that reason. Now the roles were reversed, as the Labour leaders and the other opponents of the Popular Front took their stand on the purity of their socialist doctrine.

The opponents of the Popular Front saw its roots in pre-war progressivism more clearly than its supporters. For the former this was one of the Popular Front's most grievous faults. A prospective Labour candidate outlined the objections:

Over a generation ago, a small body of Trade Unionists and Socialists decided that a new Parliamentary Party was necessary; today we are being asked to reverse that decision – the decision that "Liberal Democracy" has nothing of final value to offer to the working classes, or at least that the achievement of Socialism was not possible through co-operation with the Liberal Party ... Workers ... have built up an organisation inspired by a belief in Socialism, an organisation that is so necessary to win this country for Socialism, and one not likely to be cast aside, because some faint hearts fear we might not be able to win alone.[41]

Another correspondent drew the same historical lesson: 'We never had a virile party in the House or in the country till we had weaned the majority of Trade Unionists from attachment to the "Progressive" alliance as a policy.'[42] These taunts flew thicker and faster as the dispute within the Labour Party developed into outright war. As it did so, the opponents of the Front placed an ever increasing emphasis on the importance of the integrity of their organisation.

All was relatively quiet on the Popular Front in the summer months of 1938. Cripps took a long-planned holiday in Jamaica, and Labour Party members were preoccupied with the escalating Czech crisis. The eventual 'resolution' of that crisis – the infamous Munich agreement – directly triggered the next move towards concerted progressive efforts to remove the Chamberlain Government. This was the 'Independent Progressive' candidature of A. D. Lindsay, Master of Balliol, in the Oxford City by-election on 27 October. The candidature was not, strictly speaking, a part of the Popular Front campaign, although Lindsay's platform, which was concerned purely with foreign policy, bore all its hallmarks. It came about only after the local Liberal and Labour Parties agreed to withdraw their candidates. The national Liberal leadership gave its blessing; the national Labour leadership grudgingly offered its neutrality.

Lindsay drew amazingly wide support.[43] Local Liberal and Labour activists worked energetically for the campaign, as did many members of the university. From outside Oxford, many prominent Liberals, thirty-nine Labour MPs, and the wayward Conservative MP, Harold Macmillan, came to speak for Lindsay. Although he lost, the fact that the government majority had been halved to just over 3,500 votes in a campaign lasting only a fortnight gave great heart to the government's opponents. Some, including the Hammonds, were especially pleased that the election had been conducted 'without any party stuffing'.[44] The victory of the Liberal journalist, Vernon Bartlett, who stood as an Independent Progressive at Bridgwater on 17 November, raised these hopes even higher.

Cole and Brailsford both had reservations about the Independent Progressive candidatures. While Brailsford thought that in the absence of a genuine Popular Front, the Independent Progressives were 'a sign of health',[45] he was concerned about the implications of support from Conservatives, whose 'prime concern,' he maintained, was 'not to make a stand for democracy against Fascism: [but] to defend the Empire they own'.[46] Cole shared this view, and was also concerned that the Independent Progressives were attempting something that could only result in disarray: 'There is no time to set about the long process of disrupting parties in order to re-form them on different lines. The only possible alternative Government, as matters stand, is one either composed exclusively of Labour Party members or dominated by them'.[47] Cole need not have worried. There were no more Independent Progressive candidatures.

Cripps had remained aloof from the Independent Progressives, but not from the Popular Front campaign. He had returned from Jamaica on 2 October, two days after the announcement of the

Munich agreement. His first step was to help organise another conference on Spain for 23 October. The meeting was chaired by Brailsford, and Trevelyan was the principal speaker. Unlike the meeting in April, which had moved a resolution only for united action on Spain and had been content merely to cheer for a Popular Front, this meeting passed a concrete resolution calling for 'a People's Government, led by the Labour Party, based upon a broad union of all the progressive forces in the country'.[48]

In the light of the publication of *Labour and the Popular Front*, this could be seen as a breach of party discipline on the part of the organisers and the representatives of 120 Divisional Labour Parties who took part. The next major development in the campaign – the circulation of the Cripps Memorandum in January – was a still clearer breach. From that point onwards the focus of the dispute within the Labour Party shifted from the merits of the Popular Front to the question of party loyalty.

Briefly, the events were these. On 9 January, Cripps wrote to Middleton, secretary of the Labour Party, requesting a special meeting of the Executive to consider a memorandum which he enclosed. In it he advanced the usual arguments for a Popular Front with renewed urgency, and proposed that the Party call a special conference to adopt his manifesto. The Executive meeting was held on 14 January and rejected the manifesto by fourteen votes to three, with only Pritt and Ellen Wilkinson supporting Cripps. Cripps reserved his right to continue to promote his views within the Labour Party. In fact he had already prepared for the Executive's decision, and on the same evening posted a copy of the memorandum to 100 Labour MPs and every Divisional Labour Party in the country.

The Executive took the view that this was a serious breach of party rules and requested Cripps to reaffirm his allegiance to the Party and to withdraw the memorandum. Cripps refused and was expelled on 25 January. On 30 March the Executive also expelled five other supporters of the Popular Front campaign for their continued agitation for the memorandum. Among them were Trevelyan and the MPs Aneurin Bevan and G. R. Strauss, although inexplicably, no action was taken against Brailsford.[49]

Following Cripps's expulsion the rebels continued the campaign by launching a petition addressed to the Labour, Liberal, and Co-operative Parties asking them to form a Popular Front. The aim of the petition was to place pressure on the Labour Party conference scheduled for Whitsuntide (29 May–2 June). The Labour Executive threatened members with expulsion if they supported the campaign. It also produced two pamphlets once again outlining its opposition to the Popular Front and explaining its reasons for expelling Cripps.[50] Although some Labour Party members supported the Petition Campaign, and although it produced some spectacular meetings, most Labour people stayed away. At the Party conference the Executive's positions on both the Popular Front and Cripps were overwhelmingly endorsed.[51] Cripps announced the end of the campaign in June and sought readmission to the Party.

The expulsion unleashed a storm of protest, some of it from opponents of the Popular Front who nevertheless saw the Executive's actions as heavy-handed and undemocratic. The debate is instructive, for it illustrates the extent to which the advocates of the Popular Front were indebted to the organisational norms of pre-Versailles progressivism as well as to its political ideals. As Cripps put it, 'Loyalty is a matter of conviction, not of discipline.'[52]

One writer to the *New Statesman and Nation* itemised the 'only three possible reasons' he could see for the Executive's actions. These were '1. Jealousy of its most able member. 2. A determination that Party discipline shall override all wider issues. 3. A faith in the capacity of "pure Socialism" alone to retrieve the rapidly declining fortunes of this country.' The writer offered no comment on the first point, and in dealing with the third merely reiterated the usual arguments for a Popular Front. The second point, he argued, 'can only be valid when the rebellious member opposes the fundamental principles for which his Party stands. I have never yet heard it suggested that Sir Stafford has given up a single one of his Socialist ideals.'[53]

This argument was frequently employed in Cripps's defence, as was the argument that the Executive had suppressed healthy democratic debate within the Party. As Strauss put it,

The argument that to initiate discussion in the Party on a vital tactical proposal, which may be defeated, means splitting the Party is a denial of democracy in our movement. Such discussion is more likely to have an invigorating effect. What may split the Party is the action of the Executive in abusing their powers by expelling those who disagree with them.[54]

Trevelyan described Cripps's expulsion as 'the most petty, ungenerous and preposterous piece of heresy hunting', and asked 'Who are these inquisitors at Transport House who because Stafford Cripps challenges their uninspiring strategy come down on him and declare that he is not fit for their impeccable and orthodox society?'[55]

This revulsion against orthodoxy was common and embraced not just the Cripps issue but the whole Popular Front debate:

Between such Progressives as Mrs Corbett-Ashby [a Liberal candidate] and similar people in the Labour Party what a splendid united programme . . . might there not be formed! But no. Mr Greenwood has said, and the Labour Executive has endorsed it by expelling Sir Stafford Cripps, that it is useless to think of co-operating with anyone . . . unless they can pronounce correctly the magic words "Socialism" and "Nationalisation".[56]

Such attitudes were anathema to the Labour leadership and to many of the rank and file. Party loyalty and party independence were the central themes of the two relevant debates at the 1939 conference. Speaking on Cripps's expulsion one delegate came very close to arguing for 'my party right or wrong' when he reminded the rebels 'that the part is not greater than the whole, and while we as members of the Party and the Executive may be a pack of idiots, once we have decided we are, we may as well go forward'.[57] In the Popular Front debate one delegate echoed the sentiments of many when he claimed that to accept the Popular Front was to be 'disloyal to the pioneers of the Party, Keir Hardie and the rest; disloyal to the electors and the working class of the country'.[58] Another delegate spoke of the 'grave risk of the disappearance of the Labour Party', and, as others had done, affirmed his 'burning conviction . . . that we must be independent of the other political parties'.[59]

Just after Cripps's expulsion R. H. S. Crossman, who supported the Popular Front, analysed the dispute in terms of generational conflict:

The National Executive is largely composed of men and women who have devoted their lives to building up an independent Labour Party. Their ideas moulded by pre-war conditions, they have worked to create a great Socialist political machine . . . It is only natural that such people should view with the deepest suspicion a movement which seems to ask them to collaborate with life-long enemies and to surrender the objective for which the Labour Party was formed . . . [The young] are unable to understand the feuds between Liberal, Labour, and Communist politicians, because they have never known a time when the two-party system was working properly, and so do not hanker after a return to the "normalcy" which still haunts the minds of pre-war politicians.[60]

There was doubtless a great deal of truth in Crossman's analysis. But it overlooks the important fact that many of the most active supporters of the Popular Front – most notably Trevelyan, Cole, and Brailsford – also had their ideas 'moulded by pre-war conditions'. These prominent supporters were by no means unusual among their generation. Morgan Phillips Price – the man who as the *Manchester Guardian*'s Moscow correspondent in 1918 had been responsible for the first English publication of the notorious 'secret treaties' – used the same paper to express his qualified support for the campaign. Another member of the Labour Party, Harrison Barrow, who, like Price, was a veteran of the UDC, publicised his enthusiasm for the campaign in both the *Manchester Guardian* and the *New Statesman and Nation*. W. Lyon Blease, who thirty years earlier had committed to paper a definition of the nature of Liberalism which I borrowed much earlier in this study to help define progressivism, was a co-signatory, with Leonard Barnes, to a letter which laid down a set of UDC style preconditions for Liberal and Labour support for a war against fascism.[61] More ambiguously, Alfred Beesly, who had been a member of the LLAAM, wrote from the Reform Club against the expulsion of Cripps in tones reminiscent of the progressives who had remained in the Liberal Party after the First World War: 'It appears to be laid down as a fundamental principle of the Labour party that nobody can become or remain a member of it unless he will refrain from advocating any policy about anything which conflicts with the policy on that subject laid down by the party. The minority must be effectively silenced.'[62] Another supporter of the Popular Front, Sydney Silverman MP, who had been a conscientious objector in the First World War, was moved by Cripps's expulsion to shift from opposition to support of the Front. This was tactical lunacy, but his reasons were typical of the importance progressives placed on the maintenance of an arena of free discourse. The argument against the Popular Front, he believed, rested 'upon the capacity of the Labour Party, acting alone, to win the support of all those who desire an alternative to a British Government which is a European calamity'. The Labour Executive's unwillingness to permit free discussion, however, made him 'wonder whether they are really measured to the exigencies of the times or whether they are merely flotsam and jetsam upon a fatal tide of history'.[63]

Crossman could not account for these older progressives' support for the Popular Front because he overlooked the possibility that more than one conclusion could be drawn from pre-war conditions. As the early chapters of this book have shown, pre-war (or more accurately, pre-Versailles) progressive politics were characterised by institutional fluidity and by a multiplicity of organisations and informal groupings that transcended party divisions as a matter of course. Within that milieu, progressive intellectuals worked assid-uously to maintain these arenas of progressive discourse and vehicles of political action. Participation in the milieu was ultimately subject to one criterion: a faith in the possibility and desirability of political progress.

In 1900–1 and in 1914–20 the one issue that proved capable of refashioning the internal boundaries of the milieu was foreign policy. In 1938–9 a crisis of foreign policy again precipitated a widespread desire to redraw those boundaries – at least temporarily. But the walls had been built too high. In place of an open progressive discourse, there were three mutually hostile parties, each of which claimed – in different ways and for different reasons – to be the only true heir to the progressive tradition. The progressives of the Labour left, who after 1931 adopted an uncharacterstic insistence on rigid ideological criteria for their evaluation of other political groupings and beliefs were partly responsible for this. But if the Labour Party had stronger grounds to claim the progressive heritage than any other party, it was due in part to the work of people like Brailsford and Trevelyan, whose subordination of party to their progressive values had taken them into the Party in a more intellectually open era.

Conclusion

The most obvious point to emerge from this study is that the Popular Front campaign, being nothing more than a means of uniting the political efforts of progressives in a shared and urgent cause, had ample precedents within the history of the British progressive tradition. In the earlier crises of British foreign policy engendered by the Boer War and the First World War, progressives had united across party lines without any need to agonise and without any objection from the leaders of their parties.

A number of the progressives of the Labour left who supported the Popular Front, most conspicuously Brailsford and Trevelyan, had themselves played a role in these earlier united efforts. More than this, however, it is clear that united action and open, inter-party discourse was an established feature of the everyday life of progressives. This is very obvious in the period before the First World War, but it continued to be so in the 1920s and beyond, when men like Cole and Laski came to take their positions of leadership within the progressive milieu.

Placed in this context, the Popular Front campaign presents few difficulties. It can be readily understood by the historian's customary procedure of studying the past of the individuals and institutions involved, and there is no need to have recourse to elaborate theories of Communist manipulation. In the late 1930s, the aims of the Labour and Liberal supporters of the Popular Front partially coincided with those of the Communists. Given that socialism, in all its forms, was long established as a legitimate strand in the progressive tradition, it is hardly surprising that those who desired progressive unity were willing to accept whatever contribution the Communists might be able to make to the fight against appeasement. In the same way, Liberal and Labour opponents of the Boer War had been willing, before Bolshevism existed, to accept the support of the revolutionary Marxists of the SDF.

It could still reasonably be argued, however, that the belief that the Communists belonged in the British progressive tradition was fundamentally mistaken. Not only did the CPGB give unquestioning support to a regime whose repressive brutality was repugnant to the democratic faith of British progressives, it also demanded from its members absolute adherence to orthodoxy, a demand completely at odds with progressives' established habits of free thought and discussion. From this point of view, the Labour leftists' support for a United Front, which was to include Communists and exclude Liberals, becomes particularly difficult to understand if the Labour left is to be understood as belonging to the progresssive tradition.

The explanation nevertheless should be sought in the history of the progressive tradition rather than in the idea that the entire Labour left was in thrall to the Communists. As I have argued, the United Front campaign is to be understood in the light of the fact that the Labour left and the Communist Party shared a common analysis of the major political problems then confronting all progressives, and proposed similar, although not identical, strategies with which to meet those problems. To recapitulate, both regarded fascism as an outcome of the imperialist phase of capitalism, and regarded the policies of the National Government, as well as the circumstances of its birth, as evidence that fascism was implicit in the mainstream of British politics. Both believed that the risk of fascism could not be removed without a socialist transformation of British society. They differed, as we have seen, only on the means by which the transformation was to be achieved.

These differences were no greater than some of the other differences which have been evident at various times within the progressive tradition. Around the turn of the century, progressive discussion groups such as the Rainbow Circle, and more formally constituted bodies such as the South Place Ethical Society and the Fabian Society contained, more or less comfortably, people whose opinions differed on seemingly fundamental questions. There were those such as the Webbs, Ramsay MacDonald, and Brailsford who were ultimately committed to the social ownership of the means of production, distribution, and exchange; there were those such as Trevelyan, Samuel, and Asquith who believed that private enterprise was an essential feature of any free and prosperous society.

The philosophical differences between Labour leftists and Com-. munists in the 1930s also were no wider than those which existed within pre-war progressivism. Indeed, they were no wider than the differences within the Labour left itself. In both, we have identified philosophical ideas derived from Mill, Bentham, Green, and, significantly, Marx. In seeking an alliance with Communists, the progressives of the Labour left were thus casting their net no wider than it had customarily been cast in the heyday of the Progressive Movement. The truly peculiar feature of the united Front, considered in the context of the progressive tradition, was not its breadth, but its narrowness. It is not the proposed inclusion of Communists which requires special explanation, but its exclusion of Liberals.

The hostility towards Liberalism expressed by many on the Labour left in the 1930s was based on the simple ideological consideration that Liberals did not share a commitment to socialism. This was the first and last time within the whole period we have considered that any significant group of progressives chose to define themselves and to determine the limits of political alliance in purely ideological terms. The attempt was short-lived, partial, and for some progressives of the Labour left, obviously uncomfortable. Brailsford, for example, wanted to move on to a broader progressive alliance even before the United Front campaign was properly under way.

The progressive tradition cannot be defined in ideological terms any more than it can be defined in terms of membership of any particular political organisation or commitment to any specific philosophical creed or political programme. Still less can progressivism be thought of merely as the sum total of the parties opposed to conservatism. Within the Liberal Party there was, during the whole period of this study, a significant, perhaps dominant, group which remain irrevocably committed to the continuation of the existing system of property relations. It was the existence of this group within the Liberal Party which led many progressives to join the Labour Party, and which formed the basis of many of Labour progressives' criticisms of Liberalism. Conversely, the existence within the Labour Party of certain trade unionists who conceived their role in purely sectional terms was enough to deter Liberals like Gilbert Murray and Hobhouse from joining it.

Here then are two of the negative defining characteristics of the progressive tradition. Progressives have not been prepared to ally themselves blindly with any particular interest or to uphold any particular economic system for its own sake. They have always taken the common good as the starting-point of their political thought and the ultimate objective of their political action.

The progressive tradition is, as I have suggested earlier, a discourse. Within that discourse many different political opinions have been uttered. Its existence as a discourse has depended not upon the ability of its participants to produce uniform answers, but on the nature of the questions they have discussed and the assumptions upon which they have done so. In the period I have considered progressives of various viewpoints have concerned themselves with the same cluster of questions: the necessity for state intervention to ensure social justice; the relationship between socialism, capitalism, and liberty; the potential of British institutions to enable social and political reform; imperialism.

Progressives have assumed that the purpose of political institutions and political activity should be to enlarge freedom. They have therefore been inherently and inevitably opposed to the possessors of arbitrary power, whether derived from ancestral privilege, bureaucratic position, or wealth. In 1900, Sidney Webb defined the 'progressive instinct' as 'opposition to the party which strives to maintain the vested interests of the existing order'.[1] This is the barest possible definition. Even as Webb wrote, however, the progressive tradition was in the process of establishing for itself the more specific touchstone of anti-imperialism.

The reasons for the centrality of anti-imperialism to the progressive tradition in the twentieth century are fairly obvious. It became clear, to progressives at least, that empire had become the exclusive preserve of the possessing classes, and the most concrete, systematic, and naked expression of the domination of man by man. Even here there are exceptions and qualifications. The Fabian and Liberal Imperialists obviously did not share this view of the nature of imperialism. They did not thereby disappear altogether from the progressive stage; they merely moved from the centre to the wings, some to take up new leading parts at a later date, as Asquith did during the struggle with the House of Lords in 1909-11. One might even go a step further and suggest that Winston Churchill, who also played a leading role in that struggle, returned after years backstage to play an even bigger role in the 'people's war', but that would be to stretch the meaning of progressivism beyond the limits that most of its participants could comprehend.

Although the progressive tradition cannot be defined and its participants cannot be categorised, it has, nevertheless, constituted an important and enduring feature of the British political landscape. Many political organisations, campaigns, newspapers, and magazines – far more than I have been able to consider – which have influenced British political parties and events belong within the progressive tradition, and cannot be fully understood without reference to it. The Popular Front, at a moment in history when the values most central to that tradition were more than ever before under direct threat, was unequivocally an expression of it.

Notes

INTRODUCTION

1. *Unity Manifesto of the Socialist League, the Independent Labour Party and the Communist Party*, reproduced in G. D. H. Cole, *The People's Front*, Gollancz, 1937, pp. 357–9.
2. E. P. Thompson, 'Outside the Whale', in *The Poverty of Theory and Other Essays*, Merlin, 1978, deals with the issues raised here from a different perspective. The germ of this book was sown originally by my reading of Thompson's essay.
3. G. Orwell, 'Spilling the Spanish Beans', in *Collected Essays, Journalism and Letters*, Harmondsworth, Penguin, 1970, pp. 301–9; B. Crick, *George Orwell: a Life*, Secker & Warburg, 1980, pp. 227–8.
4. *NS & N*, 22 May 1937, pp. 837–9; 15 May 1937, pp. 801–2.
5. Orwell, *Essays*, vol. 1, p. 335.
6. Crick, *Orwell*, p. 210.
7. E. P. Thompson, 'The Moral Economy of the English Crowd in the Eighteenth Century', *Past and Present*, 50 (Feb. 1971), pp. 77–8.
8. ibid., p. 78.
9. ibid., p. 76.
10. ibid.
11. See, e.g., A. J. P. Taylor, *English History 1914–1945*, Harmondsworth, Pelican, 1975, pp. 488, 510; L. C. B. Seaman, *Post-Victorian Britain 1902–1951*, Methuen, 1966, p. 298.
12. A. Sherman, 'The Days of the Left Book Club', *Survey*, 41 (April 1962), pp. 75–85 *et passim*; J. Symons, *The Thirties: a Dream Revolved*, Faber & Faber, 1975, chs 10, 12–13; N. Wood, *Communism and British Intellectuals*, New York, Columbia University Press, 1959, pp. 60–2 *et passim*. D. Caute, *The Fellow Travellers*, Weidenfeld & Nicolson, 1973, pp. 157–65.
13. A. J. A. Morris, *C. P. Trevelyan 1870–1958: Portrait of a Radical*, Belfast, Blackstaff Press, 1977.
14. F. M. Leventhal, *The Last Dissenter: H. N. Brailsford and his World*, Oxford, Clarendon Press, 1985, provides a full and rich account of Brailsford's life.

15. There are a number of studies of both Cole and Laski, none of them altogether satisfactory. For Cole the best is M. I. Cole, *The Life of G. D. H. Cole*, Macmillan, 1971. The best account of Laski's life is still Kingsley Martin, *Harold Laski*, Gollancz, 1953, although the student of Laski's ideas should also see H. A. Deane, *The Political Ideas of Harold J. Laski*, New York, Columbia University Press, 1955.

16. Of the three biographies of Cripps, by far the best is C. A. Cooke, *The Life of Richard Stafford Cripps*, Hodder & Stoughton, 1957.

17. M. Foot, *Aneurin Bevan*, Frogmore, Granada, 1975, vols. I & II, is a splendid study by Bevan's most distinguished disciple. It is only occasionally marred by Foot's desire to justify Bevan's every act.

18. ibid., p. 133.

19. P. F. Clarke, *Lancashire and the New Liberalism*, Cambridge University Press, 1971, p. 397.

20. P. F. Clarke, 'The Progressive Movement in England', *Transactions of the Royal Historical Society*, fifth series, vol. 24, 1974, p. 181.

21. P. F. Clarke, *Liberals and Social Democrats*, Cambridge University Press, 1978.

22. J. Hinton, *Labour and Socialism*, Brighton, Wheatsheaf Books, 1983, p. 104.

23. D. Howell, *British Social Democracy*, Croom Helm, 1976, p. 26

24. H. H. Asquith, 'Introduction' to H. Samuel, *Liberalism: an Attempt to State the Principles and Proposals of Contemporary Liberalism in England*, Grant Richards, 1902, p. ix.

25. T. H. Green, *Works of Thomas Hill Green*, R. L. Nettleship (ed.), New York, Kraus Reprint Co., 1969 (London, Longmans, Green & Co., 1906), vol. III, p. 367.

26. W. L. Blease, *A Short History of Liberalism*, T. Fisher Unwin, 1913, p. 3.

1 THE PROGRESSIVE SIDE OF POLITICS

1. T. Kirkup, *A History of Socialism*, Adam and Charles Black, 1909, pp. 7, 4–5.

2. W. Wolfe, *From Radicalism to Socialism*, New Haven, Yale University Press, 1975.

3. J. R. MacDonald, *The Socialist Movement*, Williams & Norgate, 1911, p. 28n.

4. H. Perkin, 'Individualism versus Collectivism in Nineteenth-Century Britain: a False Antithesis', *Journal of British Studies*, XVII (Fall, 1977), pp. 111–12 (emphasis in the original).

5. ibid., pp. 114–17.

6. ibid., p. 117 (emphasis added).

7. J. B. Brebner, 'Laissez-faire and State Intervention in Nineteenth-Century Britain', *Journal of Economic History, Supplement*, VIII (1968), p. 61.

8. ibid. (emphasis in the original).
9. D. G. Ritchie, *Principles of State Interference*, 1902, Freeport, Books for Libraries Reprints, 1969, p. 136.
10. M. Blaug, 'The Classical Economists and the Factory Acts – a Re-examination', *Quarterly Journal of Economics*, LXXII (1958), pp. 211–26 *et passim*.
11. ibid., pp. 217–18.
12. ibid., pp. 213–14.
13. Brebner, 'Laissez-faire', p. 64, describes Chadwick as 'Bentham's most stubbornly orthodox disciple ... with his finger in every interventionist pie'. W. H. Greenleaf, *The British Political Tradition*, Methuen, 1983, vol. I, pp. 222, 256, gives a more measured view.
14. Greenleaf, *Tradition*, I, pp. 124-7.
15. F. W. Hirst, 'Liberalism and Wealth', in *Six Oxford Men, Essays in Liberalism*, Cassell & Co., 1897, pp. 82–3.
16. Mill to Carlyle, 11 and 12 April 1833, cited in Wolfe, *Radicalism to Socialism*, p. 41.
17. Mill, 'Chapters on Socialism', *Collected Works*, Routledge & Kegan Paul, 1967, vol. V, p. 710.
18. Mill, *Works*, III, pp. 956–7.
19. ibid., p. 939.
20. ibid., V, p. 753.
21. ibid., pp. 745–6.
22. M. Richter, *The Politics of Conscience: T. H. Green and his Age*, Weidenfeld & Nicolson, 1964, p. 212.
23. Green, 'Liberal Legislation and Freedom of Contract', *Works*, III, p. 371.
24. ibid., p. 372.
25. ibid., p. 373.
26. Seven of the sixteen chapter headings of *Principles of Political Obligation* are explicitly concerned with the rights of the state. This, perhaps more neatly than anything else, indicates the distance Green had travelled from Mill. Green, *Lectures on the Principles of Political Obligation and Other Writings*, ed. P. Harris & J. Morrow, Cambridge University Press, 1986.
27. Richter, *Green*, p. 210.
28. Green, *Political Obligation*, pp. 176–7.
29. ibid., p. 175.
30. F. Inglis, *Radical Earnestness*, Oxford, Martin Robertson, 1982, p. 38.
31. M. Freeden, *The New Liberalism*, Oxford, Clarendon Press, 1978, pp. 55–60, has argued both that Green was an individualist and that his influence on the New Liberalism was small. The present discussion negates the former claim; later discussion of the New Liberals will negate the latter.

32. R. Plant & A. Vincent, *Philosophy, Politics and Citizenship*, Oxford, Basil Blackwell, 1984, pp. 28, 32.

33. P. Thompson, *Socialists, Liberals and Labour: the Struggle for London, 1885–1914*, Routledge & Kegan Paul, 1967, p. 21.

34. Plant & Vincent, *Citizenship*, p. 105, quoting B. Bosanquet, *Charity Organisation Review*, 69 (1890), p. 363.

35. B. Bosanquet, *The Philosophical Theory of the State*, Macmillan, 1965, p. 177.

36. Asquith, in Samuel, *Liberalism*, p. x.

37. Samuel, *Liberalism*, pp. 23–4.

38. Freeden, *New Liberalism*, p. 111.

39. ibid., p. 110; Hobson, *Work and Wealth: a Human Valuation*, New York, 1914, p. 304.

40. *Progressive Review*, i, p. 2.

41. Freeden, *New Liberalism*, p. 59, appears to accept Hobson's assessment at face value. Plant & Vincent, *Citizenship*, pp. 90–3, provide a telling qualification of this view.

42. Ritchie, *State Interference*, p. 143.

43. L. T. Hobhouse, *Democracy and Reaction*, Brighton, Harvester, 1972 (first published 1904), p. 78.

44. Hobhouse, *The Metaphysical Theory of the State*, George Allen & Unwin, 1918, p. 24.

45. ibid., pp. 120, 118.

46. Jones to Macmillan, 22 Feb. 1918, Macmillan archive (readers' reports), vol. MCCII, pp. 116–18. I am grateful to Dr David Boucher of the Australian National University for drawing this and other documents relating to Jones to my attention.

47. *Nation*, 10 June 1916, p. 308.

48. Hobson, *The Crisis of Liberalism: New Issues of Democracy*, P. S. King & Son, 1909, p. 106.

49. A. F. Mummery & J. A. Hobson, *The Physiology of Industry*, New York, Kelley & Millman, 1956, p. iv.

50. ibid., p. 106 *et passim*.

51. Hobson, *Crisis*, p. 77.

52. Freeden, *New Liberalism*, pp. 76–9. Ch. 3 is a detailed account of New Liberals' uses of biological arguments.

53. Hobhouse, *Social Evolution and Political Theory*, New York, Columbia University Press, 1911, p. 155.

54. Ritchie, 'Evolution and Democracy', in S. Coit (ed.), *Ethical Democracy: Essays in Social Dynamics*, Society of Ethical Propagandists, 1900, p. 7.

55. Freeden, *New Liberalism*, p. 98.

56. Hobson, *Crisis*, p. 76.

57. A. Toynbee, *Lectures on the Industrial Revolution of the Eighteenth Century in England*, Longmans, Green & Co., 1908, p. 223.

58. Samuel, 'The Independent Labour Party – II', *PR*, I, iii, p. 255.
59. *PR*, I, iii, p. 210.
60. Samuel, 'The Independent Labour Party – II', *PR*, I, iii, p. 259.
61. Hobhouse, *Democracy and Reaction*, p. 237.
62. ibid., p. 229.
63. ibid., p. 227.
64. ibid., p. 229.
65. G. B. Shaw in M. I. Cole (ed.), *The Webbs and their Work*, Frederick Muller Ltd, 1949, p. 7.
66. E. R. Pease, *The History of the Fabian Society*, Frank Cass & Co., 1963 (first published 1918), pp. 18–21.
67. Shaw, in Cole, *The Webbs*, p. 6. Mill's influence on Webb is well known. For Webb's positivism see Wolfe, *Radicalism to Socialism*, ch. 6. For the influence of positivism on the milieu from which the early Fabians emerged, see Pease, *History*, pp. 18–19.
68. *The Diary of Beatrice Webb*, Virago, 1983, II, p. 200.
69. M. J. Weiner, *Between Two Worlds: the Political Thought of Graham Wallas*, Oxford, Clarendon Press, 1971, p. 15.
70. ibid., pp. 8–13.
71. Wolfe, *Radicalism to Socialism*, p. 242.
72. ibid., p. 232, *et passim* for a full discussion of the Fabians' intellectual histories. See also A. M. McBriar, *Fabian Socialism and English Politics 1884–1914*, Cambridge University Press, 1966, pp. 7–19.
73. G. Wallas, 'Property Under Socialism', in G. B. Shaw (ed.), *Fabian Essays in Socialism*, George Allen & Unwin, 1962, p. 165.
74. W. Clarke, in *Fabian Essays*, p. 115. Cf. K. Marx, *The Communist Manifesto*, in R. C. Tucker (ed.), *The Marx–Engels Reader*, New York, W. W. Norton, 1972, p. 339.
75. H. Bland, in *Fabian Essays*, p. 247 and pp. 237–55 *passim*.
76. Shaw, in M. Cole, *The Webbs*, p. 218.
77. A. Besant, in *Fabian Essays*, p. 184.
78. ibid., p. 185. This idea is remarkably similar to the ideas of the Marxist theorists of the Second International. The chief difference is that the Fabians anticipated that the whole process would be slower than even the most cautious leaders of the Second International imagined.
79. See S. Webb, p. 63; Clarke, pp. 94–5; S. Olivier, p. 161; Wallas, p. 165; and Bland, pp. 237–9, in *Fabian Essays*.
80. Olivier, *Fabian Essays*, p. 138.
81. Wallas, *Men and Ideas*, Allen & Unwin, 1940, p. 135.

2 THE COLOURS OF THE RAINBOW

1. Fabian Society, Minutes of the Executive Committee, 20 May 1890.
2. FS: membership books, undated MS list [1891].

3. This is only to count each type of organisation once. Many Fabians were members of several Liberal and Radical associations. These plural memberships have not been counted in this analysis.

4. Although it is impossible to know how many of the Fabians on the register joined organisations or acquired influence in them before or after they joined the Fabian Society, it is unlikely that new members rushed off to join organisations such as the Temperance Society or the Balloon Society in order to become effective permeators.

5. McBriar, *Fabian Socialism*, p. 95. For a discussion of the concrete effects of permeation see ibid., chs. 7–11.

6. For an example of a pessimistic view of permeation in the particular sense, see Bland, in *Fabian Essays*, pp. 246–53.

7. McBriar, *Fabian Socialism*, pp. 95–7.

8. [Shaw], *Report on Fabian Policy*, Fabian Tract 70, 1896, p. 6.

9. FS:EC minutes, 5 Feb. 1886.

10. Ritchie to Pease, 1 Nov. 1896, FS: corres.

11. McBriar, *Fabian Socialism*, pp. 19–22. See also E. P. Thompson, *William Morris: Romantic to Revolutionary*, New York, Pantheon Books, 1976, pp. 538–49 and 605–10.

12. Shaw, *The Fabian Society: its Early History*, Fabian Tract 41, p. 12.

13. Pease, *History*, p. 67.

14. Shaw, *Early History*, p. 14.

15. FS:EC minutes, 20 Oct. 1893.

16. FS:EC minutes, 27 Oct. 1893.

17. In 1908, Wilson returned to active work in the Fabian Society and was instrumental in the formation of the Fabian Women's group, of which she was secretary until ill-health forced her resignation in 1914 (Pease, *History*, pp. 189–90). She was a member of the Fabian Executive 1911–15.

18. Fabian Society Minutes, 5 Nov. 1886.

19. W. Morris, *Communism*, Fabian Tract 113.

20. FS:EC minutes, 28 Oct. 1892.

21. This line of argument has an obvious corollary: the SDF was not the 'alien' body that it has often been held to be.

22. Shaw, *Early History*, pp. 24–5.

23. The Fabian Society [S. Webb & Shaw], 'To Your Tents O Israel', *Fortnightly Review*, CCCXXIII (1 Nov. 1893), p. 584. Shaw maintained, in Pease, *History*, p. 112, that he and Webb had initially devised the Newcastle programme. McBriar, *Fabian Socialism*, pp. 238–41, argues that this claim is exaggerated.

24. *The Fabian Election Manifesto*, Fabian Tract 40, 1892, pp. 6, 9, 14.

25. *BWD*, vol. II, p. 41 (25 Dec. 1893).

26. Massingham to Pease, 18 Oct. FS: corres., A/8/2 f.11.

27. Massingham to Shaw, 20 Oct. 1893, Passfield papers, II.4.9/15.

28. Massingham to S. Webb, 3 Nov. 1893, Passfield papers, II.4.9/19.

29. Ritchie to Pease, 31 Oct. 1893, FS: corres., A/8/4 ff.15–18.
30. Ritchie to Pease, 18 Nov. 1893, FS: corres., A/8/4 f.21.
31. Samuel to Pease, 8 May 1892, FS: corres., A/9/1 f.25.
32. D. Powell, 'The New Liberalism and the Rise of Labour, 1886–1906', *Historical Journal*, 29, 2 (1986), pp. 369–93. From this perspective the decline of the Liberal Party can be explained by the New Liberals' failure to convert the Party, and by the persistence (and after 1910 the upsurge), particularly at the local level, of sharp class confrontation in which Liberals were either 'neutral' or hostile to the workers' cause. (See A. Howkuns, 'Edwardian Liberalism and Industrial Unrest: a Class View of the Decline of Liberalism', *History Workshop*, 3–4 (1977), pp. 143–61.) I am inclined to accept this last part of the argument, but should stress that the problem it addresses is outside the scope of this study.
33. FS:EC minutes, 6 Feb. 1891.
34. Leventhal, *Last Dissenter*, p. 24. Brailsford, a star pupil of the Idealist philosopher Edward Caird, was one of those involved. The distinction between Fabianism and the ILP branches outside London was very fine. Before the formation of the ILP the local Fabian Societies, which were entirely autonomous and generally more proletarian than the London body, tended to concern themselves chiefly with labour representation questions. Many later became ILP branches (Pease, *History*, pp. 101–3).
35. *BWD*, vol. II, p. 45 (12 Mar. 1894).
36. See Table 1. All figures have been rounded to the nearest 0·5%.
37. It is not until we consider groups within the register that are too small to be of any statistical value that any significant variations in rates of departure appear. In these groups, while there are some spectacular percentage differences from the average, these would disappear had one or two individuals left rather than stayed or vice versa. Nevertheless it is interesting to note that only four of the eight who claimed influence in the SDF had left the Fabian Society by 1897; and it is an eloquent testimony to the Fabians' adherence to the principles of Tract 70, that of the seven who claimed influence in Christian Socialist or Christian reform bodies, and the three who claimed influence in secularist organisations, all were still Fabians in 1897.
38. Tracts 53 and 56–8. In accordance with the usual Fabian practice, Samuel's Tracts were published anonymously. His authorship was no secret however. Samuel had Tract 56 reprinted under his own name for distribution in Oxfordshire (Samuel to Pease, FS: corres., 21 May 1894, A/9/1, f.29).
39. *BWD*, vol. II, p. 83 (18 Oct. 1895). Samuel's and Trevelyan's professed differences with the Fabian Society over ulterior ends only partly account for their failure to join it. Samuel's views on the matter, which may have been given extra weight in his mind by his

careerism, have already been discussed. It is possible that both men feared ructions within their prominently and traditionally Liberal families.

40. *BWD*, vol. II, p. 66 (23 Jan. 1895).
41. P. F. Clarke, 'Progressive Movement', p. 175.
42. Helen Bosanquet was a philosopher and a key figure in the COS along with her husband Bernard Bosanquet. She and Beatrice Webb both served on the Royal Commission on the Poor Law of 1905–9. The Commission's majority report, inspired by COS principles, was subjected to severe and sustained attack by supporters of its minority report, led by Beatrice Webb.
43. The fullest account of the Rainbow Circle is M. Freeden (ed.), *Minutes of the Rainbow Circle 1894–1924*, Royal Historical Society, 1989, pp. 1–15.
44. MacDonald suggested *Evolutionary Socialism* as the title for the English edition of Bernstein's *Die Voraussetzung des Sozialismus und die Aufgaben der Sozialdemokratie*.
45. *PR*, i, p. 2.
46. *PR*, i, p. 8. While its ends may have been admirable, the policy is a heavy blow for the historian trying to analyse the ideas of individuals.
47. Freeden (ed.), *Rainbow Circle*, pp. 27–38.
48. S. Webb, *The Difficulties of Individualism*, Fabian Tract 69, 1896, p. 3.
49. ibid., p. 14. Cf. Clement Attlee: 'It is necessary to get rid of the tyranny of capital, just as formerly it was necessary to restrain the tyranny of kings and princes.' Speech reported in *Manchester Guardian*, 24 Sept. 1936.
50. Webb, *Difficulties*, p. 15.
51. ibid., p. 16. Cf. Mill, p. 32, above.
52. [Shaw], *Report on Fabian Policy*, Fabian Tract 70, 1896, p. 6.
53. MacDonald to Pease, 8 Apr. 1896, FS: corres., A/8/1 f.9.
54. *PR*, i, p. 20.
55. *PR*, i, p. 98.
56. P. F. Clarke, *Liberals and Social Democrats*, p. 60.
57. W. Clarke to Pease, 4 July 1899, FS: corres., A/7/1 f.6.
58. Clarke to MacDonald, n.d. [1896] in B. Porter, *Critics of Empire*, Macmillan, 1968, p. 165.
59. Clarke to Pease, 12 July 1897, Fabian Society corres., A/7/1 f.4.
60. P. F. Clarke, 'Progressive Movement', p. 166.
61. ibid.
62. Olivier to Pease, 14 Oct. 1899, FS:EC minutes, 20 Oct. 1899.
63. FS:EC minutes, 15 Dec. 1899.
64. No relation to J. A. Hobson.
65. FS:EC minutes, 20 Oct. 1899.
66. Both resolutions are reproduced in full in McBriar, *Fabian Socialism*, pp. 122–3.

67. Pease, *History*, p. 131.
68. FS:EC minutes, 12 Jan. 1900.
69. FS:EC minutes, 23 Jan. 1900.
70. Olivier to Pease, (14 Oct. 1899), FS:EC minutes, 20 Oct. 1899.
71. FS:EC minutes, 20 Apr. 1900. Leventhal, *Last Dissenter*, p. 95. For Salt, the war was only the final straw. He had already instructed Pease to remove him during the next routine purge of inactive members as a consequence of the leadership's endorsement of the Jubilee celebrations (Salt to Pease, 4 June 1897, 30 Oct. 1899), FS: corres., A/9/1 ff.19–20.
72. Another three members of the SACC and the LLAAM actually joined the Fabian Society during the Boer War.
73. SACC, List of Members, March 1900. LLAAM, *First Annual Report*, April 1901.
74. ibid., p. 3.
75. Robert Waite (per Cadbury) to MacDonald, 3 Aug. 1900, Cadbury to MacDonald, 15/5/1900, PRO 30/69/1144.
76. S. Coit to MacDonald, 16 Apr. 1900, ibid.
77. Crane to MacDonald, 25 Feb. 1900, ibid.
78. I. MacKillop, *The British Ethical Societies*, Cambridge University Press, 1986, chs 2–3.
79. ibid., p. 62.
80. *Ethical World*, 28 July 1900, pp. 433–4.
81. ibid., 28 July 1900, p. 465.
82. Hobhouse to Trevelyan, 24 June 1901, Trevelyan papers, pkt 135.
83. FS:EC minutes, 14 June 1901.
84. *BWD*, vol. II, p. 166 (30 Oct. 1900).
85. ibid., p. 213 (9 July 1901).
86. ibid., p. 215 (26 July 1901).
87. S. Webb, 'Lord Rosebery's Escape from Houndsditch', *Nineteenth Century*, Sept. 1901, p. 369.
88. ibid., pp. 371–2.
89. K. E. Miller, *Socialism and Foreign Policy: Theory and Practice in Britain to 1931*, The Hague, Martinus Nijhoff, 1967, p. 5. Ibid., pp. 5–15, provides a useful discussion of the Liberal tradition in foreign policy.
90. P. Magnus, *Gladstone*, John Murray, 1963, p. 288.
91. J. Bright, speech on the Principles of Foreign Policy, in E. R. Jones (ed.) *Selected Speeches on British Foreign Policy 1738–1914*, Oxford University Press, 1914, p. 336.
92. S. Webb, 'Houndsditch', p. 374.
93. ibid., p. 370.
94. ibid., p. 375. The echoes of Asquith's old tutor, T. H. Green, can be heard clearly, cf. p. 34, above.
95. The most thorough treatment of the phenomenon is G. R. Searle, *The Quest for National Efficiency*, Oxford, Basil Blackwell, 1971.

96. Fabian Tract 70, p. 6. See p. 49, above.
97. [Shaw], *Fabianism and the Fiscal Question: an Alternative Policy*, Fabian Tract 116, 1904.
98. Wallas to Pease, 21 Jan. 1904, FS: corres., A/9/2 ff.48–51.

3 IMPERIALISM AND WAR

1. McBriar, *Fabian Socialism*, pp. 253–6, provides an account of the many reasons for the brevity of the alliance.
2. J. A. Hobson, *Imperialism: a Study*, James Nisbet & Co., 1902.
3. Hobson's attitude to Cobden approached worship. See Hobson, *Richard Cobden: the International Man*, Ernest Benn, 1968 (T. Fisher Unwin, 1919).
4. See p. 40, above.
5. For discussions of nineteenth-century liberal views on foreign policy of particular relevance in this context, see Miller, *Foreign Policy*, pp. 5–14; Porter, *Critics*, pp. 5–18; A. J. P. Taylor, *The Troublemakers: Dissent over Foreign Policy 1792–1956*, Hamish Hamilton, 1957, chs. 2, and 3.
6. Hobson, 'Socialistic Imperialism', *International Journal of Ethics*, XII (October 1901), p. 45.
7. ibid. This was no mere rhetorical flourish. Hobson's later work on international government attempted strenuously to find a workable basis for the establishment of such a 'mode of expression'. See ch. 4, below.
8. Hobson, 'Socialistic Imperialism', p. 47.
9. ibid., pp. 47–9.
10. ibid., p. 56.
11. ibid., cf. p. 38, above.
12. Hobson, 'Socialistic Imperialism', p. 57.
13. ibid., pp. 50–3.
14. This line of argument was very close to one frequently advanced by E. D. Morel, who in turn was strongly influenced by the anthropological studies of Mary Kingsley, which are referred to several times in *Imperialism*. The fullest discussion of the influence of Kingsley's work on anti-imperialist thought is to be found in Porter, *Critics*, ch. 8. J. Allett, *The New Liberalism: the Political Economy of J. A. Hobson*, Toronto, University of Toronto Press, 1981, p. 140, suggests that Hobson's 'concern for cultural diversity' stemmed also from his reading of the works of Gustav Le Bon.
15. Hobson, 'Socialistic Imperialism', p. 57. A few months earlier, one of Hobson's friends from the Rainbow Circle had employed biological analogy more directly to the same effect. 'Biological science has drawn the inference that "the greater the differentiation of organ, the greater is the concentration of action and purpose." This inference can, with

equal justification, be drawn from the facts of social and political life.'
J. A. Murray MacDonald, 'The Liberal Party and Imperial Federation', *Contemporary Review*, vol. 77 (May 1900), p. 653.

16. ibid., pp. 56, 58. This argument reappears, refined and expanded, in *Imperialism*, part II, ch. 2, 'The Scientific Defence of Imperialism'.

17. A near identical argument can be found in *Imperialism: its Meaning and its Tendency*, (*City Branch Pamphlets, No. 3*), City Branch, ILP, 1900, pp. 13–14. P. Thompson, *London*, p. 233, describes the City branch as being composed of intellectuals. It is almost inconceivable that none of its members had read Hobson's articles.

18. See pp. 61–2, above.

19. Hobson, *Imperialism*, p. 153.

20. ibid., p. 158.

21. ibid., p. 160.

22. ibid., p. 158.

23. ibid., ch. 2, pp. 34–8 *et passim*.

24. ibid., p. 72.

25. Hobson to E. T. Scott, 10 Feb. 1930, Scott papers, A/H69/17.

26. 'I formally resigned my membership [of the Liberal Party] when during the [First World] War Liberals of the Government abandoned Free Trade.' Hobson, *Confessions of an Economic Heretic*, George Allen & Unwin, 1938 (Hassocks, Harvester, 1976), p. 126.

27. ibid.

28. Hobson, 'Free Trade and Foreign Policy', *Contemporary Review*, vol. 74 (August, 1898), p. 167.

29. ibid., p. 168, quoting Cobden in 1850.

30. It is interesting to note also that Philip Snowden, one of the few Labour Party ministers who had followed MacDonald into the National Government in 1931, resigned when the government adopted a system of imperial protection in the following year. The Liberals Herbert Samuel and Archibald Sinclair went with him.

31. Hobson, *Imperialism*, part I, ch. 2, 'The Commercial Value of Imperialism'.

32. ibid., p. 38; 'Free Trade', pp. 171–5.

33. Hobson, *Imperialism*, pp. 51–2.

34. L. Courtney, *The War in South Africa*, speech delivered at Birmingham, 10 Feb. 1900 (SACC pamphlet).

35. '*The War!*' (*Spread the Light – No. 2.*), Labour Leader, n.d. [1900?].

36. E. Carpenter, *Boer and Briton*, Labour Press Leaflet, 1900, pp. 3–4. For a fuller discussion of the proponents of this view, see Porter, *Critics*, pp. 62–9.

37. Hobson, *The War in South Africa: its Causes and Effects*, James Nisbet & Co., 1900, p. 197.

38. On this point see Allett, *Hobson*, pp. 132–3.

39. ibid., p. 189.

40. Hobson, 'Capitalism and Imperialism in South Africa', *Contemporary Review*, vol. 77 (Jan. 1900), pp. 1–2.
41. ibid., p. 86.
42. *Imperialism: its Meaning and its Tendency*, pp. 14–15.
43. Hobson, *Imperialism*, pp. 52–3.
44. Porter, *Critics*, pp. 40–8.
45. Hobson, *Imperialism*, p. 171.
46. Leventhal, *Last Dissenter*, pp. 51–5.
47. Brailsford to Millicent Garret Fawcett, 25 Jan. [1910], Millicent Garret Fawcett papers, M50/2; 1/292.
48. Conciliation Committee, *Manifesto*, 1910, Millicent Garret Fawcett papers, M50/2; 1/304.
49. Brailsford to Fawcett, 26 Nov. 1911, ibid., 1/341.
50. Taylor, *Troublemakers*, p. 124, suggests that these articles may have been the result of a collaboration between Brailsford and Hobson. Whether this is true or not hardly matters. The two men had first worked together in 1906 and were soon close.
51. Brailsford, *The War of Steel and Gold: a Study of the Armed Peace*, G. Bell & Sons, 1915 (first published May 1914), p. 41.
52. ibid., pp. 219–20.
53. ibid., p. 219. This line of argument makes Brailsford's version of the theory of capitalist imperialism somewhat less vulnerable than Hobson's (or Lenin's, see ch. 5, below) to the penetrating criticisms to which the theory has been subjected in D. K. Fieldhouse, 'Imperialism: an Historiographical Revision', *Economic History Review*, second series, XIV, 2 (1961), pp. 187–209. See also Fieldhouse, *Economics and Empire 1830–1914*, Weidenfeld & Nicolson, 1973, ch. 3 *et passim*.
54. Brailsford, *Steel and Gold*, p. 165.
55. ibid., p. 235.
56. ibid., p. 209.
57. ibid., pp. 172–3.
58. ibid., p. 45. Henry Nevinson left the Liberal Party in 1907 because of the Russian Entente: H. W. Nevinson, *Fire of Life*, James Nisbet & Co., 1935, pp. 234–5.
59. C. A. Cline, *E. D. Morel 1873–1924: the Strategies of Protest*, Belfast, Blackstaff Press, 1980, ch. 2. See also F. S. Cocks, *E. D. Morel: the Man and his Work*, Allen & Unwin, 1920.
60. E. D. Morel, *Red Rubber*, T. Fisher Unwin, 1907, pp. 202–3.
61. ibid., pp. 205–6.
62. See p. 77, above. Porter, *Critics*, p. 182, points out that Kingsley gave two lectures at the South Place Ethical Society in 1897–8; it is likely that Hobson heard them.
63. ibid., p. 205.
64. See p. 79, above.
65. ibid., p. 150.

66. ibid., p. 160.
67. ibid., p. 181. Morel clearly saw himself as a successor to Wilberforce. See Cline, *Morel*, p. 40.
68. Cline, *Morel*, p. 52.
69. ibid., pp. 68–74.
70. ibid., p. 69.
71. Morel, *Great Britain and the Congo*, New York, H. Fertig, 1969 (Smith, Elder & Co., 1909), p. 256.
72. Morel, *Ten Years of Secret Diplomacy: an Unheeded Warning*, National Labour Press, 1915, p. 168. The text originally appeared as *Morocco in Diplomacy*, Smith, Elder & Co., 1912.
73. ibid., p. 170.
74. ibid., p. 64.
75. ibid., p. 171.
76. ibid.
77. J. D. B. Miller, *Norman Angell and the Futility of War*, Basingstoke, Macmillan, 1986, p. 7.
78. Sir Frank Lascelles, speech at Glasgow, 21 Sep. 1912, quoted in endpaper to Angell, *Foundations of International Polity*, Heinemann, 1914.
79. Angell, *The Great Illusion*, Heinemann, 1911, p. vi.
80. ibid., p. 146.
81. ibid., pp. 157–8.
82. Angell, *Foundations*, p. 84.
83. ibid., p. 108.
84. ibid., pp. 113–15.
85. Angell, *Illusion*, p. 89.
86. ibid., pp. 79–80.
87. Angell, *Foundations*, p. 119.
88. *Nation*, 18 Apr. 1914, p. 89.
89. *Nation*, 18 Dec. 1909, p. 491.
90. *Nation*, 18 Apr. 1914, p. 90. The idea that there was a necessary link between capitalism and national sovereignty was to assume growing importance in Brailsford's thought, and was to inform much of his post-war criticism of the League of Nations.
91. *Nation*, 27 June 1914, p. 489.
92. ibid.
93. It is not proposed here to offer even a potted history of the UDC. The standard work is M. Swartz, *The Union of Democratic Control in British Politics during the First World War*, Oxford, Clarendon Press, 1971. H. M. Swanwick, *Builders of Peace*, George Allen & Unwin, 1924, is an informative partisan account.
94. Here I differ from Swartz, pp. 17–18, who suggests that the UDC was founded by Trevelyan, Morel, and Arthur Ponsonby MP, who then recruited MacDonald in order to tap Labour support. This is

inconsistent with the fact that on 18 August 1914, exactly a fortnight after Britain entered the war, Trevelyan wrote to Graham Wallas informing him, 'MacDonald and I have set on foot an organisation . . . for preparing literature against the time when the public will want to think again' (Wallas papers, 1/56). Ponsonby, on Swartz's own account, did not join until 'a few weeks' after the outbreak of war (p. 14). Furthermore, the sequence of events offered by Swartz cannot account for the fact that while MacDonald (together with Trevelyan, Morel, and Angell) was a signatory to the UDC's first circular, Ponsonby was not (p. 41).

95. J. Hannam, *Isabella Ford*, Oxford, Basil Blackwell, 1989; A. Tyrell, *Joseph Sturge and the Moral Radical Party in Early Victorian Britain*, Christopher Helm, 1987. Ford was E. R. Pease's cousin. A biography of Joseph Sturge was written by another Quaker, Stephen Hobhouse, cousin of L. T. and Emily Hobhouse and Stafford Cripps, nephew of Beatrice Webb and Kate Courtney, and member of the No Conscription Fellowship.

96. [Lt. R. L. Tawney], *The War to End War: a Plea to Soldiers by a Soldier*, UDC pamphlet no. 21, 1917.

97. [E. D. Morel et al.], *The Morrow of the War*, UDC pamphlet No. 1, n.d. [1914], p. 1.

98. The UDC's four Cardinal Points appeared on the inside cover of most of its pamphlets. They are reproduced in full in Swanwick, *Builders*, p. 39.

99. Taylor, *Troublemakers*, p. 103.

100. Swartz, *UDC*, p. 22.

101. Angell, *The Prussian in our Midst*, UDC pamphlet No. 13, n.d. [1915]; Hobson, *Labour and the Costs of War*, UDC pamphlet No. 16a, 1916; Morel, *The African Problem and the Peace Settlement*, UDC pamphlet No. 22, 1917; *War and Diplomacy*, UDC pamphlet No. 11, n.d.

102. Swanwick, *Women and War*, UDC pamphlet No. 11, n.d. [1915]; MacDonald, *War and the Workers: a Plea for Democratic Control*, UDC pamphlet No. 8, n.d. [1915].

103. Brailsford, *Turkey and the Roads of the East*, UDC pamphlet No. 18a, 1916, pp. 22–4.

104. *The Morrow of the War*, p. 5. Swartz has pointed out that this pamphlet was toned down by Ponsonby, Trevelyan, and Angell who feared that Morel's and MacDonald's harsh criticism of the government would antagonise possible Liberal supporters. This is a rare case of UDC writers being obliged to modify their views for public consumption by anyone but the government censor, but it is important to note that this was for tactical rather than ideological reasons.

105. Swanwick, *Builders*, p. 50.

106. R. E. Dowse, 'The Entry of Liberals into the Labour Party: 1910–1920', *Yorkshire Bulletin of Economic and Social Research*, XIII, 2 (1961).

4 THE PILGRIMS' PROGRESS

1. R. B. Haldane, *Richard Burdon Haldane*, Hodder & Stoughton, 1929, p. 309.
2. C. A. Cline, *Recruits to Labour*, Syracuse, Syracuse University Press, 1963. In an appendix, Cline gives biographical profiles of about seventy prominent 'recruits'. In so far as precise figures can be gleaned from this source, they show that of the forty who were definitely members of the Liberal Party before the war (as opposed to those who merely came from Liberal families) fourteen changed their allegiance in 1914–18, another nineteen in 1919–23, at least eight of them in 1919 alone. The remainder joined the Labour Party at the rate of about one a year until 1930.
3. R. E. Dowse, *Left in the Centre*, Longmans, Green & Co., 1966, p. 32.
4. Nevinson, *Fire*, p. 213.
5. Clarke, *Liberals and Social Democrats*, p. 171.
6. Swartz, *UDC*, pp. 136–40.
7. The Fourteen Points are reproduced in full in L. L. Snyder, *Fifty Major Documents of the Twentieth Century*, New York, Van Nostrand Rheinhold, 1955, pp. 26–8. Ibid., pp. 29–51, reproduces the armistice terms, the Covenant of the League of Nations, and extracts from the Treaty of Versailles.
8. *Nation*, 13 July 1918, p. 381. 'Never-Endians' was Massingham's term for the advocates of a punitive peace.
9. Asquith, *A Clean Peace and National Reconstruction*, Liberal Party, 1918.
10. Asquith, *The League of Nations: the True Crusade*, Liberal Party, 1918, p. 8.
11. Dickinson was a close friend of Edward Carpenter, whom he had met in 1885 while engaged in the quintessentially progressive occupation of University Extension lecturer. E. M. Forster, *Goldsworthy Lowes Dickinson*, Edward Arnold & Co., 1934, p. 57.
12. Brailsford, *The Covenant of Peace: an Essay on the League of Nations*, Headley Bros., 1918, p. 4.
13. See p. 76, above.
14. D. Martin, *Pacifism*, Routledge & Kegan Paul, 1965, pp. 91–3, discusses the variety of opinion on sanctions.
15. L. S. Woolf, 'Suggestions for the Prevention of War', special supplement to *New Statesman*, part 1, 10 July 1915, p. 23.
16. ibid.
17. ibid., p. 19.
18. ibid., pp. 2–3.
19. ibid., part 2, 17 July 1915, p. 2.
20. H. R. Winkler, *The League of Nations Movement in Great Britain 1914–1919*, Scarecrow Reprint Corporation, 1967, p. 7.
21. G. L. Dickinson, *The Choice Before Us*, George Allen & Unwin, n.d. [1917], p. 172.

22. ibid., p. 173.
23. *Mr. Asquith on Liberalism after the War*, speech to office-bearers of the London Liberal Federation, 15 Jan. 1918, Liberal Party, 1918, p. 1.
24. *Nation*, 29 May 1920, pp. 272–3.
25. A. Henderson, *The Peace Terms*, Labour Party, 1919, p. 3.
26. MacDonald, *Nation*, 29 May 1920, p. 272.
27. M. P. Price, *Blue Blood and Bolshevism*, Gloucester, ILP, 1920, p. 5.
28. C. P. Trevelyan, *From Liberalism to Labour*, George Allen & Unwin, 1921, p. 36.
29. Letter to *Nation*, 15 Nov. 1919, p. 238. See also Morel, *Pre-War Diplomacy – Fresh Revelations*, ILP, 1919, for an example of Morel's zeal in hounding Asquith and Grey.
30. This is the estimate provided in Dowse, 'Entry', xiii, 2, 1961, p. 84.
31. Brailsford to Trevelyan, 2 Dec. 1920, Trevelyan papers, pkt 135.
32. Trevelyan, *From Liberalism*, pp. 19, 20.
33. ibid., p. 45.
34. ibid., pp. 43, 45.
35. ibid., p. 31.
36. *Nation*, 15 Nov. 1919, p. 238.
37. Loreburn to Trevelyan, 26 Mar. 1921, Trevelyan papers, pkt 103.
38. Dowse, 'Entry', p. 84.
39. See pp. 131–2, below.
40. See pp. 126–8, below.
41. Angell, *The British Revolution and the American Democracy*, New York, 1919, quoted in Angell, *After All*, Hamish Hamilton, 1951, p. 232. The section of this autobiography in which Angell discusses his political activities in the inter-war years is called 'Left Turn with Doubts'. It is rich in anti-socialist tirades.
42. 'Socialism and New Liberalism', ts. of speech, n.d., Trevelyan papers, pkt 135.
43. Trevelyan, *From Liberalism*, p. 70. Taylor, *Troublemakers*, quite wrongly asserts that this book contained, 'not a word ... about nationalisation or the capital levy', an error which leads him to the mistaken conclusion that 'Foreign affairs alone carried him into the Labour Party.' (Taylor dates the work 1920. The first and only edition was in 1921.)
44. Trevelyan, *From Liberalism*, p. 20.
45. ibid., p. 22.
46. *Nation*, 19 July 1919, p. 469.
47. *Nation*, 23 Nov. 1918, p. 215.
48. Burns resigned from the government on the outbreak of war.
49. *Nation*, 23 Nov. 1918, p. 216.
50. *Nation*, 27 Sep. 1919, p. 752.
51. See p. 53, above.

52. *Nation*, 22 May 1920, p. 244.
53. C. F. G. Masterman, *The New Liberalism*, Leonard Parsons, 1921, p. 245.
54. Miller, *Foreign Policy*, p. 98.
55. *Nation*, 29 May 1920, p. 273. Trevelyan had put forward a similar argument, *From Liberalism*, p. 64.
56. Masterman, *New Liberalism*, p. 198.
57. Hobhouse to C. P. Scott, 16 Nov. [1924], Scott papers, 132/317.
58. G. Murray, *What Liberalism Stands For*, Liberal Party, 1925, p. 16.
59. ibid., p. 11.
60. J. M. Robertson, *Liberalism and Labour*, Liberal Party, 1921, pp. 7–8.
61. Hobson, *Confessions*, p. 126.
62. A. F. Havighurst, *Radical Journalist: H. W. Massingham*, Cambridge University Press, 1974, p. 308. For Massingham's loathing of Lloyd George, see ibid., pp. 287–8.
63. P. Snowden, *What is the Labour Party? A Reply to Liberal Misrepresentations*, Labour Party, 1922, p. 2. The 'Liberal misrepresentations' were contained in B. Musgrave, *What is the Labour Party?*, Liberal Party, 1922. Interestingly, 'The Labour Party is a Class Party' was Musgrave's first point, ahead of his criticisms of its socialism.
64. Massingham, *Join the Labour Party: My Advice to Liberals*, Labour Party, 1923 (reprinted from *Daily Herald*), p. 2.
65. *Nation*, 24 Aug. 1918, p. 466.
66. Murray, *Stands*, p. 13.
67. ibid., p. 14.
68. ibid., p. 15.
69. Hobhouse to C. P. Scott, 7 Nov. [1924], Scott papers, 132/318.
70. Hobhouse to Scott, 16 Nov. [1924], ibid.
71. Robertson, *Liberalism and Labour*, pp. 12–13. Of all the Liberals discussed in this chapter Robertson was the least attuned to the contemporary mood and ideas of the Labour Party. His remoteness from new developments is perhaps best attested by his pamphlet's repeated references to G. D. H. Cole as 'Mr. Coles'.
72. ibid., p. 13.
73. Murray, *Stands*, p. 19. It is interesting that Murray did not mention a purely Liberal Government; presumably he realised that it was not a possibility.
74. Masterman, *New Liberalism*, p. 195.
75. ibid.
76. ibid., pp. 196–7.
77. *Nation*, 20 Mar. 1920.
78. *Nation*, 9 Oct. 1920, p. 40.
79. *Nation*, 16 Oct. 1920, p. 71.
80. S. Hodgson, letter to *Nation*, 23 Oct. 1920, p. 130.
81. *Nation*, 23 Oct. 1920.

82. Trevelyan to Ponsonby, 30 Dec. 1918, Ponsonby papers, c.667.
83. Clarke, *Liberals and Social Democrats*, p. 235.
84. M. Freeden, *Liberalism Divided: a Study in British Political Thought 1914–1939*, Oxford, Clarendon Press, 1986, pp. 88–94.
85. Havighurst, *Massingham*, pp. 293–302.
86. ibid.; Clarke, *Liberals and Social Democrats*, p. 216.
87. Leventhal, *Last Dissenter*, p. 176.
88. Woolf to Hammond, 19 Dec. 1928, Hammond papers, 21:185.
89. *Political Quarterly*, 1 (1930), p. 3.

5 INSIDE THE LEFT

1. J. Lee, *My Life with Nye*, Harmondsworth, Penguin, 1981.
2. Laski, *Nationalism and the Future of Civilisation*, Watts & Co., 1932, pp. 16, 35–6, 39–40, 46–7, 49, 52.
3. Martin, *Laski*, p. 12. The following account of Laski's early life is drawn mainly from ibid., chs. 1–3.
4. Laski to Graham Wallas, 27 June 1918, Wallas papers, 1/61.
5. Haldane at the time was 'trying to find a new outlook which will serve Liberalism and Labour equally without prejudicing their special programmes'. Haldane to Laski, 7 April 1920, Laski papers (Hull).
6. 'Mr George and the Constitution', *Nation*, Oct. 1920–Jan. 1921, pp. 38, 124, 184, 269.
7. Martin, *Laski*, p. 56.
8. Laski wrote an affectionate notice of Robertson for the *Dictionary of National Biography*.
9. Laski to C. P. Scott, 14 Nov. 1927, Scott papers, A/L10/13.
10. Deane, *Laski*.
11. Freeden, *Liberalism Divided*, pp. 307–8.
12. Laski, *A Grammar of Politics*, Allen & Unwin, 1967, pp. 39–40.
13. ibid., p. 176.
14. Laski, *Communism*, Williams & Norgate, 1927, p. 78.
15. ibid., p. 80.
16. Freeden, *Liberalism Divided*, pp. 295–313, discusses the relationships between Laski and Hobhouse and Hobson.
17. G. D. H. Cole, quoted in M. I. Cole, *G. D. H. Cole*, p. 33.
18. See B. Holton, *British Syndicalism 1900–1914*, Pluto Press, 1976.
19. McBriar, *Fabian Socialism*, p. 104.
20. Cole to B. Webb, 14 Mar. 1917, Passfield papers, 11.4.g.30.
21. B. Webb to Cole, 14 Mar. 1917, Passfield papers, 11.4.g.29.
22. M. I. Cole, *G. D. H. Cole*, p. 70.
23. Cole to C. P. Scott, 30 Oct. 1924, Scott papers, A/C68/4; Lindsay to Scott, [May 1912], ibid., A/C68/2.
24. Cole to Scott, 10 July 1921, Scott papers, A/C68/13. The offer was accepted.

25. Cole, *Self-Government in Industry*, G. Bell & Sons, 1918, p. 5. The fact that Cole himself tended to use 'collectivism' and 'state socialism' interchangeably does not, given the argument of ch. 1 above, invalidate the following remarks.
26. ibid., p. 24.
27. ibid., pp. 78, 82.
28. ibid., p. 109.
29. G. D. H. & M. I. Cole, *A Guide to Modern Politics*, Gollancz, 1934, p. 401.
30. G. D. H. Cole, *What Marx Really Meant*, New York, Alfred A. Knopf, 1934, p. 25.
31. *New Clarion*, 18 Mar. 1933, p. 291.
32. G. D. H. Cole, in O. H. Ball (ed.), *Sydney Ball: Memories and Impressions of 'an Ideal Don'*, Oxford, Basil Blackwell, 1923, p. 228.
33. S. Ball to O. H. Ball, February 1891, quoted ibid., p. 43. The influence of Mill, Green, and Hobson is clearly seen in S. Ball, *The Moral Aspects of Socialism* (Fabian Tract 72, reprinted with some omissions and additions from the *International Journal of Ethics*, April 1896).
34. Cole, 'John Atkinson Hobson', (obit.), *Economic Journal*, vol. 50 (June–Sep. 1940), pp. 352–3.
35. G. D. H. & M. I. Cole, *A Guide to Modern Politics*, p. 442.
36. ILP, *Report of Annual Conference* 1922, p. 57 (R. C. Wallhead, chairman's address). See Dowse, *Left*, ch. 3 *et seq.* for an elaboration of the post-war role of the ILP.
37. Dowse, 'The Left-Wing Opposition during the First Two Labour Governments', part 1, *Parliamentary Affairs* (Winter 1960–1), pp. 80–93.
38. Cline, *Recruits*, pp. 102–5.
39. ILP, *Report of Annual Conference*, 1921, p. 139.
40. Labour Party, *Report of Annual Conference*, 1921, p. 207.
41. MacDonald, *Labour and the Empire*, George Allen, 1907, pp. 18–20.
42. G. L. Dickinson, *The Choice Before Us*, pp. 135–6 (my emphasis).
43. ibid., p. 138. Cf. Hobson's insistence that neither a socialist nor a *laissez-faire* nation could gain from imperialist ventures, p. 82, above.
44. Angell, *Hands off Russia*, Adelaide, Australian Freedom League, 1920, p. 2.
45. See p. 93, above.
46. ibid., p. 3.
47. Angell, *Foreign Policy and Our Daily Bread*, W. Collins & Co., 1925, p. 7.
48. Leventhal, *Last Dissenter*, p. 112.
49. Foot, *Bevan*, p. 209.
50. *New Leader*, 31 Mar. 1921, p. 3.
51. ILP, *How to End War: ILP View on Imperialism and Internationalism*, n.d. [1922], p. 8.

52. *New Leader*, 28 Sep. 1922, p. 1.
53. Leventhal, *Last Dissenter*, pp. 188–90.
54. Creech-Jones papers, Box 1 f.3.
55. This profile of Wise is based largely on a conversation with his daughter, Mrs Margaret Jenner.
56. Hobson et al., *The Living Wage*, ILP, 1926, pp. 11–12.
57. ibid., pp. 13–19.
58. ibid., p. 37.
59. ibid., pp. 3–4.
60. ibid., p. 53.
61. ibid., pp. 52–3.
62. W. T. Symons, *A Living Wage or a Living Income*, ILP, n.d. [1926], p. 1.
63. ibid., p. 7.
64. Bevin to Brailsford, quoted in Leventhal, *Last Dissenter*, p. 193.
65. *Living Wage*, p. 5.
66. ibid., p. 7.
67. Hobhouse to C. P. Scott, 7 Nov. and 16 Nov. [1924], Scott papers, 132/317, 318; see pp. 115–16, above.
68. Keynes to Brailsford, 27 Oct. 1926, Keynes papers, L/26.
69. See Clarke, *Liberals and Social Democrats*, pp. 226–34, for a full discussion of the complexities of this relationship.
70. Keynes to Hobson, 23 April 1930, Keynes papers, EJ/13.
71. ibid.; see also R. Skidelsky, *Politicians and the Slump*, Harmondsworth, Pelican, pp. 67–72.
72. *New Leader*, 7 June 1929, p. 6. Simon was a progressive Liberal of the *Nation* group. Samuel in 1925–6 had chaired a commission of inquiry into the coal industry and produced recommendations generally favourable to the miners; the Baldwin Government's failure to implement its proposals was one of the triggers of the coal lockout of 1926.
73. E. A. Richards, letter to *New Leader*, 21 June 1929, p. 13.
74. ILP, 'NAC Annual Report', in ILP, *Report of Annual Conference*, 1930, p. 45.
75. E. Parker, letter to *New Leader*, 14 June 1929, p. 2.
76. R. P. Dutt, *Socialism and the Living Wage*, CPGB, 1927, p. 134.
77. ibid., p. 146.
78. ibid., p. 98.
79. S. F. Macintyre, *A Proletarian Science*, Cambridge University Press, 1980, p. 163. Macintyre also points out that Dutt's theoretical criticism of *The Living Wage* was extremely perfunctory.
80. Dutt, *Living Wage*, p. 8.
81. ibid., p. 190.
82. ibid., quoting Lenin. The passage appears, in a somewhat different translation, in V. I. Lenin, *Imperialism, the Highest Stage of Capitalism*, Peking, Foreign Languages Press, 1973, p. 115.

83. Macintyre, *Science*, p. 69.
84. Lenin, *Imperialism*, p. 110.
85. ibid., p. 142.
86. This is given a full discussion in Allett, *Hobson*, pp. 154–7.
87. Lenin, *Imperialism*, p. 173.
88. This ignores those members of the ILP who joined the Communist Party and were thus briefly members of both the CPGB and the Labour Party. This was only possible until the Labour Party proscribed the CPGB in 1924. W. Kendall, *The Revolutionary Movement in Britain 1900–1921: the Origins of British Communism*, Weidenfeld & Nicolson, 1969, p. 276, estimates that 500–1,000 members of the ILP participated in the formation of the CPGB in 1921.
89. ILP, *Report of Annual Conference*, 1921, p. 122.
90. ibid., p. 123.
91. ibid., p. 114.
92. Lee, *Nye*, pp. 34–5.
93. Laski, *Communism*, p. 235.
94. ibid., p. 50.
95. ibid., p. 51.
96. B. Russell, *The Practice and Theory of Bolshevism*, New York, Simon & Schuster, 1964, p. 100.
97. ibid., p. 11.
98. ibid., p. 10.
99. *New Statesman*, 7 Aug. 1920, p. 495.
100. ibid., p. 127.
101. Brailsford, *The Russian Workers' Republic*, George Allen & Unwin, 1921, p. 7.
102. ibid., pp. 115–17.
103. *New Leader*, 21 Nov. 1924
104. ibid., 14 Nov. 1924, p. 2.
105. Brailsford, chairman's address, in Laski, *Nationalism and the Future of Civilisation*, pp. 13–14.

6 FASCISM, UNITY AND LOYALTY: 1932–1937

1. The fullest study of the Socialist League is R. G. Dare, 'The Socialist League 1932–1937', Oxford, unpublished D.Phil. thesis, 1973.
2. B. Pimlott, *Labour and the Left in the 1930s*, Cambridge University Press, 1977, p. 43.
3. Dowse, 'Left-Wing Opposition'.
4. W. J. Brown, *The Crisis and the Labour Movement: Where I Stand*, ILP, 1931, pp. 5, 7. Brown was a co-founder of Mosley's New Party, but left it on the same day.
5. ibid., pp. 4–5.
6. Brockway was a leading working-class member of the ILP. He

replaced Brailsford as editor of the *New Leader* in 1926, after a long dispute about Brailsford's salary and the paper's 'highbrow' tone.

7. A. F. Brockway, *The ILP and the Crisis*, ILP, 1931, p. 5. Norman was the Governor of the Bank of England.

8. Brailsford, *The 'City' or the Nation?*, ILP, 1931, p. 1.

9. This argument was acted out repeatedly between Jennie Lee, who stayed in the ILP, and Aneurin Bevan, who stayed in the Labour Party, J. Lee, *This Great Journey*, New York, Farrar & Rhinehart, 1942, pp. 120, 140–2. It did not prevent their marrying, nor did it disrupt her earlier affair with Frank Wise.

10. *New Clarion*, 13 Aug. 1932.

11. ibid.

12. Mellor had been a friend of Cole's since their undergraduate days and had been prominent in the Guild Socialist revolt against the Fabian leaders. In 1920 he helped found the CPGB, but left within a few years.

13. See M. Cole, 'The Society for Socialist Inquiry and Propaganda', in A. Briggs & J. Saville (eds.), *Essays in Labour History*, Croom Helm, 1977, for a good account of the brief history of the SSIP.

14. *SSIP News*, June 1932, (roneo) p. 1 (Cole papers, B3/5/E, Box 5).

15. Trevelyan to Cole, 28 July 1932; Hobson to Cole, 28 July 1932, ibid.

16. Nevinson to Cole, 28 July 1932, ibid.

17. M. Cole, 'SSIP', p. 200.

18. Cole to D. N. Pritt, A. Pugh, Cripps, and Attlee, 19 Sept. 1932, Cole papers, B3/5/E, Box 5.

19. Cole to Cripps, 19 Sep. 1932, ibid.

20. ibid.

21. Cripps to Cole, 21 Sep. 1932, ibid. Cripps's concern was shared by Pethick-Lawrence, who nevertheless joined the League 'on the strength of [Cripps's] signature'. Pethick-Lawrence to Cripps, 28 Sep. 1932, Pethick-Lawrence papers, 4/43.

22. Bevin to Cole, 24 Sep. 1932, Cole papers, B3/5/E, Box 5.

23. Bevan to Wise, quoted in Foot, *Bevan*, vol. 1, p. 156.

24. M. Cole, 'SSIP', p. 196.

25. *New Clarion*, 24 Sep. 1932.

26. P. Seyd, 'Factionalism within the Labour Party: the Socialist League 1932–1937', in Briggs & Saville (eds.), *Labour History*, pp. 217–19.

27. Cripps, 'Can Socialism Come by Constitutional Methods?' in C. Addison *et al.*, *Problems of a Socialist Government*, Gollancz, 1934. This text, which was the substance of Cripps's original lecture, was earlier published as a pamphlet by the Socialist League.

28. Socialist League, *Report of the First Annual Conference Whitsun*, 1933.

29. NEC minutes, 25 Jan. 1933.

30. Laski, *New Clarion*, 3 Feb. 1934.

31. Labour Party Research Department, *What is this Fascism?*, Labour Party, 1934, pp. 3, 4, 5.
32. ibid., p. 11.
33. Socialist League, *Forward to Socialism*, 1934, p. 4.
34. ibid.
35. Cripps, 'Democracy – Real or Sham?' in Cripps et al., *Problems of the Socialist Transition*, Gollancz, 1934, p. 16.
36. G. R. Mitchison, *Socialist Leaguer*, July–Aug. 1935, p. 201.
37. *New Clarion*, 2 Jan. 1933. Visc. Sidmouth was Home Secretary in the Government of Lord Liverpool, which in 1817 suspended habeas corpus and suppressed seditious meetings and publications. For an account of the Sidmouth regime see E. P. Thompson, *The Making of the English Working Class*, Harmondsworth, Pelican, 1968, chs. 14, 15.
38. ibid.
39. *New Clarion*, 23 Sep. 1933.
40. ibid.
41. Brailsford, *Property or Peace?*, Gollancz, 1934, p. 63. The comparison with Orwell's prediction of 'a slimy Anglicized form of Fascism, with cultured policemen [a reference to Trenchard's reforms?] instead of Nazi gorillas and the lion and the unicorn instead of the swastika' is irresistible, G. Orwell, *The Road to Wigan Pier*, Harmondsworth, Penguin, 1962, p. 203.
42. Letter to *Socialist Leaguer*, 15 Feb. 1935, p. 142.
43. Brailsford, 'The Labour Party and India', *Socialist Leaguer*, 15 Jan. 1935, p. 121.
44. Brailsford, *Property or Peace?*, p. 54.
45. See ch. 4, above.
46. *New Clarion*, 26 Aug. 1933.
47. Brailsford, *Property or Peace?*, p. 233.
48. Laski, *New Clarion*, 23 Sep. 1933.
49. See ch. 3, above.
50. Socialist League, *Forward to Socialism*, p. 3.
51. See, e.g., G. D. H. Cole and R. S. Postgate, *War Debts and Reparations*, *NS & N*, n.d. [1932].
52. Hobson, *Property and Improperty*, Gollancz, 1937, p. 151.
53. ibid., pp. 135–6.
54. ibid., p. 136.
55. ibid., p. 143.
56. ECCI (13th Plenum), 'Fascism and the Maturing of the Revolutionary Crisis, in J. Degras (ed.), *The Communist International 1919–1943: Documents*, Frank Cass & Co., 1971, vol. III, p. 299.
57. ibid., p. 296.
58. R. P. Dutt, *Fascism and Social Revolution*, Martin Lawrence Ltd, 1935, p. xiv.
59. *Socialist Leaguer*, June–July 1934, p. 1.

60. *International Press Correspondence*, ix, 26 (31 May 1929), p. 557.
61. See H. Pelling, *The British Communist Party: a Historical Profile*, Adam and Charles Black, 1975, ch. 4.
62. ECCI, 'Statement on the German Situation and the United Front', in Degras, *Communist International*, iii, pp. 253–4.
63. Labour Party (National Joint Council), *Democracy v. Dictatorship*, 1933, p. 2.
64. ibid.
65. R. P. Dutt, *Democracy and Fascism*, CPGB, 1933, p. 7.
66. L. Elvin, *New Clarion*, 25 Mar. 1933.
67. ibid.
68. Dutt, *Fascism*, p. 168.
69. ibid., p. 155.
70. Laski, *Communism*, p. 210.
71. J. T. Murphy, *Socialist Leaguer*, Aug.–Sep. 1934, p. 47.
72. Cripps, *The Choice for Britain*, Socialist League, n.d. [1934], p. 5.
73. Brailsford, *Property or Peace?*, p. 250.
74. Orwell, *Collected Essays, Journalism and Letters*, vol. iv, p. 212.
75. Trevelyan, *Soviet Russia: a Description for British Workers*, Gollancz, 1935, p. 30.
76. ibid., pp. 44–5.
77. ibid., p. 16.
78. S. Glynn & J. Oxborrow, *Interwar Britain: a Social and Economic History*, George Allen & Unwin, 1976, pp. 145, 151.
79. J. Lee to Trevelyan, 31 July 1935, Trevelyan papers, pkt 149.
80. See p. 34, above.
81. *New Clarion*, 1 Apr. 1933.
82. Trevelyan, *Soviet Russia*, p. 31.
83. ibid., p. 27.
84. G. D. H. & M. I. Cole, *Modern Politics*, p. 226.
85. ibid., p. 236.
86. *New Clarion*, 27 May 1933.
87. ibid.
88. Laski to B. Webb, 9 Mar. 1935, Passfield papers, ii.4.c.53a.
89. Trevelyan to Cripps, 15 Sep. 1935, Cripps papers, 590.
90. Cripps to Trevelyan, 16 Sep. 1935, ibid.
91. Trevelyan to M. P. Price, 16 Dec. 1934, Trevelyan papers, pkt 69.
92. Brailsford, 'Roosevelt versus Anarchy', *New Clarion*, 22 July 1933.
93. ibid.
94. Laski, *The Roosevelt Experiment*, Socialist League, n.d. [1933], p. 1.
95. *Socialist Leaguer*, May 1935, p. 170.
96. *Socialist Leaguer*, June–July 1934, p. 6.
97. N. Thompson, *The Anti-Appeasers: Conservative Opposition to Appeasement in the 1930s*, Oxford, Clarendon Press, 1971, ch. 7.
98. *Socialist Leaguer*, Aug.–Sep. 1934.

99. *Socialist*, March 1936.
100. Labour Party, *Report of Annual Conference*, 1936, pp. 210–11.
101. ibid.
102. *Unity Manifesto*. The voting on the Unity Campaign at the Socialist League conference was 56 in favour, 38 against, and 23 abstentions; Pimlott, *Labour and Left*, p. 97.
103. J. S. Middleton, *The Labour Party and the So-Called 'Unity Campaign'*, Labour Party, 1937, p. 1.
104. NEC, *Labour Party Loyalty: an Appeal to the Movement*, Labour Party, n.d. [1936].
105. Barbara Betts 1911–, MP 1945–79, held (as Barbara Castle) various cabinet posts in the Wilson and Callaghan Governments.
106. *Socialist*, Sep. 1935, p. 2.
107. Pimlott, *Labour and Left*, p. 5.

7 THE POPULAR FRONT

1. Cole, *People's Front*, p. 24.
2. *Socialist*, Sep. 1935, p. 1.
3. J. T. Murphy, *New Horizons*, John Lane, 1941, p. 318.
4. ibid.
5. ibid., p. 319.
6. Aneurin Bevan was invited, but apparently did not attend, Layton papers (8/64).
7. J. V. Delahaye, 'The People's Front', ts. of item for publication in 'the leading weeklys [*sic*]', encl. Delahaye to Layton, 2 July 1936, Layton papers (8/60).
8. ibid.
9. Speech at joint meeting of Oxford University Liberal and Labour Clubs, reported in *Oxford Mail*, 2 Feb. 1937.
10. Labour Party, *Report of Annual Conference*, 1936, p. 253.
11. ibid., p. 255.
12. ibid.
13. ibid., p. 256.
14. Brailsford had been doubtful about the Popular Front proposal when Murphy had proposed it to the Socialist League (Murphy, *New Horizons*, p. 318).
15. Brailsford to Cripps, 31 July 1936, Cripps papers (504).
16. Brailsford, *Spain's Challenge to Labour*, Socialist League, n.d. [1936], p. 12.
17. *Nazi Germany and Fascist Italy Have Invaded Spain*, Labour Party, 1938, p. 15.
18. Martin, *Pacifism*, pp. 114–17.
19. Brailsford to Cripps, 31 July 1937, Cripps papers, (504).
20. Brailsford, *Challenge*, p. 12.

21. Brailsford, 'The International People's Front', *Plan*, Nov. 1936, p. 9.
22. Neither Cripps's papers nor his biographers shed any light on precisely why or when he changed his position on the Popular Front question. It is possible that Brailsford persuaded him, or that he was alarmed by the possibility of a Liberal-led front.
23. *Tribune*, 14 Apr. 1938, p. 1.
24. *National Report of the Emergency Conference on Spain*, 1938, p. 17.
25. ibid., p. 27.
26. *Labour and the Popular Front*, Labour Party, 1938, pp. 4–6.
27. ibid., p. 8.
28. Brailsford to Cripps, 31 July 1936, Cripps papers (504).
29. Cole, *People's Front*, p. 17.
30. *Tribune*, 6 May 1938, p. 14.
31. Brailsford, letter to *NS & N*, 26 Nov. 1938, p. 868.
32. Cripps, 'Memorandum', encl., Cripps to Middleton, 9 Jan. 1939, Labour Party archive, JSM/LP/247.
33. See ch. 1, above.
34. Cole, in *Northern Daily Mail*, 3 Oct. 1938, Cole papers, fo. 59.
35. Notes for speech at Leith Hall, 22 May 1938, Trevelyan papers, pkt 183.
36. J. M. Keynes, interview with Kingsley Martin, *NS & N*, 28 Jan. 1939, p. 122.
37. Anon., *NS & N*, 23 April 1938, p. 678.
38. Cripps, 'Memorandum', p. 7.
39. *Tribune*, 3 June 1938, p. 1.
40. *Tribune*, 14 April 1939, p. 5.
41. R. S. G. Rutherford, letter to *NS & N*, 7 May 1938, p. 763.
42. F. Hughes, letter to *NS & N*, 18 Feb. 1939, p. 247.
43. The fullest account of the campaign is to be found in D. Scott, *A. D. Lindsay: a Biography*, Oxford, Basil Blackwell, 1971, ch. 14. R. Eatwell, 'The Labour Party and the Popular Front Movement in Britain in the 1930s', Oxford, unpublished D.Phil. thesis, 1975, ch. 6, provides a full account of both the Oxford and the later Bridgwater campaign.
44. B. Hammond to Jean Lindsay, quoted in Scott, *Lindsay*, p. 255.
45. Brailsford, letter to *NS & N*, 26 Nov. 1938, p. 868.
46. ibid.
47. Cole, *NS & N*, 19 Nov. 1938.
48. *Tribune*, 28 Oct. 1938, p. 5.
49. Labour Party, *Annual Report of the Executive*, 1939, pp. 44–53. One can only guess that Brailsford was protected by his extraordinarily high stature as an elder statesman of the Party.
50. *Socialism or Surrender* and *Unity: True or Sham?*, Labour Party, 1939.
51. Although the notorious block vote system inflated the majorities, it is important to note that the Constituency Parties supported the Executive in the proportion of about three to one.

52. *Tribune*, 6 Jan. 1939, p. 1.
53. K. F. A. Johnston, letter to *NS & N*, 4 Feb. 1939, p. 172.
54. G. R. Strauss, letter to *NS & N*, 11 Feb. 1939, p. 207.
55. Trevelyan, speech notes, 'Cripps Meeting', 5 Feb. 1939, Trevelyan papers, pkt 184.
56. W. B. Graham, letter to *NS & N*, 11 Feb. 1939, p. 207.
57. Labour Party, *Report of Conference*, 1939, p. 235.
58. ibid., p. 296.
59. ibid., p. 297.
60. R. H. S. Crossman, *NS & N*, 28 Jan. 1939, p. 117.
61. *Manchester Guardian*, 29 Sep. 1939.
62. *Manchester Guardian*, 15 March 1939.
63. *Manchester Guardian*, 30 Jan. 1939. Silverman's later career demonstrates some of the longer continuities of the progressive tradition. Despite his resistance to the First World War, he supported the Second, but after the war was expelled from the Labour Party for his objections to its stance on nuclear weapons. He was instrumental in the abolition of capital punishment.

CONCLUSION

1. Webb, 'Houndsditch', p. 368.

Bibliography

1 MANUSCRIPT SOURCES

Bryce papers, Bodleian Library, Oxford
G. D. H. Cole papers, Nuffield College, Oxford
Creech-Jones papers, Rhodes House Library, Oxford
Cripps papers, Nuffield College, Oxford
Fabian Society minutes and correspondence (microform)
Millicent Garrett Fawcett papers, Manchester Public Library
Hammond papers, Bodleian Library, Oxford
Hobson papers, Brynmoor Jones Library, University of Hull
Independent Labour Party archives (microform)
Keynes papers, King's College, Cambridge
Labour Party archive, Labour Party Headquarters, London
Laski papers, Brynmoor Jones Library, University of Hull
Laski papers, International Institute of Social History, Amsterdam
Layton papers, Trinity College, Cambridge
MacDonald papers, Public Record Office, Kew
Gilbert Murray papers, Bodleian Library, Oxford
Passfield papers, British Library of Political and Economic Science
Pethick-Lawrence papers, Trinity College, Cambridge
Ponsonby papers, Bodleian Library, Oxford
Scott papers, Manchester Guardian archives, John Rylands Library, University of Manchester
Trevelyan papers, University of Newcastle-upon-Tyne
Wallas papers, British Library of Political and Economic Science

2 NEWSPAPERS AND PERIODICALS

Contemporary Review
Daily Herald
Daily Worker
Ethical World
Foreign Affairs
International Press Correspondence

Labour Leader
Manchester Guardian
Nation
New Clarion
New Leader
New Statesman
New Statesman & Nation
Nineteenth Century
Plan
Political Quarterly
Progressive Review
Socialist
Socialist Leaguer
Speaker
Tribune

3 BIOGRAPHIES, MEMOIRS, PUBLISHED DIARIES

Angell, N., *After All*, Hamish Hamilton, 1951.

Attlee, C. R., *As It Happened*, New York, Viking, 1954.

Ball, O. H. (ed.), *Sydney Ball: Memories and Impressions of 'an Ideal Don'*, Oxford, Basil Blackwell, 1923.

Brockway, F., *Inside the Left*, Allen & Unwin, 1942.

Carpenter, E., *My Days and Dreams: Being Autobiographical Notes*, George Allen & Unwin, 1916.

Carpenter, L. P., *G. D. H. Cole: an Intellectual Biography*, Cambridge University Press, 1973.

Cline, C. A., *E. D. Morel 1873–1924: the Strategies of Protest*, Belfast, Blackstaff Press, 1980.

Cocks, F. S., *E. D. Morel: the Man and his Work*, Allen & Unwin, 1920.

Cole, M. I., *Growing up into Revolution*, Longmans, Green & Co., 1949.
   The Life of G. D. H. Cole, Macmillan, 1971.

Cooke, C. A., *The Life of Richard Stafford Cripps*, Hodder & Stoughton, 1957.

Crick, B., *George Orwell: a Life*, Secker & Warburg, 1980.

Dalton, H., *The Fateful Years – Memoirs 1931–45*, Frederick Muller, 1957.

Eastwood, G., *Harold Laski*, A. R. Mowbray, 1977.

Edsall, N. C., *Richard Cobden Independent Radical*, Cambridge, Mass., Harvard University Press, 1986.

Estorick, E., *Stafford Cripps: a Biography*, Heinemann, 1949.

Foot, M., *Aneurin Bevan*, Frogmore, Granada, 1975.

Forster, E. M., *Goldsworthy Lowes Dickinson*, Edward Arnold & Co., 1934.

Goldring, D., *The 1920s: a General Survey & Some Personal Memories*, Nicholson & Watson, 1945.

Haldane, R. B., *Richard Burdon Haldane*, Hodder & Stoughton, 1929.

Hannam, J., *Isabella Ford*, Oxford, Basil Blackwell, 1989.
Havighurst, A. F., *Radical Journalist: H. W. Massingham*, Cambridge University Press, 1974.
Hobhouse, S., *Forty Years and an Epilogue: an Autobiography 1881–1951*, J. Clarke, 1951.
Hobson, J. A., *Confessions of an Economic Heretic*, Allen & Unwin, 1938 (Hassocks, Harvester, 1976).
Hoggart, S. and Leigh, D., *Michael Foot*, Hodder & Stoughton, 1981.
Housman, G. L., *G. D. H. Cole*, Boston, Twayne Publishers, 1979.
Hyde, D., *I Believed*, Heinemann, 1950.
Koestler, A., *The Invisible Writing*, Collins, 1954.
Lee, J., *My Life with Nye*, Harmondsworth, Penguin, 1981.
This Great Journey, New York, Farrar & Rhinehart, 1942.
Leventhal, F. M., *The Last Dissenter: H. N. Brailsford and his World*, Oxford, Clarendon Press, 1985.
Magnus, P., *Gladstone*, John Murray, 1963.
Mahon, J., *Harry Pollitt*, Lawrence & Wishart, 1976.
Marquand, D., *Ramsay MacDonald*, Jonathan Cape, 1977.
Martin, K., *Harold Laski*, Gollancz, 1953.
Miller, J. D. B., *Norman Angell and the Futility of War*, Basingstoke, Macmillan, 1986.
Morris, A. J. A., *C. P. Trevelyan 1870–1958: Portrait of a Radical*, Belfast, Blackstaff Press, 1977.
Muirhead, J. H., *Reflections of a Journeyman in Philosophy*, George Allen & Unwin, 1942.
Murphy, J. T., *New Horizons*, John Lane, 1941.
Nevinson, H. W., *Fire of Life*, James Nisbet & Co., 1935.
Nichols, H. D. et al., *C. P. Scott 1846–1932*, Frederick Muller, 1946.
Samuel, H., *Memoirs*, Cresset Press, 1945.
Scott, D., *A. D. Lindsay: a Biography*, Oxford, Basil Blackwell, 1971.
Spender, S., *World within World*, Hamish Hamilton, 1951.
Strauss, P., *Cripps: Advocate and Rebel*, Gollancz, 1943.
Terril, R., *R. H. Tawney and His Times: Socialism as Fellowship*, Cambridge, Mass., Harvard University Press, 1973.
Thompson, E. P., *William Morris: Romantic to Revolutionary*, New York, Pantheon Books, 1976.
Tyrell, A., *Joseph Sturge and the Moral Radical Party in Early Victorian Britain*, Christopher Helm, 1987.
Vernon, B. D., *Margaret Cole, 1893–1980: a Political Biography*, Croom Helm, 1986.
Wallas, G., *Men and Ideas*, Allen & Unwin, 1940.
Webb, B., *The Diary of Beatrice Webb*, Virago, 1983.
Wedgewood, J. C., *Memoirs of a Fighting Life*, Hutchinson & Co., 1940.
Wilson, D., *Leonard Woolf: a Political Biography*, Hogarth Press, 1978.
Wilson, J., *CB: A Life of Sir Henry Campbell-Bannerman*, Constable, 1973.

Wright, A. W., *G. D. H. Cole and Socialist Democracy*, Oxford, Clarendon Press, 1979.

4 CONTEMPORARY PUBLICATIONS

(1) BOOKS, SIGNED PAMPHLETS AND JOURNAL ARTICLES

Addison, C. et al., *Problems of a Socialist Government*, Gollancz, 1934.
Angell, N., *Can Trade be Captured?*, War and Peace, 1915.
    Foreign Policy and our Daily Bread, W. Collins & Co., 1925.
    Foundations of International Polity, Heinemann, 1914.
    The Great Illusion, Heinemann, 1911.
    Hands off Russia, Adelaide, Australian Freedom League, 1920.
    The Peace Treaty and the Economic Chaos of Europe, The Swarthmore Press, 1919.
    The Prussian in our Midst, UDC, n.d. [1915].
    Shall this War End German Militarism?, UDC, n.d. [1914].
    War Aims: the Need for a Parliament of the Allies, Headley Bros, n.d. [1917].
    War and the Essential Realities, Watts & Co., 1913.
Angell, N. et al., *Does Capitalism Cause War?*, H. & E. R. Brinton, 1935.
Asquith, H. H., *A Clean Peace and National Reconstruction*, Liberal Party, 1918.
    The League of Nations: the True Crusade, Liberal Party, 1918.
    Liberalism after the War, Liberal Party, 1918.
Attlee, C. R., *The Labour Party in Perspective*, Gollancz, 1937.
Ball, S., *The Moral Aspects of Socialism*, Fabian Society (Tract 72), 1896.
Barnes, L., *Empire or Democracy*, Gollancz, 1939.
Blease, W. L., *A Short History of Liberalism*, T. Fisher Unwin, 1913.
Bosanquet, B., *The Philosophical Theory of the State*, Macmillan, 1965.
Brailsford, H. N., *The 'City' or the Nation?*, ILP, 1931.
    The Covenant of Peace: an Essay on the League of Nations, Headley Bros., 1918.
    India in Chains, Socialist League, n.d. [1932?].
    A League of Nations, Headley Bros., 1917.
    The Nazi Terror, Socialist League, n.d. [1934].
    The Origins of the Great War, UDC, n.d. [1914].
    Property or Peace?, Gollancz, 1934.
    The Russian Workers' Republic, George Allen & Unwin, 1921.
    A Share in your Motherland, The Herald Book Service, 1918.
    Socialism for To-Day, ILP, 1925.
    Spain's Challenge to Labour, Socialist League, n.d. [1936].
    Turkey and the Roads of the East, UDC, 1916.
    The War of Steel and Gold: a Study of the Armed Peace, G. Bell & Sons, 1915.
Brailsford, H. N. et al., *The Living Wage*, ILP, 1926.
Braunthal, J., *In Search of the Millennium*, Gollancz, 1945.
Brockway, A. F., *The ILP and the Crisis*, ILP, 1931.
Brown, W. J., *The Crisis and the Labour Movement: Where I Stand*, ILP, 1931.

Bryce, J. (Viscount) et al., *Proposals for the Prevention of Future Wars*, George Allen & Unwin, 1917.

Burns, E., *The People's Front*, Labour Research Department, 1936.

Burns, J., *The New Imperialism*, 'Stop the War' Committee, 1900.

    The Trail of the Financial Serpent, 'Review of Reviews' Office, 1900.

Buxton, C. R., *The Secret Agreements*, ILP, 1918.

Carpenter, E., *Boer and Briton*, Labour Press, 1900.

    Towards Democracy, Swan Sonnenschein, 1911.

Channing, F. A., *Is War to the Bitter End Worthwhile?*, South Africa Conciliation Committee, n.d. [1901?].

    The Transvaal War and Democracy, P. S. King & Son, 1899.

Clifford, J., *Socialism and the Teaching of Christ*, Fabian Society (Tract 78), 1897.

Cobden, R., *The Political Writings of Richard Cobden*, Cassell & Company, 1886.

Coit, S. (ed.), *Ethical Democracy: Essays in Social Dynamics*, Society of Ethical Propagandists, 1900.

Cole, G. D. H., *Guild Socialism Restated*, Parsons, 1920.

    The Intelligent Man's Guide through World Chaos, Gollancz, 1932.

    The People's Front, Gollancz, 1937.

    Self-Government in Industry, G. Bell & Sons, 1918.

    Socialism in Evolution, Harmondsworth, Penguin, 1938.

    A Study-Guide on Socialist Policy, Socialist League, n.d. [1933].

    What is Ahead of Us?, Allen & Unwin, 1937.

    What Marx Really Meant, New York, Alfred A. Knopf, 1934.

Cole, G. D. H. & Cole, M. I., *A Guide to Modern Politics*, Gollancz, 1934.

Cole, G. D. H. & Mitchison, G. R., *The Need for a Socialist Programme*, Socialist League, n.d. [1933?].

Cole, G. D. H. & Postgate, R. S., *War Debts and Reparations*, New Statesman and Nation, n.d. [1932].

Courtney, L., *The War in South Africa*, Birmingham, South Africa Conciliation Committee, 1900.

Cripps, R. S., *Are You a Worker?*, Labour Research Department, 1933.

    The Choice for Britain, Socialist League, n.d. [1934].

    The Economic Planning of Agriculture, Labour Party, 1934.

    Fight Now against War, Socialist League, 1935.

    The Struggle for Peace, Gollancz, 1936.

    Why this Socialism?, Gollancz, 1934.

Cripps, R. S. et al., *Problems of the Socialist Transition*, Gollancz, 1934.

Degras, J. (ed.), *The Communist International 1919–1934: Documents*, Frank Cass & Co., 1971, vol. III.

Dickinson, G. L., *The Choice before Us*, George Allen & Unwin, n.d. [1917].

    Economic War after the War, UDC, n.d. [1916].

Dutt, R. P., *Democracy and Fascism*, CPGB, 1933.

    Fascism and Social Revolution, Martin Lawrence Ltd, 1935.

    Socialism and the Living Wage, CPGB, 1927.

What Next for the Labour Party?, CPGB, 1936.

Green, T. H., *Lectures on the Principles of Political Obligation and Other Writings*, ed. P. Harris & J. Morrow, Cambridge University Press, 1986.

The Works of Thomas Hill Green, New York, Kraus Reprint Co., 1969.

Groves, R., *East End Crisis! Socialism, the Jews and Fascism*, Socialist League, n.d. [1936].

Trades Councils in the Fight for Socialism, Socialist League, n.d. [1936?].

Headlam, S., *Christian Socialism*, Fabian Society (Tract 42), 1892.

Henderson, A., *Labour and Foreign Affairs*, Labour Party, n.d. [1917].

The Peace Terms, Labour Party, 1919.

Hicks, G., *Poverty from Plenty*, Social Democratic Federation, 1933.

Hirst, F. W. et al., *Six Oxford Men, Essays in Liberalism*, Cassell & Co., 1897.

Hobhouse, L. T., *Democracy and Reaction*, ed. P. F. Clarke, Brighton, Harvester, 1972 [1904].

'The Ethical Basis of Collectivism', *International Journal of Ethics*, VIII, 1989.

Liberalism, Williams & Norgate, n.d.

The Metaphysical Theory of the State, George Allen & Unwin, 1918.

Social Evolution and Political Theory, New York, Columbia University Press, 1911.

Hobson, J. A., 'Capitalism and Imperialism in South Africa', *Contemporary Review*, vol. 77, Jan. 1900, pp. 1–17.

The Crisis of Liberalism: New Issues of Democracy, P. S. King & Son, 1909.

Democracy after the War, George Allen & Unwin, 1918.

The Economics of Reparation, George Allen & Unwin, 1921.

The Evolution of Modern Capitalism, Allen & Unwin, 1926 [1894].

Forced Labour, National Council of Civil Liberties, 1917.

'Free Trade and Foreign Policy', *Contemporary Review*, vol. 74, Aug. 1898, pp. 167–80.

The German Panic, Cobden Club, 1913.

Imperialism: a Study, James Nisbet & Co., 1902.

The Importance of Instruction in the Facts of Internationalism, National Peace Council, 1912.

Labour and the Costs of War, UDC, 1916.

A League of Nations, UDC, 1915.

The New Protection, Cobden Club, 1916.

Property and Improperty, Gollancz, 1937.

Richard Cobden: the International Man, Ernest Benn, 1968 (T. Fisher Unwin, 1919).

Saving and Spending, ILP, 1929.

'Socialistic Imperialism', *International Journal of Ethics*, XII, October 1901, pp. 44–58.

Towards International Government, George Allen & Unwin, 1915.

Traffic in Treason, George Allen & Unwin, 1914.

The War in South Africa: its Causes and Effects, James Nisbet & Co., 1900.

Work and Wealth: a Human Valuation, Macmillan, 1914.

Humphrey, A. W., *The Allies' Crime against Russia*, ILP, 1919.

Jennings, I., *The Sedition Bill Explained*, Unwin Bros, 1934.

Jones, A. S. D. et al., *Report of a Group of Anglican and Free Churchmen who visited Spain*, Henry Brinton, 1937.

Jones, E. R. (ed.), *Selected Speeches on British Foreign Policy 1738–1914*, Oxford University Press, 1914.

Jones, H., 'The Corruption of the Citizenship of the Working Man', *Hibbert Journal*, 10 (1911–12), pp. 155–78.

Keynes, J. M., *The Economic Consequences of the Peace*, Macmillan, 1920.

King, J., *Soviets and Soviet Government*, Glasgow, Reformers' Bookstall, 1919.

Why Does Killing Go On in Russia, Glasgow, Reformers' Bookstall, n.d. [1919].

Kirkup, T., *A History of Socialism*, Adam and Charles Black, 1909.

Kneeshaw, J. W., *From Versailles to Conscription and ???*, Forward, 1939.

Langdon-Davies, J., *Behind the Spanish Barricades*, Secker & Warburg, 1936.

Laski, H. J., *Communism*, Williams & Norgate, 1927.

The Crisis and the Constitution: 1931 and After, L. & V. Woolf at the Hogarth Press, 1932.

The Dangers of Obedience and Other Essays, Harper & Row, 1930.

Democracy at the Crossroads, National Council of Labour Colleges, n.d. [1933?].

Democracy in Crisis, Allen & Unwin, 1933.

A Grammar of Politics, George Allen & Unwin, 1967 [1925].

The Labour Party and the Constitution, Socialist League, n.d. [1933?].

Nationalism and the Future of Civilisation, Watts & Co., 1932.

Parliamentary Government in England, George Allen & Unwin, 1938.

The Roosevelt Experiment, Socialist League, n.d. [1933].

Lenin, V. I., *Collected Works*, Moscow, Progress Press, 1964, vol. xxi.

Imperialism, the Highest Stage of Capitalism, Peking, Foreign Languages Press, 1973.

Lenin on War and Peace, Peking, Foreign Languages Press, 1960.

Lewis, C. D. (ed.), *The Mind in Chains: Socialism and the Cultural Revolution*, Muller, 1937.

Lloyd George, D. et al., *The Foreign Policy of the Liberal Party*, Liberal Party, 1929.

MacDonald, J. R., 'The "Corruption" of the Citizenship of the Working Man: A Reply', *Hibbert Journal*, 10 (1911–12) pp. 345–61.

Labour and the Empire, George Allen, 1907.

Labour's Policy versus Protection, Labour Party, n.d. [1923].

Socialism After the War, ILP, 1919.

The Socialist Movement, Williams & Norgate, 1911.

War and the Workers: a Plea for Democratic Control, UDC, n.d. [1915].

What I Saw in South Africa, The Echo, n.d. [1902].

Mann, T., *Tom Mann and the ILP*, CPGB, 1938.

Massingham, H. W., *Join the Labour Party: my Advice to Liberals*, Labour Party, 1923.

Masterman, C. F. G., *The New Liberalism*, Leonard Parsons, 1920.

McGovern, G., *Terror in Spain*, ILP, n.d. [1938].

Middleton, J. S., *The Labour Party and the So-Called 'Unity Campaign'*, Labour Party, 1937.

Mill, J. S., *Collected Works*, Routledge & Kegan Paul, 1967.

Mitchison, G. R., *The First Workers' Government*, Gollancz, 1934.

Morel, E. D., *The African Problem and the Peace Settlement*, UDC, 1917.

The Alsace–Lorraine Problem, ILP, 1918.

Great Britain and the Congo, New York, H. Fertig, 1969 (Smith, Elder & Co., 1909).

Pre-War Diplomacy – Fresh Revelations, ILP, 1919.

Red Rubber, T. Fisher Unwin, 1907.

Ten Years of Secret Diplomacy: an Unheeded Warning, National Labour Press, 1915.

War and Diplomacy, UDC, n.d.

Morris, W., *Communism*, Fabian Society (Tract 113), 1903.

Political Writings of William Morris, Lawrence & Wishart, 1973.

Morrison, H. et al., *The League and the Future of the Collective System*, George Allen & Unwin, 1937.

Mummery, A. F. & Hobson, J. A., *The Physiology of Industry*, New York, Kelley & Millman, 1956.

Murphy, J. T., *Fascism! The Socialist Answer*, Socialist League, n.d. [1936].

Preparing for Power, Pluto Press, 1974.

The Workers' Committee: an Outline of its Principles & Structure, Pluto Press, 1972 (Sheffield Workers' Committee, 1917).

Murray, G., *What Liberalism Stands For*, Liberal Party, 1925.

Murry, J. M., *The Defence of Democracy*, Jonathan Cape, 1939.

Musgrave, B., *What is the Labour Party?*, Liberal Party, 1922.

Myers, T., *Liberalism and Socialism*, Labour Party, 1923.

Newbold, J. T. W., *Bankers Bondholders and Bolsheviks*, ILP, 1919.

The Next Five Years Group, *The Next Five Years: an Essay in Political Agreement*, Macmillan, 1935.

Noel-Baker, P., *Hawkers of Death*, Labour Party, n.d. [1934?].

Orwell, G., *Collected Essays, Journalism and Letters*, Harmondsworth, Penguin, 1970, vols. I–IV.

Homage to Catalonia, Harmondsworth, Penguin, 1979.

The Road to Wigan Pier, Harmondsworth, Penguin, 1962.

Pethick-Lawrence, F. W., *The Capital Levy*, Labour Party, n.d. [1920].

Pitcairn, F. (C. Cockburn, pseud.), *Reporter in Spain*, Lawrence & Wishart, 1936.

Pointing, H. B., *A Countryman Talks about Socialism*, n.d. [1933?].

Pollitt, H., *Save Spain from Fascism*, CPGB, 1936.
  Spain and the TUC, CPGB, 1936.
Ponsonby, A., *Parliament and Foreign Policy*, UDC, n.d. [1914].
Price, M. P., *Blue Blood and Bolshevism*, Gloucester, ILP, 1920.
Pritt, D. N. & Smith, E., *They Helped Hitler*, LRD, 1936.
Ritchie, D. G., *Principles of State Interference*, 1902, Freeport, Books for Libraries Reprints, 1969.
Robertson, J. M., *Liberalism and Labour*, Liberal Party, 1921.
Rowse, A. L., *Mr Keynes and the Labour Movement*, Macmillan, 1936.
Russell, B., *War: the Offspring of Fear*, UDC, n.d. [1914].
  The Practice and Theory of Bolshevism, New York, Simon & Schuster, 1964.
Samuel, H., *Britain and the Dictators*, Liberal Party, 1938.
  The Liberal Party and the International Crisis, Liberal Party, 1935.
  Liberalism: an Attempt to State the Principles and Proposals of Contemporary Liberalism in England, Grant Richards, 1902.
Shaw, G. B., *The Fabian Society: its Early History*, Fabian Society (Tract 41).
Shaw, G. B. (ed.), *Fabian Essays in Socialism*, George Allen & Unwin, 1962.
Sinclair, A., *10 Points for Progressives*, Liberal Party, 1939.
Smith, C. A., *The Crime of Empire*, ILP, n.d. [1925].
Snowden, P., *What is the Labour Party? A Reply to Liberal Misrepresentations*, Labour Party, 1922.
Spencer, H., *The Man versus the State*, Harmondsworth, Pelican, 1969.
Spender, S., *Forward from Liberalism*, Gollancz, 1937.
Strachey, J., *The Coming Struggle for Power*, Gollancz, 1933.
  The Menace of Fascism, Gollancz, 1933.
  The Theory and Practice of Socialism, Gollancz, 1936.
Swanwick, H., *Women and War*, UDC, n.d. [1915].
Symons, W. T., *A Living Wage or a Living Income*, Blackfriars Press, n.d. [1926].
Tait, F., *The Jugglers of Finance Are Bleeding the Nation White*, ILP, 1932.
Tawney, R. H., *The Acquisitive Society*, Fontana, 1961.
  The Attack and Other Papers, George Allen & Unwin, 1953.
  The British Labour Movement, Cambridge, Mass., Harvard University Press, 1925 (New York, Greenwood, 1968).
  Equality, Unwin Books, 1964.
  R. H. Tawney's Commonplace Book ed. J. H. Winter & D. M. Joslin, Cambridge University Press, 1972.
  The Radical Tradition, George Allen & Unwin, 1964.
Toynbee, A., *Lectures on the Industrial Revolution of the Eighteenth Century in England*, Longmans, Green & Co., 1908.
Trevelyan, C. P., *From Liberalism to Labour*, George Allen & Unwin, 1921.
  Soviet Russia: a Description for British Workers, Gollancz, 1935.
Tucker, R. C. (ed.), *The Marx–Engels Reader*, New York, W. W. Norton, 1972.
Webb, S., *The Difficulties of Individualism*, Fabian Society (Tract 69) 1896.

'Lord Rosebery's Escape from Houndsditch', *Nineteenth Century*, September 1901.
Socialism: True and False, Fabian Society (Tract 51), 1894.
[Webb, S. & Shaw, G. B.], 'To Your Tents O Israel', *Fortnightly Review*, CCXXIII, 1 November 1893.
Wilkinson, E. C., *The Terror in Germany*, British Committee for the Relief of the Victims of Fascism, n.d. [1937?].
Wilkinson, E. C. & Conze, E., *Why Fascism?*, Selwyn & Blunt, 1934.
Williams, T. R., *Should the Labour and Liberal Parties Unite?*, Arthur J. Cooper, 1903.
Woolf, L. S., *Barbarians at the Gate*, Gollancz, 1939.
International Economic Policy, Labour Party, n.d. [1920?].
Woolf, L. S. (ed.), *The Intelligent Man's Way to Prevent War*, Gollancz, 1933.
Zangwill, I. et al., *Russia Free! Ten Speeches Delivered at the Royal Albert Hall, London*, Friends of Russian Freedom, 1917.

(II) UNSIGNED PAMPHLETS

Communist League
Forward against Fascism, n.d. [1935?].
Communist Party of Great Britain
Hitler's Friends in Britain, 1938.
The March of English History, 1936.
The Party & the Workers, 1935.
The Plain Man's Guide to the Coronation (3 parts), 1937.
Report on the Crisis Policy of the Labour Party, the TUC General Council and the ILP, 1932.
Fabian Society
Fabian Election Manifesto, (Tract 40), 1892.
[Shaw, G. B.], *Fabianism and the Fiscal Question: an Alternative Policy*, (Tract 116), 1904.
[Shaw, G. B.], *Report on Fabian Policy*, (Tract 70), 1896.
Independent Labour Party
How to End War: ILP View on Imperialism and Internationalism, n.d. [1922].
The ILP and the 3rd International, 1920.
Imperialism: its Meaning and its Tendency, ILP (City Branch), 1900.
The Independent Labour Party Platform, Pamphlet Series c. 1900–1903.
Six Months' of Liberalism: a Record of Mess, Muddle and Make-Belief, n.d. [1925].
What the ILP Stands For, n.d. [1935?].
Labour Party
The Communist Solar System, 1933.
Control of Foreign Policy: Labour's Programme, 1921.
Democracy v. Dictatorship, 1933.
Inter-Allied Labour and Socialist Conference, 1918.

Labour and The Popular Front, 1938.
Labour and the War Debt, n.d. [1923].
The Labour Party and the So-Called 'Unity Campaign', n.d. [1937].
Labour Party Loyalty: an Appeal to the Movement, n.d. [1936].
Labour's Policy for a True League of Nations, 1921.
Labour's Russian Policy, n.d. [1920].
Liberals and the Capital Levy: a Comedy in 3 Acts, 1923.
Nazi Germany and Fascist Italy Have Invaded Spain, 1938.
The 'Popular Front' Campaign, 1939.
The Proposed 'United Front', 1934.
Socialism or Surrender, 1939.
The United Front, 1934.
Unity: True or Sham?, 1939.
What is this Fascism?, 1934.
Labour Representation Committee
Why We Are Independent, 1903.
Labour Research Department
Capitalism in Crisis, n.d. [1933?].
Dividends from Defence, 1939.
National Service and the Workers, n.d. [1939].
The People's Front, 1936.
Standards of Starvation, 1936.
League against Imperialism and for National Independence
Abyssinia, n.d. [1936?].
The British Empire, n.d. [1935?].
League of Liberals against Aggression and Militarism
First Annual Report, April 1901.
Liberal Party
Labour's Debt to Liberalism, 1920.
Peace in our Time, 1928.
What Liberalism Has Done for Labour, 1920.
Why Did Eden Go?, 1938.
National Report of the Emergency Conference on Spain, 1938.
National United Front Congress of Action
The Workers' United Front, 1934.
People's Front Propaganda Committee
A People's Front for Britain, n.d. [1936].
The Voice of the People, n.d. [1936].
Socialist League
Forward to Socialism, 1934.
Trades Union Congress
The Spanish Problem, 1936.
Union of Democratic Control
The Balance of Power, n.d. [1915].
The Eastern Menace, 1936.

The International Industry of War, n.d. [1915].
[Morel, E. D. et al.], *The Morrow of the War*, n.d. [1914].
Patriotism Ltd: an Exposure of the War Machine, 1936.
The Secret International, 1932.
[Tawney, Lt. R. L.], *The War to End War: a Plea to Soldiers by a Soldier*, 1917.
Why We Should State the Terms of Settlement, n.d. [1915].

5 SECONDARY SOURCES

(1) PUBLISHED WORKS

Addison, P., *The Road to 1945*, Quartet, 1975.
Allett, J., *The New Liberalism: the Political Economy of J. A. Hobson*, Toronto, University of Toronto Press, 1981.
Benewick, R., *The Fascist Movement in Britain*, Allen Lane, The Penguin Press, 1972.
Bentley, M., *The Liberal Mind 1914–1929*, Cambridge University Press, 1977.
Blaug, M., 'The Classical Economists and the Factory Acts – a Re-examination', *Quarterly Journal of Economics*, LXXII, 1958.
Brebner, J. B., 'Laisser-faire and State Intervention in Nineteenth-Century Britain', *Journal of Economic History, Supplement*, VIII, 1968.
Briggs, A. & Saville, J. (eds.), *Essays in Labour History*, Croom Helm, 1977.
Brown, K. D. (ed.), *Essays in Anti-Labour History*, Macmillan, 1974.
Bullock, A. & Shock, M. (eds.), *The Liberal Tradition from Fox to Keynes*, Oxford, Clarendon Press, 1967.
Carr, R., *The Republic and the Civil War in Spain*, Macmillan, 1971.
Caute, D., *The Fellow Travellers*, Weidenfeld & Nicholson, 1973.
Challinor, R., *The Origins of British Bolshevism*, Croom Helm, 1977.
Clarke, P. F., *Lancashire and the New Liberalism*, Cambridge University Press, 1971.
Liberals and Social Democrats, Cambridge University Press, 1978.
'The Progressive Movement in England', *Transactions of the Royal Historical Society*, fifth series, vol. 24, 1974.
Cline, C. A., *Recruits to Labour*, Syracuse, Syracuse University Press, 1963.
Cole, G. D. H., *A History of Socialist Thought*, (7 vols.), Macmillan, 1953–1960.
Cole, G. D. H. & Postgate, R. S., *The Common People 1746–1946*, Methuen, 1961.
Cole, M. I. (ed.), *The Webbs and their Work*, Frederick Muller Ltd, 1949.
Collini, S., *Liberalism and Sociology: L. T. Hobhouse and Political Argument in England, 1880–1914*, Cambridge University Press, 1979.
Cook, C., *A Short History of the Liberal Party: 1900–1976*, Macmillan, 1976.
Dangerfield, G., *The Strange Death of Liberal England*, New York, Perigee, 1980.

Deane, H. A., *The Political Ideas of Harold J. Laski*, New York, Columbia University Press, 1955.

Deli, P., 'The Image of the Russian Purges in the Daily Herald and the New Statesman', *Journal of Contemporary History*, vol. xx (1985), pp. 261–82.

    'The Manchester Guardian and the Soviet Purges 1936–38', *Survey*, 28, 1 (120), pp. 119–65.

Douglas, R., *In the Year of Munich*, Basingstoke, Macmillan, 1977.

Dowse, R. E., 'The Entry of Liberals into the Labour Party: 1910–1920', *Yorkshire Bulletin of Economic and Social Research*, xiii, 2, 1961.

    Left in the Centre, Longmans, Green & Co., 1966.

    'The Left-Wing Opposition during the First Two Labour Governments', *Parliamentary Affairs*, Winter 1960–1 & Spring 1961.

Eatwell, R. & Wright, A., 'Labour and the Lessons of 1931', *History*, 63/1, 1978.

Fieldhouse, D. K., *Economics and Empire 1830–1914*, Weidenfeld & Nicolson, 1973.

    ' "Imperialism": an Historiographical Revision', *Economic History Review*, second series, vol. xiv, 2 (1961) pp. 187–209.

Foot, M., *Debts of Honour*, Davis-Poynter, 1980.

Freeden, M., *Liberalism Divided: a Study in British Political Thought 1914–1939*, Oxford, Clarendon Press, 1986.

    The New Liberalism, Oxford, Clarendon Press, 1978.

    (ed.) *Minutes of the Rainbow Circle 1894–1924*, Royal Historical Society, 1989, pp. 1–15.

Gannon, F. R., *The British Press and Germany 1936–1939*, Oxford, Clarendon Press, 1971.

Gilbert, M., *Britain and Germany between the Wars*, Longmans, Green & Co., 1964.

Glynn, S. & Oxborrow, J., *Interwar Britain: a Social and Economic History*, George Allen & Unwin, 1976.

Graubard, S. R., *British Labour and the Russian Revolution 1917–1924*, Cambridge, Mass., Harvard University Press, 1956.

Greenleaf, W. H., *The British Political Tradition* (vols. i & ii), Methuen, 1983.

Groves, R., *The Balham Group: How British Trotskyism Began*, Pluto Press, 1974.

Gupta, P. S., *Imperialism and the British Labour Movement 1914–1964*, New York, Holmes & Meier, 1975.

Halsey, A. H., *Traditions of Social Policy*, Oxford, Basil Blackwell, 1976.

Harvie, C., *No Gods and Precious Few Heroes*, Edward Arnold, 1981.

Himmelfarb, G., *Victorian Minds*, New York, Alfred A. Knopf, 1967.

Hinton, J., *Labour and Socialism*, Brighton, Wheatsheaf Books, 1983.

Holton, B., *British Syndicalism 1900–1914*, Pluto Press, 1976.

Howard, M., *War and the Liberal Conscience*, Temple Smith, 1978.

Howell, D., *British Social Democracy*, Croom Helm, 1976.

Howkuns, A., 'Edwardian Liberalism and Industrial Unrest: a Class View of the Decline of Liberalism', *History Workshop*, 3–4 (1977), pp. 143–61.

Inglis, F., *Radical Earnestness*, Oxford, Martin Robertson, 1982.

Jupp, J., *The Radical Left in Britain 1931–1941*, Frank Cass & Co., 1982.

Kendall, W., *The Revolutionary Movement in Britain 1900–1921: the Origins of British Communism*, Weidenfeld & Nicolson, 1969.

Laquer, W. & Mosse, G. L. (eds.), *The Left-Wing Intellectuals between the Wars*, New York, Harper & Row, 1966.

Letwin, S., *The Pursuit of Certainty*, Cambridge University Press, 1965.

Lewis, J., *The Left Book Club: an Historical Record*, Gollancz, 1970.

Macintyre, S. F., *A Proletarian Science*, Cambridge University Press, 1980.

MacKillop, I., *The British Ethical Societies*, Cambridge University Press, 1986.

Martin, D., *Pacifism*, Routledge & Kegan Paul, 1965.

Marwick, A., *The Deluge: British Society and the First World War*, Macmillan, 1973.

McBriar, A. M., *Fabian Socialism and English Politics 1884–1914*, Cambridge University Press, 1966.

McKibbin, R. I., 'James Ramsay MacDonald and the Problem of the Independence of the Labour Party', *Journal of Modern History*, 42, 2 (1970), pp. 216–35.

Miller, K. E., *Socialism and Foreign Policy: Theory and Practice in Britain to 1931*, The Hague, Martinus Nijhoff, 1967.

Milliband, R., *Parliamentary Socialism*, Allen & Unwin, 1961.

Mirsky, D., *The Intelligentsia of Great Britain*, Gollancz, 1935.

Mommsen, W. J., & Kettenacher, L. (eds.), *The Fascist Challenge and the Policy of Appeasement*, Allen & Unwin, 1982.

Morris, A. J. A. (ed.), *Edwardian Radicalism 1900–1914*, Routledge & Kegan Paul, 1974.

Morrow, J., 'British Idealism, "German Philosophy" and the First World War', *Australian Journal of Politics and History*, 28, 3 (1982), pp. 380–90.

Muggeridge, M., *The Thirties*, Quality Book Club, n.d.

Newman, M., ' "Democracy versus Dictatorship": Labour's Role in the Struggle against British Fascism, 1933–1936', *History Workshop*, 5 (Spring 1978), pp. 67–88.

Noonan, L. G., 'The Decline of the Liberal Party in British Politics', *Journal of Politics*, February, 1954.

Northedge, F. S. & Wells, A., *Britain and Soviet Communism: the Impact of a Revolution*, Macmillan, 1982.

Pease, E. R., *The History of the Fabian Society*, Frank Cass & Co., 1963.

Peele, G. & Cook, C., *The Politics of Reappraisal 1918–1939*, Macmillan, 1975.

Pelling, H., *The British Communist Party: a Historical Profile*, Adam and Charles Black, 1975.

The Origins of the Labour Party, Oxford University Press, 1965.

Perkin, H., 'Individualism versus Collectivism in Nineteenth-Century Britain: a False Antithesis', *Journal of British Studies*, XVII (Fall, 1977).

Pimlott, B., *Labour and the Left in the 1930s*, Cambridge University Press, 1977.

'The Socialist League: Intellectuals and the Labour Left in the 1930s', *Journal of Contemporary History*, vol. VI (1971) pp. 12–38.

Plant, R. & Vincent, A., *Philosophy, Politics and Citizenship*, Oxford, Basil Blackwell, 1984.

Plumb, J. H., *Studies in Social History*, Longmans, Green & Co., 1955.

Poirier, P. P., *The Advent of the Labour Party*, Allen & Unwin, 1958.

Porter, B., *Critics of Empire*, Macmillan, 1968.

Powell, D., 'The New Liberalism and the Rise of Labour, 1886–1906, *Historical Journal*, 29, 2 (1986), pp. 369–93.

Richter, M., *The Politics of Conscience: T. H. Green and his Age*, Weidenfeld & Nicolson, 1964.

Seaman, L. C. B., *Post-Victorian Britain 1902–1951*, Methuen, 1966.

Searle, G. R., *The Quest for National Efficiency*, Oxford, Basil Blackwell, 1971.

Sherman, A., 'The Days of the Left Book Club', *Survey*, 41 (April 1962), pp. 75–85.

Shinwell, E., *The Labour Story*, Macmillan, 1963.

Sked, A. & Cook, C., *Crisis and Controversy*, Macmillan, 1976.

Skidelsky, R., *Politicians and the Slump*, Harmondsworth, Pelican, 1970.

Somervell, D. C., *English Thought in the Nineteenth Century*, Methuen, 1929.

Spear, S., 'Pacifist Radicalism in the Post-War British Labour Party: the Case of E. D. Morel, 1919–1923', *International Review of Social History*, 23, 2 (1978), pp. 193–223.

Stevenson, J., *Social Conditions in Britain between the Wars*, Harmondsworth, Penguin, 1977.

Swanwick, H. M., *Builders of Peace*, George Allen & Unwin, 1924.

Swartz, M., *The Union of Democratic Control in British Politics during the First World War*, Oxford, Clarendon Press, 1971.

Symons, J., *The Thirties: a Dream Revolved*, Faber & Faber, 1975.

Taylor, A. J. P., *English History 1914–1945*, Harmondsworth, Pelican, 1975.

The First World War, Harmondsworth, Penguin, 1966.

The Origins of the Second World War, Harmondsworth, Penguin, 1964.

The Troublemakers: Dissent over Foreign Policy 1792–1956, Hamish Hamilton, 1957.

Thomas, H., *The Spanish Civil War*, Harmondsworth, Penguin, 1968.

Thompson, E. P., 'The Moral Economy of the English Crowd in the Eighteenth Century', *Past and Present*, 50, Feb. 1971.

The Making of the English Working Class, Harmondsworth, Pelican, 1968.

The Poverty of Theory and Other Essays, Merlin, 1978.

Thompson, N., *The Anti-Appeasers: Conservative Opposition to Appeasement in the 1930s*, Oxford, Clarendon Press, 1971.

Thompson, P., *Socialists, Liberals and Labour: the Struggle for London, 1885–1914*, Routledge & Kegan Paul, 1967.

Ulam, A., *Philosophical Foundations of English Socialism*, New York, Octagon, 1964.

Viner, J., 'The Intellectual History of Laissez-Faire', *Journal of Law and Economics*, vol. III (1960), pp. 45–69.

Weiner, M. J., *Between Two Worlds: the Political Thought of Graham Wallas*, Oxford, Clarendon Press, 1971.

Wilford, R. A., 'The "Federation of Progressive Societies and Individuals"', *Journal of Contemporary History*, 11, 1 (1976), pp. 49–82.

Wilson, T., *The Downfall of the Liberal Party, 1914–1935*, Collins, 1966.

Winkler, H. R., *The League of Nations Movement in Great Britain 1914–1919*, Scarecrow Reprint Corporation, 1967.

Winter, J. M., 'Arthur Henderson, the Russian Revolution, and the Reconstruction of the Labour Party', *Historical Journal*, xv, 4 (1972), pp. 753–73.

'R. H. Tawney's Early Political Thought', *Past and Present*, vol. 47, May 1970.

Wolfe, W., *From Radicalism to Socialism*, New Haven, Yale University Press, 1975.

Wood, N., *Communism and British Intellectuals*, New York, Columbia University Press, 1959.

(II) UNPUBLISHED THESES

Dare, R. G., 'The Socialist League 1932–1937', Oxford, D.Phil., 1973.

Eatwell, R., 'The Labour Party and the Popular Front Movement in Britain in the 1930s', Oxford, D.Phil., 1975.

McCulloch, G., 'The Politics of the Popular Front 1935–1945', Cambridge, Ph.D., 1980.

Index